CARL PRUSCHA
SINGULAR PERSONALITY

CARL PRUSCHA SINGULAR PERSONALITY

ARCHITECT, BOHEMIAN, ACTIVIST

Edited by
Lars Müller
Arno Ritter
Eva Schlegel

With texts by
Natalie Lettner
Michael Sorkin
Manjushree Thapa

Lars Müller Publishers

If Frank Lloyd Wright had stayed in Wisconsin or Charles-Édouard Jeanneret-Gris in La Chaux-de-Fonds, we might expect that they would have lived ordinary lives, maybe becoming architects or master builders, perhaps renowned and successful within the framework of rural communities. But they set out to create a wider world for themselves. While most stay, or return to, where they were raised, others are drawn to faraway places, by twists of fate or an effort of will. That already is something quite singular.

When Carl Pruscha left the mountains of Tyrol, found his way to Vienna, and continued his education in the United States, he had long left the beaten path and embarked on an unsettled life. It is fully out of the ordinary when, on top of that, dreams and long-held plans are called into question overnight, for instance by an offer to take up a career representing the exact opposite of one's own perspective. Usually, people will find good reasons to decline such a proposal, regardless of its singular appeal, to forego adventure and stay on the safe and narrow path. Not Carl Pruscha. Having set up shop fairly successfully in cosmopolitan New York and cultivating the image of a dandy, he decided on the spur of the moment to relocate to Kathmandu as an architect on assignment by the United Nations. Kathmandu? The contrast to New York could not have been greater—the same goes for the challenges the young architect had to overcome.

Life at the foot of the Himalayas meant freedom and a curse, the city was both a Moloch and a hippie paradise. Pruscha found his way around, explored, inventoried, drew up development plans for the valley and brought architecture in the form of a distinctive type of building that wedded tradition with Modernism.

After ten years, Pruscha settled down in Vienna again. Not so much as a homecomer, more as a repeat newcomer. His unusual experience gave him the perfect background to become a teacher who shakes up conventions, shows young people the world as well as their options, and exerts influence on academic institutions. At the same time, it gave him the ability to see the potential in existing conditions or structures and realize remarkable architectural projects in a historical context.

This book sets out to tell the story of architect Carl Pruscha and document his work, highlighting numerous surprising facets along the way, because, strikingly, both are so much about precisely not walking a straight line. Pruscha made the world of architecture richer with his idiosyncratic personality and encouraged its denizens to stray from ostensibly chalked out career paths.

Manjushree Thapa's essay vividly describes the years in Kathmandu without glossing over the difficulties that crossed the path of the expatriate. Natalie Lettner traces the architect's many-facetted path from his childhood in Tyrol to faraway destinations and back to Vienna where he navigated his way through the inner workings of the city's cultural and architectural circles. In his trenchant style and with little mercy, Michael Sorkin reflects on the Vienna he came to know as a professor at the Academy of Fine Arts in the early 1990s. In every aspect, his subtle portrait of Carl Pruscha paints him as what he really is, which is to say, an singular architect.

Lars Müller
Arno Ritter
Eva Schlegel

Impressions of Kathmandu,
1970s and 1980s

PRUSCHA IN NEPAL

Manjushree Thapa

Carl Pruscha explains his concept for the CEDA building to ministers and chief engineers of Nepal

AUTHOR'S NOTE

Amid the thicket of roads and concrete-block buildings by the grand stupa of Boudhanath, in Kathmandu, lies the Taragaon Museum, a charming, offbeat brick complex of barrel-vaulted rooms connected by stairways leading to multilevel open-air platforms. It is a hushed idyll. Unlike anything in the vicinity, it recalls the traditional Buddhist monastic cell, as well as the *pati*, or pilgrims' rest house of Kathmandu's indigenous Newar architecture. It also brings to mind a futuristic space station, albeit one that feels intimate and human for being built predominantly of brick. Rumor has it that Jay A. and Cindy Pritzker, whose family founded the Pritzker Architecture Prize, have stayed there while visiting Kathmandu.

I have been to Taragaon throughout my life: first as a child in the 1970s, on a family outing to see the newfangled hostel, which had caused quite a stir in Kathmandu, and then on a date in my twenties, when it was a discreet and forgotten—and failing—restaurant. I went there in 2016 to take in the Kathmandu Triennale, when the Saraf Foundation had restored the complex and converted it into a smart new museum. Taragaon has always been a part of my Kathmandu, weaving in and out of consciousness somewhere in the background. An acquaintance working at the museum had even enthused to me about the Austrian architect who had designed it in 1971. What I did not know—or I forgot—was that his name was Carl Pruscha.

I came to write this account of Pruscha's work in Nepal after interviewing him at his home in Gattendorf, Austria, in 2018, where he was living with his wife, the artist Eva Schlegel, in a late-Renaissance building that he renovated and refitted upon returning to Austria from Nepal. Pruscha's Gattendorf home is his architectural manifesto, and it is a rousing one. Its elegant preserved exterior honors the building's humble past as a granary, while its interior fuses together an eclectic mix of vernacular and modern elements, including syncretic Hindu and Buddhist Tantric iconography. The result is a habitable art installation, one that is both highly conceptual and arrestingly sensual, continually intriguing and awakening those who move through it.

It was in Kathmandu that Pruscha honed the creative vision that he has since showcased in Gattendorf. This is the story of how he developed this vision, growing out of an early fascination with Futurism to arrive at a poised and considered response to the call of his age: critical regionalism.

Upon returning to Austria, Pruscha went on to teach at the Academy of Fine Arts in Vienna, first as a professor for architecture and planning, then as the vice chancellor, and finally as the chair for habitat, environment and conservation. He was retired when I met him. He, his family, and a few of his acquaintances in Vienna are my sources for this account, as are several of the publications that cover his life's work: *The Physical Development Plan for the Kathmandu Valley* (His Majesty's Government of Nepal, Kathmandu, 1969); *Kathmandu Valley, the Preservation of Physical Environment and Cultural Heritage: Protective Inventory*, vols. 1 and 2 (first published by Anton Schroll & Co., Vienna, 1975, and reissued by Vajra Books, Kathmandu, 2015); *Himalayan*

Vernacular (Akademie der bildenden Künste, Vienna, 2004); and *Mein Haus in Lajtakatta* (Carl Pruscha, 2016).

Writing about Pruscha has allowed me to deepen my knowledge of an aspect of Kathmandu of which I was only glancingly aware: its modern planning and architecture. As I got to know his work, I realized that Taragaon was not the only building of Pruscha's that I had grown up with. I recall my father, who worked in government, talking about the new CEDA building at Tribhuvan University, which Pruscha designed. Pruscha got Kenzo Tange involved in the Lumbini Master Plan, and this still generates great pride in Nepal. He also got Louis Kahn to design a building for the Maternal Child Health and Family Planning Program. My mother headed that program: I learned about modern architecture through this building. And I grew up hearing about everything that Pruscha was vitally concerned with during his years in Nepal: the preservation of the Kathmandu Valley in the face of enormous economic pressure for rapid expansion and growth.

Writing about Pruscha has taught me about my own hometown. Kathmandu is a palimpsest, a dense accrual of countless fine layers of artifacts, both material and intellectual. The 475-square-kilometer area of the valley contains a wealth of cultural riches, from the oldest known inscriptions from the fifth century AD to the resplendent Licchavi- and Malla-era towns for which Kathmandu is renowned. These exist alongside the city's grittier manifestation as the burgeoning, overstressed capital of a politically fractious modern nation.

I find it moving that Pruscha's work and ideas endure in present-day Kathmandu. They may be difficult to locate, scattered as they are in the urban sprawl, but they are very much present: one building here and another one there, some groundbreaking plans and conceptual notes, a comprehensive inventory of the cultural and natural heritage of the Kathmandu Valley, and a vision of a modern vernacular style of Nepali architecture that Pruscha left behind, as a legacy, for future architects to take up should they so desire. Though he spent a scant decade there, Pruscha became part of the palimpsest of Kathmandu. That is, perhaps, all a creative artist might hope for.

I would like to thank Carl Pruscha for talking to me candidly about his experience. Thank you also to Eva Schlegel for all of her energy in setting up my interviews in Vienna. Alexandra Surendra Pruscha talked to me about her family life in Nepal. Tom Dove filled me in on a few aspects of Carl's work in Nepal and the atmosphere in Kathmandu in the 1960s and 1970s. I am grateful to them and to Aradhana Seth for introducing us to each other. In addition to interviewing Carl, I also relied on the writings of architect Biresh Shah, information on the Taragaon Museum's website and UNESCO's (the United Nations Educational, Scientific and Cultural Organization's) website, as well as a number of *Nepali Times* reports to fill in the historical details of Kathmandu—and Nepal in general—in the 1960s and 1970s. Many of the conservation architects named in this account—and many ordinary residents of the Kathmandu Valley—still encounter Carl's work, concepts, or legacy in their lives today. There is a new generation of Nepali

Aerial view of the CEDA building, 2017

Aerial view of Taragaon, 2017

Aerial view of Lumbini, 2017

Paul L. Wiener

Wallace K. Harrison

Lewis Mumford

architects who are grappling with the ideas that Carl introduced there in the 1960s. There are debates going on about heritage conservation. My hope is that this account will add to those debates and revive a sense of possibility about what might still be done.

In the spring of 1965, Carl Pruscha, age thirty, born in Innsbruck, raised in Tyrol, and trained at the Academy of Fine Arts in Vienna, arrived in Kathmandu from New York, where he had practiced architecture amid mounting frustration after obtaining a master's degree in urban design at the Harvard Graduate School of Design. He had not won the approval of many clients in New York. Deeming his vision too lofty, they had overlooked his bright proposals for the offices of Paul Lester Wiener and Wallace Harrison—an urban space in Boston, a plaza at Brandeis University, a center for humanistic studies in Aspen—in favor of simpler, more practical proposals. To Pruscha's deep disappointment, the Rockefeller Center's lead architect, Wallace Kirkman Harrison, had also rejected his proposal to refashion the watershed area from Battery Park to the World Trade Center into a series of man-made islands in the Hudson River. At a loss, Pruscha had returned to academia, pursuing a Ph.D. on planning for developing countries. It genuinely puzzled him that the most urbane, educated Americans who readily embraced the Bauhaus and the International Style should draw the line at his particular passion, Futurism.

He was spending his days at the United Nations' library poring over books on planning. Pruscha had learned in his youth of Swedish explorer Sven Hedin's expeditions to Central Asia and Tibet. Seeing the explorer's writings, drawings, and maps from 1894 to 1908 made him yearn to go to Tibet.

It also prompted him to rethink his own views on architecture and on regionalism in particular. He had been exposed to regionalism throughout his studies: the preservation of traditional architecture was heavily emphasized, and even romanticized, in the postwar Europe that Pruscha emerged from. As a student in Vienna, Pruscha had been a member of Roland Rainer's research team on the architecture of the eastern region of Burgenland, including the hamlet of Gattendorf. He had helped to document the elaborate thatched roofs, mud walls, and sturdy woodwork of the buildings in that region. Pruscha was not himself interested in the romantic ethos of architectural preservation that prevailed in Vienna. He was wary of the nostalgic nationalism that could arise from such an ethos, the kind of nationalism that had blighted the Austria of his childhood. He harbored quite a divergent, unsentimental utopian vision.

Yet at Harvard, he had heard the lectures of Lewis Mumford, the historian and critic who had reinvented regionalism with a call for organic humanism. Mumford had championed the work of Frank Lloyd Wright and other architects who fused regional architecture with internationalism, which had heretofore been considered irreconcilable. This fusion of the local and global had intrigued Pruscha, though his own sensibilities had remained firmly Futurist. In one of his more heady theoretical projects in New York, he had sketched out a bold vision of "global urbanization,"

an experimental habitat for humankind with cities expanding beyond Earth into space, based on technologies that were yet to be invented.

Pruscha began to dream of going to Tibet: perhaps he could even respond creatively to Mumford's call for critical regionalism in Tibet. He began to consider the possibilities of an architecture that did not preserve the regional style but reinvented it instead, so that it was very much of its locale and yet open to the modern.

This was New York in the early 1960s, an era of lingering optimism despite the prevailing racial tensions leading up to the civil-rights movement and the escalation of the Cold War with the widening military engagement in Vietnam. Mankind was traveling to outer space, after all, and in the years before his assassination, President John F. Kennedy had infused the world with a giddy idealism. Pruscha had embraced this idealism in choosing to settle in the United States. He had left Austria to make his mark in the world.

Upon consulting with Josep Lluís Sert, the dean of the Harvard Graduate School of Design, Pruscha went to meet Ernest Weissmann, who headed the United Nations' Department of Housing, Building, and Planning. Weissmann was an architect who had worked with Le Corbusier. Sert had told Pruscha that he would understand him. But when Weissmann learned of Pruscha's research methodology, he chided him: "You're a young man, you should be ashamed to research your Ph.D. thesis in a library! You should go to the field and conduct firsthand research!" Weissmann was in a position to offer him a UN job. Pruscha told him that he would accept it if he could go to work in Tibet. This Weissmann could not do.

Pruscha returned to researching his Ph.D., but his mind kept wandering to the far reaches of the world. At the Museum of Modern Art, he took in Bernard Rudofsky's iconoclastic exhibition, *Architecture without Architects*. The exhibition highlighted Indigenous structures that were still in use—sophisticated, innovative architecture—in regions yet unknown to the West, and had sparked considerable debate in architectural circles. It fired Pruscha's imagination. He began to realize that in order to look into the future, he may have to first look at the past.

Not long after their meeting, Weissmann called Pruscha to tell him that although he couldn't send him to Tibet, he had looked for alternatives: "Would Nepal be all right for you?" he asked. The country had opened up to the world in 1950, and had joined the United Nations five years later. "It's the closest alternative I could find," Weissmann told Pruscha. But there was a caveat: If he wanted the job, he would have to leave for Nepal in two weeks. Pruscha turned for advice to another Harvard professor, Eduard Sekler. He knew Sekler had been to Nepal a few years earlier, to the town of Patan in the Kathmandu Valley. "Should I quit my Ph.D. and go to Nepal?" Pruscha asked him. Sekler encouraged Pruscha to do just that.

It was a challenge, a dare, to leave New York, and the United States, with all of its rich promise, and to head off to a country that no one knew about. But Pruscha was given to making bold

Carl Pruscha with students in Harvard, 1963

Stupa in Boudhanath, Nepal, between 1964 and 1974

Nyatapola Temple in Bhaktapur, Nepal, between 1964 and 1974

Ashoka-type stupa in Patan, Nepal, between 1964 and 1974

decisions. Less so was his wife. Edda Velim was the daughter of his landlord in Vienna who had ended up sharing his studio apartment and then his life. Edda had been content in Austria, and had been reluctant to move to the United States in the first place. Having made the move, she had developed an interest in art restoration. She was also pregnant with their first child. She was not keen to move again, and especially not to Nepal. Pruscha persuaded her using every argument he could think of, and added that in any case the assignment was a short-term one. They could come back to New York in a year.

Once they made up their mind, leaving was easy. There was little to tie them to New York. The Porsche that Pruscha had bought in Germany when he had left Vienna had been destroyed in a crash. Their apartment on the sixteenth floor of a building in Washington Square was furnished with discards that he and Edda had picked up curbside. The terms of their lease required that they give the landlord three months' notice. They were unable to do so, choosing, instead, to abandon their furniture and steal away overnight.

There was no easy route to Kathmandu. The journey took Pruscha and Velim first to Japan, where they saw the some of the early masterpieces of modern architecture that were rebuilding and transforming postwar Tokyo. They also visited the temples of Kyoto and bought a Nikon camera along the way to document their adventures in Nepal. Their next stop was in Hong Kong, where they ordered chic, tailored outfits: white suits for him and dresses for her. From there, their journey took them to India: Calcutta first, and then onward to Patna. Only then could they board their final flight to Nepal.

They strained to look out of the window as the fixed-wing DC-3 airplane lowered into the lush green Kathmandu Valley and landed, improbably, in a grassy cow pasture. When they disembarked, they saw that the airport building was barely more than a hut. The scenery beyond was breathtaking, with blue hills lining the valley, and above them, the ethereal, shimmering Himalayas. It was springtime. They happened to arrive on the day of the Hindu festival of Holi. The sight of Nepalis tossing balloons and vividly colored powder reminded Pruscha of a happening by Carolee Schneemann, which he had seen a couple of months earlier in New York. But this, of course, wasn't a performance piece. It was life itself: the ecstasy he was witnessing was authentic. He had arrived at a culture that was touched, in all aspects, by art.

Not much about Nepal was known to outsiders at the time. James Hilton had mythologized the Himalayas as an idyll, Shangri-la, in his 1933 novel *Lost Horizon*. In 1957 Han Suyin had published *The Mountain Is Young,* a love story that featured a description of King Mahendra's coronation, which the author had attended. The Italian Orientalist Giuseppe Tucci had discarded his early belief in fascism and taken up research in Tibet, Nepal, and India. Several other Western scholars had followed suit, but for the most part, Nepal was still full of mystique.

Landscapes in the Kathmandu Valley during various seasons, 1965–1970

Pruscha relied on UN briefings to get his bearings. Nepal was ruled by an absolute monarch, King Mahendra Bir Bikram Shah, the eighth descendent of Prithvi Narayan Shah of Gorkha, who had conquered scores of kingdoms along the Himalayan foothills to found Nepal in 1768. In 1951, soon after India won its independence from Britain, King Mahendra's father, Tribhuvan Bir Bikram Shah, had overthrown the century-long rule of the Rana dynasty in Nepal. He had then opened Nepal to the world and led the country into an experiment with democracy. Upon inheriting the throne in 1955, King Mahendra briefly continued his father's democratic experiment, allowing for the country's first-ever elections to be held in 1959 before abruptly changing course and jailing the elected prime minister, Bisheshwar Prasad Koirala of the Nepali Congress party, a year later. King Mahendra had since outlawed all of Nepal's political parties and set up a polity called the Panchayat system, which kept him firmly at the helm of His Majesty's Government.

Pruscha soon learned that in addition to the family members of the ruling Shah dynasty, Nepal's governing class consisted of Ranas, Newars, and hill Brahmins. Though no longer in power, the Ranas still led the Royal Nepal Army. The wealth they had generated during their dynasty's rule, as well as their exposure to Britain, placed them at the top end of Kathmandu's high society.

Newars were indigenous to the Kathmandu Valley. The magnificent brick temples and palaces of Kathmandu, Patan, and Bhaktapur, and the myriad smaller settlements of the valley, had been built by the Newar community. Theirs was a sophisticated urban culture, with deep traditions of learning and philosophy. They spoke a Tibeto-Burmese language and observed a unique mix of Hindu and Buddhist rites with esoteric, and even secret, Tantric traditions.

Nepal's Brahmins, who were of the Hindu priestly caste, also enjoyed a strong intellectual tradition grounded in the Nepali and Sanskrit languages. Their material culture was relatively simple: they lived in Parbate houses (i.e. those of the hill people) built of mud in the outskirts and outlying hills.

The immense intricacy of Nepal's class, caste, and ethnic identities—with the 123 languages and just as many communities that are recognized today—would reveal itself to Pruscha gradually.

There were only two world-class hotels in Kathmandu in 1965. The Royal Hotel was run by Boris Lisanevich, a former ballet dancer from Russia who had moved from Calcutta to Kathmandu upon meeting King Tribhuvan and receiving an invitation. The other was the Hotel Shanker, newly founded by a prominent Newar businessman, Ram Shankar Shrestha. The UN put up Pruscha and Edda at Hotel Shanker. Like the Royal Hotel, it was an enormous Rana-era palace built in a derivative European style, part Versailles and part wedding cake in its ostentation. The Ranas had built several such palaces during their rule. They towered over their surroundings and bore no resemblance to the indigenous Newar architecture. Their absurd waste of space shocked Pruscha. They struck him as mirages, like *fata morgana* from another world. Pruscha soon settled into a work routine. Every morning, a driver

would show up in a battered old Moskvitch and take him to the government's Town Planning Office. This was housed in a roundabout with a temple to Bhadrakali, a fierce avatar of the Hindu goddess Durga, springing forth from the god Shiva, wearing a necklace of skulls and bearing weapons in each of her multiple hands: a phantasmagorical sight.

The Town Planning Office itself was modest, with only a few rooms and hardly any staff. It was headed by Krishna Raj Pandey, the chief engineer of the building department. There were not many statistics to work with, and there was only one accurate map in existence: a map of Kathmandu and Patan. The Town Planning Office did not even have a clear sense of its own mandate. The office that Pruscha had been assigned to as a UN advisor had no idea how to make use of him.

Pruscha quickly discovered that planning—even basic economic planning—was not quite a forte of Nepal's government. It was still an unfamiliar foreign practice. The Rana rulers had drafted the country's first-ever economic development plan, a twenty-year plan, in the early 1940s, but they had never implemented it. The final Rana ruler established a National Planning Committee in 1949, but its fifteen-year plan was scrapped when Rana rule ended two years later. In 1956 King Mahendra set up a new National Planning Commission and instituted the tradition of drafting five-year economic plans. The Commission's first plan met few of its targets and was openly acknowledged as a failure. After King Mahendra took absolute power in 1961, he directed the renamed National Planning Council to prepare a three-year plan. This plan had greater success, but the following plan, the five-year plan of 1965 was, once again, headed toward failure.

As for physical planning, there had been little in the modern era. The Kathmandu Valley had once been a lake, according to its origin myth, which was supported by geological evidence. Kathmandu, Patan, Bhaktapur, and the smaller Newar towns were laid out according to an invisible master plan in the form of a cosmic mandala, with boundaries demarcated by protective shrines, including those to the Astamatrika, or eight goddesses: Mahakali to the north, Mahalakshmi to the northeast, Brahmani to the east, Maheshwari to the southeast, Kaumari to the south, Bhadrakali to the southwest, Varahi to the west, and Indrani to the northwest. The shrines of other Hindu, Buddhist, and Tantric goddesses also dotted the valley: Vajrayogini, Vajravarahi, Guhyeshwari, Raktakali, Naradevi, Teleju, Sankata, Ugratara, Annapurna, and Harisiddhi. At the center stood the Shiva temple to Pashupati, the lord of animals, who forbade the use of animals for farming in the valley. This prohibition, as well as the traditional layout of the settlements, left much of the valley open. Generations of farmers had sculpted the rich alluvial soil into undulating terraced fields.

The Rana rulers had erected their European-style palaces and villas, each with their own fanciful gardens and follies, in the fields between the Newar settlements. They had constructed some roads to connect these palaces for the motor vehicles that, from 1881 onward, were carried into the valley on the backs of porters.

They had also built a few bridges and an electric power plant. A massive earthquake had struck in 1934. A rebuilding effort had followed. In 1956 Nepal's first architect, Kul Ratna Tuladhar, had overseen the construction of the Tribhuvan Highway, linking Kathmandu with the Indian border to the south. The valley's physical development had rapidly increased since then.

The Town Planning Office was itself only three years old. Nepal's government had opened it in 1962 under the directive of the jailed prime minister, Bisheshwar Prasad Koirala. Koirala had met Sweden's prime minister, Tage Erlander, at the UN General Assembly in New York two years previously. Both of their parties were affiliated with the Socialist International, and they quickly forged a bond. Grasping the importance of town planning to a newly modernizing country such as Nepal, Erlander had offered to send a Swedish planning expert to Nepal. This planner, Per Olof Lefvert, came and set up the Town Planning Office after Bisheshwar Prasad Koirala's arrest. Over the following two years, he helped to generate an accurate map of Kathmandu and Patan based on the aerial photographs of the geographer Toni Hagen, who had come to Nepal with Swiss aid projects in 1950. Lefvert had also outlined a proposal for a master plan for Kathmandu.

Given the political changes after Prime Minister Bisheshwar Prasad Koirala's arrest, there was some concern in the UN that the Town Planning Office might fall into disfavor. As he settled into his job, it dawned on Pruscha that the UN had hired him mainly to ensure the office's survival. His work there began modestly, by shifting the office at the roundabout to a new one in a run-down Rana villa nearby, in the neighborhood of Thapathali.

On the personal front, Pruscha was keen to move out of the Hotel Shanker, but found the prospect of living in a typical Nepali house, with its low, cramped dimensions, unsuitable to him and Edda. He found a European-style villa for rent in the quiet, leafy neighborhood of Maharajganj. It belonged to a "B-class" Rana, or a member of the Rana dynasty who had not been in the line of succession. The villa was shabby but pleasant, and it came with household staff. There was a cook, a young man who, to Edda's consternation, always insisted on tucking a sharp, gleaming *khukuri* knife into his belt. The cook also went to the market to shop for their food. A young woman did all of their washing and cleaning. Both were Tamangs, from the community that lived in the hills north and east of the Kathmandu Valley.

Next, Pruscha needed a car. The office driver was forever tardy, and his Moskvitch often ran out of petrol. Pruscha wanted to be as independent as possible from the UN, and he had always had a special fondness for cars. He had met, and struck up a friendship with, the outgoing director of the Peace Corps, George Zeidenstein, who had impressed him as an intellectual. Zeidenstein had a Jeep that Pruscha bought secondhand. From then on, he took to driving through the open roads of the valley, parking when he saw anything that interested him, and strolling through the settlements. Everything was novel, in equal measures arresting, mystifying, awe-inspiring, and humbling. He took in the resplendent towns

of Kathmandu, Patan, and Bhaktapur, studying not just the palaces and temples, but also the ordinary houses, brick-lined streets, private courtyards, and public squares. There was so much to see, even in the smaller settlements such as Harisiddhi and Bungamati: the *repoussé* statues in the temples; the woodwork adorning the posts; the ornate carved spouts of the water taps. At the start, it felt overwhelming, almost too intense to process. Pruscha would stare openly at everything as Nepalis, in turn, stared openly at him.

As an architect, he paid special attention, of course, to the materials and construction techniques of the buildings. In the Newar settlements, the buildings were all made of brick, even though there were no brick factories in Kathmandu. Workers had to fashion each brick individually, squeezing the clay to shape in wooden molds. It was extraordinary. Extraordinary, too, were the local bricklaying methods. To construct temples or palaces, bricklayers sun-dried some of the bricks and baked others in small makeshift kilns in the fields. They placed the harder baked bricks on the building's exterior, placing them flush atop each other, so that the surface looked smooth, with no mortar visible. But the bricks were tapered on the inside, and the bricklayers filled those gaps with clay mortar. They then placed a layer of sun-dried bricks on the interior, and treated them with cow dung and clay. The process was laborious yet completed with precision.

Newar temples and palaces also featured impressive quantities of timber, which was all brought in from the southern Tarai-Madhes flatlands. They were expensive to build. Private homes were simpler and cheaper, with rooms serving multiple purposes. They were often built around a common courtyard, with kitchens on the top floor so that the smoke protected the wood beams from rot. Pruscha could stroll around looking at the houses all day.

Just as breathtaking were the farmlands surrounding the settlements. Unlike elsewhere in Nepal, the farmers of the valley did not use bullocks. They transported all of their goods in an ingenious contraption called a *kharpan*—two baskets slung from a sturdy bamboo pole that rested on the shoulder. They ploughed their fields with a *halo,* or rudimentary hand hoe. They transformed the entire landscape into a sculpture using only their hands.

This was art—all of it. The Kathmandu Valley was a culture in the fullest sense of the word, and the people who had created it were artists of the highest caliber. Pruscha saw that saving the Kathmandu Valley was urgent—both to preserve its monuments and to find creative responses in the rest of the valley to the pressure to modernize. Any planning for Kathmandu would have to incorporate the entire valley and not just the towns, he realized. The landscape was just as precious as the settlements. Ideas began to form in Pruscha's mind, tantalizing Futurist ideas.

Besides Pruscha, the only other architect at the Town Planning Office was Shankar Man Pradhan. A Newar, Pradhan's ancestral home stood in a beautiful traditional courtyard in Patan. He had

1521

Carl Pruscha's first futuristic ideas for the development of the Kathmandu Valley, 1965

View from the Kathmandu Valley toward the High Himalayas

Carl Pruscha with bodyguard visiting the northern regions of Nepal, 1964

Carl Pruscha with a group of local *panchayat* leaders during a journey through the outer regions of Nepal, 1965

studied in India and seemed open to new ideas. Pruscha immediately took to him. The two began to discuss the need to incorporate the entire Kathmandu Valley into the process of planning. Pruscha also shared with Pradhan the Futurist plans that he was developing for the valley. Viewing Pradhan as his successor, Pruscha decided to recommend him for further studies. He arranged to send him to Philadelphia to study under the American architect Louis Kahn, whose exposed-brick buildings in Dhaka, Bangladesh, and in Ahmedabad, India, had earned him global renown. Kahn's use of traditional materials in modern buildings had blazed the trail for critical regionalism in South Asia. Pruscha was keen to bring his influence to Nepal. He could not have known that once in the United States, Pradhan would prolong his studies to pursue a Ph.D. Neither could Pruscha have anticipated that upon returning to Nepal, Pradhan would add several stories to his ancestral home and cement-plaster it in defiance of everything he had learned.

These disappointments—and the sinking realization that Nepal was rushing to modernize without much plan or preparation—were yet to come. At the start, Pruscha was optimistic and even naive. He was eager to launch into his main assignment at the Town Planning Office: to start working on a development plan for Kathmandu. Pruscha asked Pradhan to collect the maps and data for the Kathmandu Valley, but decided to concentrate his own efforts on regional planning. To create a regional plan, he needed to learn about the rest of Nepal. And for this, he needed partners, like-minded experts with whom he could collaborate.

He found one such expert in Harka Bahadur Gurung, a young Nepali university professor with a Ph.D. in geography from Edinburgh University. Gurung would go on to be a prominent figure in the country's policy-making and planning for decades to come. Another expert was Arie Beenhakker, a Ph.D. student at the Amsterdam School of Economics who went on to author *Kaleidoscopic Circumspection of Development Planning: With Contextual Reference to Nepal*. Together, Pruscha, Gurung, and Beenhakker formed a triangle incorporating the three legs of planning: the social, the economic, and the physical. The team worked independently of the Town Planning Office, and enjoyed a professional synergy that proved very productive.

Nepal's northern border with Tibet and China fell along the Himalayan belt, which was rugged and inhospitable yet inhabited, if sparsely. The country's border with India, along the east, west, and south, was open, with the free flow of citizens from both countries. The Mid-Hills were dotted with thousands of villages as well as a few towns, where the population was rising rapidly. The government had begun to clear the dense forests of the Tarai-Madhes, to resettle the hills' communities.

As for the country's larger geographic placement, Nepal falls directly north of the Great Asian Highway, or the main artery linking Europe and the Far East along the east–west contours of the Indo-Gangetic plain. In addition, the rivers that flow down from the Himalayas do not meet within Nepali territory: the country's river valleys are isolated from one another. It was therefore

Khokana, a town in the Kathmandu Valley known for its oil pressing, 1964–1973

Pruscha's proposal to introduce a new east–west "B-Route" of the Great Asian Highway through the length of Nepal. Not only would this connect the country's river valleys, it would also allow for new urban centers to develop at key north–south junctions such as Nepalgunj, Butwal, Raxaul, and Janakpur. This vision, one of a decentralized development model, began to take hold in the imagination of the team members.

As Pruscha delved into work, Edda was left by herself much of the time. The absence of a professional structure can make adjustment challenging for expatriate spouses. It did not help that in a harrowing turn, their *khukuri*-wielding cook had run away to India to enlist in that country's war against Pakistan. He had been killed almost immediately.

It was not easy to form friendships locally. Nepalis were not much given to mingling with foreigners in those days. Though their neighbors were friendly, they tended to keep to themselves. Even Pruscha's colleagues at the Town Planning Office rarely invited them out, though they themselves clearly enjoyed full social lives, attending family gatherings and festivals aplenty. As for the expatriate community, it was tiny. Officials at the American Embassy and United States Agency for International Development (USAID) related to Pruscha and Edda as fellow Americans because they held Green Cards. They reached out to them frequently. Most of the other diplomats stationed in Kathmandu, including UN officials, were formal in demeanor. Pruscha and Edda were hippies by comparison. Every day after work, Pruscha would come home and slip into a comfortable white kurta. Then he would light up a joint. Imported alcohol was not widely available in the shops then. Marijuana, which was both ubiquitous and legal, quickly became Pruscha's intoxicant of choice, so much so that his colleagues at the UN jokingly referred to him as their "marijuana advisor."

It was with fellow expatriates that Pruscha took his first trip outside of Kathmandu. Right from the start, he had been longing to see the Himalayas from closer up. Bernadette Vasseux, a young French woman who went on to spend most of her life in Nepal, was going on a trek to Helambu, in the hills north of Kathmandu, with a British painter, Peter Bennett. They invited Pruscha and Edda along. Edda was at a late stage of pregnancy and had to decline, but Pruscha was all too happy to accept. This was a purely private visit, a holiday to an entirely new and fantastical world. But it also taught Pruscha exactly how formidable it was to do any planning in Nepal. The conditions of the trek were grueling. The ups and downs of the trail exhausted Pruscha, and the jumping involved strained his knees. He had to cut holes into his cloth shoes in order to ford the rivers. The trail led the group into Tamang villages with their own Tibeto-Burmese language, as well as their distinct culture. The houses here did not resemble those in the Kathmandu Valley. Even there, there was variation between the homes of Newars and Parbates. Here, all of the buildings were made of cut stone, with simple wooden beams and sloping slate roofs, and the villages featured Buddhist stupas and monasteries.

Though everything was utterly foreign to Pruscha, every now and then he would see something—a stone house, a child herding sheep—that would transport him back to Tyrol, where his father had moved his family to keep them safe during World War II. He would remember the family's timber-frame house, where he had to gather water at the tap. As foreign as Nepal was, it was also knowable to him, somehow.

The trek focused Pruscha on his professional challenge: how to create a regional plan for a country as diverse as Nepal. Soon afterward, he, Harka Gurung, and Arie Beenhakker began to travel the country to research their regional plan. They took three field trips through the hills: to Rara in the west, through the Kali Gandaki Valley in the central mountains, and to Ilam in the east. They also visited towns in the Tarai-Madhes: Nepalgunj in the far west, Butwal and Hetauda in the center, and Janakpur in the east, to study the viability of constructing an east–west highway—the B-Route of the Great Asian Highway—through Nepal.

Ilam was accessible by road, and they could drive most of the way there. On the other trips, the team had to first fly to towns such as Biratnagar, Pokhara, and Nepalgunj, and then travel by foot or horse to the interior. Each field trip was a mini-expedition lasting about two weeks, with ten to twelve people in the team, including drivers, cooks, porters, and other support staff. They had to carry in all of their food, bedding, and tents.

The team's methodology was to speak directly to the officials of the local governments, which was called a *panchayat*, in order to gather empirical evidence and on-the-ground information to help draft the regional plan. Harka Gurung would ask the *panchayats* whether they had ever received aid: "Have you ever even applied for aid?" The team discovered that most *panchayats* lacked the wherewithal to articulate local needs, let alone to make them heard in faraway Kathmandu. The team's methodology went against the norm, given Kathmandu's top-down, centralized approach to governance. Most foreign governments and international aid organizations would send their representatives directly to the royal palace. All foreign-aid decisions were made—and all attendant financial transactions took place—at the highest levels. Many diplomats and aid officials saw little more of Nepal than their hotel rooms. Little of their aid trickled down to ordinary citizens. Pruscha was already learning that Kathmandu was very corrupt.

In between Pruscha's work and travel, Edda gave birth to their first child. After some debate, the couple had decided not to go to a hospital abroad but to rely on Nepal's first maternity ward, housed in a former Rana palace called Surendra Bhavan. It was not a state-of-the-art hospital, but it had a missionary doctor from Australia.

It was the monsoon season when they went for the delivery. The rain was pouring down onto the terraced fields, which were dense with ripening rice paddies. Water coursed through the irrigation canals onto the road. All of Kathmandu struck Pruscha as especially fecund on that day. It felt magical to bring a new life into

Views of villages in the Mugu District, 1965–1974

such fertility. The couple named their newborn daughter Alexandra Surendra Pruscha, and nicknamed her Bachcha, ("child" in Nepali). They brought in another helper at home to look after the baby.

For Pruscha, everything about that year was enchanted. But Edda was feeling some misgivings. It had not occurred to her, when marrying Pruscha, that he would become a world traveler. She did not want to be with someone so footloose.

"Your surname sounds like *purusha*," someone told him one day. "*Purusha* means 'man.' Did you know that?"

"Really?"

"Yes, your name means 'man' in Sanskrit."

He liked that a lot: Carl Purusha.

At the end of Pruscha's year in Nepal, his team presented a final report to the National Planning Commission. It outlined their decentralized vision for Nepal's development, with a new east–west highway along the Tarai-Madhes and new urban centers at key junctions. The team was well aware that the government wanted to place the highway further north, in the hills. Pruscha considered this frankly impractical: the terrain was much flatter to the south. But such decisions, of course, were not his to make. As a UN advisor, he could only offer recommendations. It was up to His Majesty's Government to follow them—or not.

With this, Pruscha's one-year term in Nepal came to an end. He had tried, without success, to extend his contract. The younger staff at the National Planning Commission were in favor of this, and had an invitation letter drafted on behalf of His Majesty's Government. The UN, however, declined. The prevailing view appeared to be that Pruscha had succeeded merely by keeping the Town Planning Office in operation. His mission in Nepal was complete. This truly disappointed Pruscha. He had fallen in love with this part of the world. Since there was no reason to return to New York, he and Edda decided to go to Vienna. They stopped in Sri Lanka on the way, renting a beachside hut. And Pruscha was awed once again by the sheer beauty of the place and the people. One day, the couple left their baby at home to go on an outing, and upon return, found her cradled in a juice vendor's arms. The vendor had heard her crying and gone to comfort her. This moved Pruscha profoundly. He felt completely at home in Asia.

Edda was ambivalent. She didn't believe that Pruscha would get back his job in Nepal, and, in any case, she wasn't entirely satisfied with their marriage. Upon returning to Vienna, she initiated a divorce. Pruscha was at a loose end when Karl Schwanzer, the head of the architecture department at the Technical University in Vienna, together with architect Günther Feuerstein invited him to lecture at the University of Technology on his Futurist ideas and his experiences in Nepal. At the lecture, Pruscha struck up a friendship with Wolf Prix, a student who would go on to found a movement for deconstructivist architecture. The university students responded well to the links that Pruscha made between Futurism and faraway places like Nepal. Afterward, they began to flock to Pruscha as though he were a guru.

Farewell after one year in Nepal, 1965

But Pruscha did not want to stay in Vienna. He turned for advice to his former employer in New York, Paul Lester Wiener, who had always treated him well, almost as a son. Wiener had studied in Vienna, and knew Adolf Loos and other Modernist and Bauhaus architects. Having married into New York's high society, he was well placed to host European artists such as Joan Miró and Marcel Duchamp when they visited the US. Wiener helped Pruscha obtain a minor teaching assignment at Columbia University.

After settling into the Hotel Owl in Washington Square, Pruscha began to immediately search for a way back to Nepal. He learned that officials at the UN's Housing Department tended to dismiss his concepts as mere intellectual games. They wanted to send someone more senior and conventional as his replacement.

For support, Pruscha reconnected with the former director of the Peace Corps in Nepal, George Zeidenstein, who had since become the director of the Ford Foundation in New York. Zeidenstein told him that the Ford Foundation could send him to Nepal for a year to research his Ph.D. Pruscha then returned to the UN and finally convinced the officials at the Housing Department to hire him back. In the end, the UN's success in any country relied on the cooperation of the host government. Pruscha's invitation letter held him in very good stead. The officials agreed that he could return to Nepal on the condition that he work under the supervision of the UN's regional office in Bangkok.

Contract in hand, Pruscha closed up in New York in the spring of 1967 and returned to Vienna via Montreal, where he went to see the Israeli-Canadian architect Moshe Safdie's Futurist housing project Habitat '67. Then he stopped by London to pick up a red Jaguar sports car that he had ordered. Dressed in voguish new clothes, he felt like a rock star, successful, glamorous, and thoroughly beloved, when he arrived in Vienna. There he persuaded Edda to remarry him and join him in Nepal. They decided that he would go first and she would follow with their daughter.

Returning to Nepal felt like a homecoming to Pruscha. This time, he flew into Kathmandu from Delhi, landing on a runway that had been freshly paved over with the Israeli government's assistance. Pruscha no longer found Kathmandu as exotic as he had on his first arrival, but he was excited to be back. He rented a bungalow on the north side of the Narayanhiti Palace, where Edda and their daughter would join him at the end of the year.

Pruscha resumed work at the Town Planning Office, collaborating more closely with Chief Engineer Krishna Raj Pandey of the Building Department this time around. The two were collegial with each other, but their visions did not quite match: Pruscha's concepts for Kathmandu's development were decidedly Futurist. As distilled into an illustration that he drew, all future settlements would be built on, and even into, the hills of the valley rim. A section of the valley would be covered with solar panels to supply electricity. The airport would have vertical takeoff and landing stations. All industries would be located outside the valley, with only two major roads being built through Kathmandu. Together,

Pruscha's own house in Bansbari, Kathmandu, 1968

these measures would prevent the valley's agricultural lands from being built on. This was Pruscha's vision for preserving not just the monument sites of the valley but the entire landscape—which he considered as a man-made sculpture—while accommodating all necessary and inevitable growth.

Pandey's focus was more pragmatic; and his pragmatism won out, as it was the prerogative of Nepal's government to set its own agenda. George Kondracki, a Polish physical planner at the UN's Regional Office in Bangkok, also steered Pruscha into line. Kondracki visited Nepal a number of times, and Pruscha, too, went to Bangkok to seek the Regional Office's cooperation. By September 1967 the Town Planning Office was ready to begin its first major undertaking: to publish a comprehensive development plan of the Kathmandu Valley. This would be a historical document: Nepal's first-ever modern urban plan.

The work began in January 1968 under Pandey and Pruscha's joint leadership.

Right off, the government restructured the Town Planning Office, placing it under the Department of Housing and Physical Planning, which was in the Ministry of Public Works, Transport, and Communications. Pruscha also hired a young US-educated architect, Madhav Bhakta Mathema, and a draftsman, P. K. Sharma, to remodel the office to give it a more functional layout. The office then set up separate mapping and statistics units. Pruscha put together a methodology for data collection and analysis. A group of Danish students who had bused into Kathmandu through Turkey and the Khyber Pass had agreed, on Pruscha's suggestion, to measure the town of Bungamati to scale. Pruscha transferred their methodology to the office and assigned Madan Man Singh Tamrakar and Wolfgang Korn to do the same for the town of Khokana. Other teams followed suit, and the mapping unit soon swelled to fifteen staff who began to measure Kathmandu by hand, using tapes, strings, markers, and levels, in groups of four or five. The statistics unit, similarly, gathered and collated all existing data from every government department. They also sent questionnaires to the *panchayats* to gather socioeconomic data and conducted firsthand field visits.

The development plan tapped into the expertise of Harka Bahadur Gurung and Arie Beenhakker, as well as thirty-two other experts in fields as diverse as archaeology, hydrology, cultural history, and meteorology. It fell to Pruscha to compile their data and analyses, as well as to oversee the preparation of the plates for publication. The work was arduous and time-consuming, and entailed much drudgery, but its value was unquestionable. For the very first time, Nepal's government was acquiring baseline information about the country.

There was no printing press in Nepal capable of publishing a document of the required format. The office had to find a press in Calcutta. The press was difficult to deal with long-distance, so Pruscha made a plan to take the plates to Calcutta and oversee the publication himself at the start of 1969.

This was the beginning of Pruscha's work as a straightforward planner. In retrospect, he would look back at his earlier Futurist

concepts as theoretical, and more suited to academia than to practice. Although he never let go of them entirely, his immersion in the nuts and bolts of planning in Nepal challenged and ultimately matured him.

Pruscha also began to work on some architectural projects on the side. This started entirely by chance. He was looking for a nicer home for his family when Krishna Raj Pandey told him he was just building one. Only the foundation had been laid. He offered it to Pruscha for rent, and said he could even supervise its construction. The idea appealed to Pruscha. He signed away half of his salary in rent. There were still no brick factories or timber mills, and all of the glass, cement, and iron rods available in Kathmandu were imported from India, China, or even further afield. Pruscha deputized someone to buy all of the materials. Then, when he received the house plans, he burned them and replaced them with a design of his own.

Though traditional Newar houses were unsuited to his needs, Pruscha appreciated their fine craftsmanship. He wanted to fuse the vernacular architecture of Kathmandu with his own global aesthetics to design a house that was thoroughly modern and yet uniquely Nepali. Modern buildings were cropping up with increasing frequency in Kathmandu. A Swiss architect, Robert Weise, had come to Nepal in 1957 with Swiss aid projects and designed a master plan for Nepal's first university, Tribhuvan University, along with several hotels, offices, and residential buildings. In 1963 King Mahendra had replaced the old Narayanhiti Palace with a modern structure designed by a Calcutta-based firm run by an Indian engineer, Binoy K. Chatterjee, with an American architect, Benjamin Polk.

Pruscha dismissed these buildings as "service station architecture," inappropriate for habitation. He especially disliked the romantic pastiche of traditional elements that evoked a nationalist aesthetic. He had seen the dangers of such nationalism in his childhood in Austria. In his design, he wanted to be true to the contemporary global moment, for Nepal was, after all, part of the present world and not a relic of the past. The house that he designed was a response to Lewis Mumford's call for critical regionalism: It was disarmingly simple, with two airy, interlocking triangles as the main structure, and a small car port to the side. Pruscha did not use cement because it offered poor insulation. Instead, he used traditional materials, mainly brick and timber.

The interior of the house was laid out according to use. The nursery and all of the public spaces, including those used by guests and the household staff, were located on the ground floor. Pruscha designed a sunken floor for the living room so that people could sit low to the ground, in the Nepali style, without having to cross their legs. The more private spaces were upstairs: separate rooms for him and Edda, and a sitting room with a terrace. None of the stairways in the house had balustrades, as Pruscha despised railings. His abiding fascination was with platforms, whether these be to sit, stand, climb up, or sleep on. He was also particularly interested in the tension between large and small

Carl Pruscha with Edda, Tom and Marge Dove, on a boat trip in the Terai, ca. 1972

scales. The big glass windows of the house allowed those inside to feel situated amid the trees and terraced fields outside.

Krishna Raj Pandey came to see the house only when its construction was complete. He did not seem to care, or indeed to notice, that the house deviated significantly from its original plans.

Edda became pregnant with their second child after they moved into the house. The couple enjoyed living there, as did their daughter. The neighboring children would come over, or she would go to play with them in their simple Nepali homes. Edda became fast friends with a neighbor, the Bhutanese Prime Minister Lhendup Dorji's sister, Tashi Dorji. They also got to know fellow neighbors Radhe Shyam Saraf, who was making a name for himself as a tourism entrepreneur. Saraf would take Pruscha horse riding some mornings, and the vision of the valley's temples and shrines, towns and open fields would shimmer before them like a dream.

This time around, Pruscha and Edda also forged closer links to diplomats. The US ambassador to Nepal, Carol Laise, had recently married US Ambassador at Large Ellsworth Bunker. She and the embassy staff—Public Affairs Officer Tom Dove and his wife, Marge, and Rod Wright and his wife, Luisa—were always kind to them. They were not even sure what Rod Wright did at the embassy; he might have been with the CIA. Such politics didn't matter to the couple. They also became close to Zenon Zielinski, a Polish engineer who had designed lightweight concrete casts in Calcutta, after he came to introduce them to Kathmandu. He and his wife, Czeslawa Bychowska, an architect, became like family.

As before, the family had a cook, Hem Bahadur Tamang, as well as a housekeeper who also did the gardening, Nara Bahadur Tamang. They also had nannies—Lali, Kalpana, and Kumari—for childcare. Edda hired a Tibetan tailor, Ngawang, for more than a year to sew curtains and drapes for the house, and Nepali-style dresses for her and her daughter. Family photographs show the mother and child dressed in graceful local attire. But the discord between Edda and Pruscha never eased: there were times when the two were close, and times when they drifted apart, taking other lovers. What they shared was a life of adventure. They visited all of the temples, even Dakshinkali during the Dashain festival, when Nepalis sacrificed buffalos, staining the grounds with blood. They observed all of the festivals, including Machhendranath, when the Newar community pulled the deity from town to town in a chariot.

At one point, the couple flew to Calcutta to pick up a white Austin-Healey that Pruscha had ordered from London. By the time they reached the port, however, all of its removable parts, including the windshield, had been stolen. Instead of driving the vehicle straight back, they decided to take a detour through Banaras. The road conditions were rough, even on the highway, and passing trucks kept driving them into the ditch. The chassis was low to the ground. The suspension was quickly damaged. Pruscha and Edda proved quite an attraction when they drove into Banaras, where crowds gathered to gawk at their odd, battered car.

The Austin-Healey broke down completely on their onward drive in the Indian border town of Muzaffarpur. A truck-repair

Carl Pruscha and his daughter Alexandra on Austin-Healey sports car, 1968

Alexandra with Lhasa Apso dogs, 1986

workshop came to their rescue, jerry-rigging a Jeep's frame onto the vehicle to raise its back high off the ground. Now they could go off-road as needed. This was the vehicle they drove for the rest of their time in Nepal.

When it came time to print *The Physical Development Plan for the Kathmandu Valley*, Pruscha went to Calcutta with the plates that had been finalized in Kathmandu. The plates contained two precious years of groundbreaking research and analysis and conceptual work.

The Ganges Printing Company was in Howrah, across town from Pruscha's hotel. The owner sent a van to pick him up, and the driver asked him to sit in the back, which had no window and only one seat: an armchair. After the driver shut the door and drove off, Pruscha wondered if he were being kidnapped. It turned out to be a precaution for his own security. There was unrest in Calcutta. Sitting in the dark in the windowless van, Pruscha could hear rioting outside on the streets.

The printing press was not well equipped to print and clothbind a book of this size. The owner kept grumbling that it was too work for too little payment, and even claimed that he had been forced to spend some of his payment on a bribe.

When the printing and binding were complete in May 1969, the result was a 196-page book offering a comprehensive background of Nepal and the Kathmandu Valley, an analysis of the physical setting, people, activities, and mobility, a series of recommendations for development, and plans for the implementation of these recommendations.

The plan began, as did all publications by His Majesty's Government, with an inspirational epigram from King Mahendra, capitalized for emphasis: "PLANS FOR THE OVERALL DEVELOPMENT OF THE COUNTRY SHOULD BE IMPLEMENTED ONLY AFTER A CAREFUL EXAMINATION OF THEIR RESOURCES, THEIR PROPER UTILIZATION, AND THEIR IMPACT ON THE NATIONAL ECONOMY." A photograph of the king graced the first page, and the facing page showed the government seal, with all the Panchayat system's chosen nationalist symbols: soldiers, a cow, a pheasant, rhododendrons, a Hindu temple, mountains, the sun and moon, *khukuri* knives, flags, and footsteps, topped by the crown. Minister for Public Works, Transport, and Communications Rudra Prasad Giri and the secretary of the same ministry, B. B. Pradhan, wrote forewords for the plan, as did the chief engineer of the Building Department, Krishna Raj Pandey, who outlined his office's history and acknowledged Pruscha's particular contribution: "Mr. Pruscha's views were that in order to plan the Capital, it was necessary to study the Kathmandu Valley as a whole, thus introducing the concept of regional physical planning."

The plan first placed Kathmandu's urban development in the context of the valley and the nation. Its conceptualization laid the foundation for all of Nepal's future plans. It distilled the country's complex topography—with the plains of the Tarai-Madhes, the low-lying Churia Hills, the higher hills of the Mahabharat range, the Himalayan range, and, in western and central Nepal,

Title page and book cover of *The Physical Development Plan for the Kathmandu Valley*, 1969

the Tibetan marginal mountains—into three broad regions: The Tarai, the Midland (or Mid-Hills), and the Himalayas. Next came a national survey of regional climates, cultural and ethnic identities, population and settlement patterns, agriculture and circulation patterns, transport infrastructure, economy, resources, and tourism. Nepal's population was 10 million at the time. Then the plan narrowed in on its primary subject: Kathmandu. *The Physical Development Plan for the Kathmandu Valley* envisioned itself as a development tool: a pilot program to be emulated throughout the country. As such, it was the launch of what was supposed to be an ongoing exercise in planning.

At the time of the latest census, from 1961, Kathmandu had a population of 459,990 living in its 475 square kilometers. About half of the population was engaged in nonagrarian employment, the highest percentage nationwide.

In its introductory section, the plan examined the geology, hydrology, and meteorology of the valley. It also reviewed the valley's history, beginning with the Kirati era (seventh century BC–second century AD), the Licchavi era (third–twelfth century AD), and the Malla era (thirteenth–eighteenth century AD), and ending with the Shah era (from 1768 onward). It noted the syncretic mix of Buddhism and Brahminism, dominated by Shiva worship, in the valley. Both faiths included Tantric traditions.

The next section, "Analysis," laid out the detailed information required for planning. Read today, it captures a Kathmandu past, one almost—though not wholly—subsumed by the present-day sprawl. The settlement patterns then were defined by Newar towns, both large and small, with less homogenous Chhetri, Brahmin, Tamang, Bhote, and Magar settlements interspersed in between. The plan compared the structure of Newar town houses with those of the freestanding houses of the Parbate people from the hills, including the Tamangs, whose houses were very rudimentary. After surveying the rural settlements, the plan offered a breakdown of caste identities, family sizes, and memberships in the traditional cooperative institutions of the Newar community, or *guthi*.

Then came carefully measured maps of individual settlements: Thankot, Khokana, Kirtipur, Bungamati, Chapagaon, Sankhu, Bauddha, and Ward No. 7 of Kathmandu's urban core. More detailed studies of Kathmandu, Patan, and Bhaktapur (then called Bhadgaon) followed, with analyses of the population, economy, land use, production and employment, and trade and commerce.

The bulk of the Analysis section was dedicated to collating data and information. After reviewing the government structure established after 1961—with 14 zones, 75 districts and local bodies called *panchayats*—it surveyed the national education and health services, and moved on to tourism. Here, with the identification of monument zones, it touched on a subject that it would return to at the end, one that was to be the central focus of Pruscha's remaining years in Nepal. The plan went on to review economic activities and land use, as well as the existing transportation and telecommunications and utilities infrastructure, before arriving at its crux: "Recommendations". Here, the plan reiterated its vision of Kathmandu as part of the valley, with its history, culture, settlement pattern, and human activity, as well as of the larger regional context. Noting that the existing population distribution was not accepted as unalterable, it clarified its goal to design infrastructure to the maximum projected level of use, given the rapid population growth rate.

As it proceeded through the various categories—urbanization and housing, circulation and utilities, public services and institutions, production and employment, culture, tourism, and recreation—the plan expressed support for the government's program to relocate part of the hill population in the Tarai-Madhes. It outlined its vision for guided growth in the Kathmandu-Patan areas, which contained the highest density in the valley, with the construction of a direct route to the Tarai-Madhes. It also called for planned growth in and around Bhaktapur, with greater vitalization and expansion. The plan recommended strengthening existing economic activities, especially agriculture, as well as strengthening services and facilities in rural areas to prevent urbanization. It promoted nontraditional means, such as bungalow-type housing in high-income areas alongside low-income housing, with development that was mindful of cultural use patterns. Its overarching vision was of multinucleated development, with compact settlements being linked through a limited number of new transportation networks.

The plan's final section, "Implementation", distilled all of the data, research, observation, and concepts of the previous sections into several action points. These began with the need to establish a Department of Housing, Building, and Physical Planning; to attain administrative approval of the plan; to have the government implement the plan swiftly; and to create a legal framework for regional and town planning, a framework that did not exist in Nepal. The plan emphasized the measures required to alleviate overcrowding in the core areas and to create a second major growth area in Bhaktapur. This required zoning for urban and rural land use, planned development for various zones, and a long-term commitment to a multinucleated development of the valley. The immediate action points that the plan called for were: the establishment of a government center, planning for Tribhuvan University, planning for Kathmandu's city core, the design of prototype houses, and the establishment of special-purpose zones and sites—including for historical districts, monument zones, temple and monument sites, and recreational zones.

In Pruscha's understanding, *The Physical Development Plan for the Kathmandu Valley* was to serve not just as a baseline study but as a resource, one that would require continual updating and rethinking. The Town Planning Office, however, treated it more as a final output and sought to move on to its implementation. Officials at the Ministry of Public Works did not invite Pruscha when they presented the plan to King Mahendra. They did involve him afterward, in an internal gathering at the Ministry to mark the plan's official release. The plan's vision for Kathmandu's development generated excitement and garnered wide praise. The government eventually followed up on many of its recommendations, including an act, the Town Planning Implementation Act, in 1972.

Daughter Czeslavia, 1971

Carl Pruscha with his daughters, 2013

The plan certainly became a baseline study, but it never became the resource that Pruscha had intended it to be.

Pruscha's and Edda's second daughter was born after the release of the plan, in the autumn of 1969. They named her Czeslavia after their friend Cseslawa Bychowska. Judy Chang, a Chinese-American Peace Corps volunteer working at the Town Planning Office, suggested they nickname the baby Meme ("younger sister" in Mandarin), or perhaps even Shaume ("beautiful younger sister"). Meme was the nickname that stuck.

Nepal was changing rapidly in the 1970s. In the two decades since it had opened to the world, the country had experienced unprecedented growth. By the 1970s the population was growing by more than 2.1 percent per year, with the Kathmandu Valley's population increasing by almost half every decade. As the government built the roads and other infrastructure outlined in *The Physical Development Plan for the Kathmandu Valley*, there was no stopping unplanned development. Side roads opened up off the major arteries, and houses went up ad hoc on the terraced fields. Pruscha's vision of the valley as an artwork, a sculpture, was vanishing rapidly.

Another major change had to do with theft. Nepal was innocent of its own cultural uniqueness in 1950. From then on, those who recognized the value of the artifacts in Kathmandu's public spaces, temples, and private homes began to steal and smuggle them to sell to private collectors and museums abroad. When Pruscha first landed in Kathmandu, rumors were already rife about art theft by aid workers, Orientalist scholars, diplomats, and world travelers. Since then, the pace of theft had only accelerated. A work of art shown off to visiting diplomats one day would disappear the next. Statues of deities at roadside shrines would go missing overnight. Entire chunks of temples would be broken off. Religious texts would no longer be found at Buddhist monasteries. People talked in hushed tones about shady smuggling rings that enjoyed the protection of Kathmandu's most powerful circles, all the way up to the royal palace.

Pruscha was acutely aware that Nepal was changing underfoot. He knew that in the absence of government will, there was little he could do to halt unplanned development. For the rest of his time in Nepal, he would turn his attention to one of the most important recommendations of *The Physical Development Plan for the Kathmandu Valley*: to inventory the valley's cultural wealth.

Maps of the Kathmandu Valley, from the publication *The Physical Development Plan for the Kathmandu Valley*, 1969

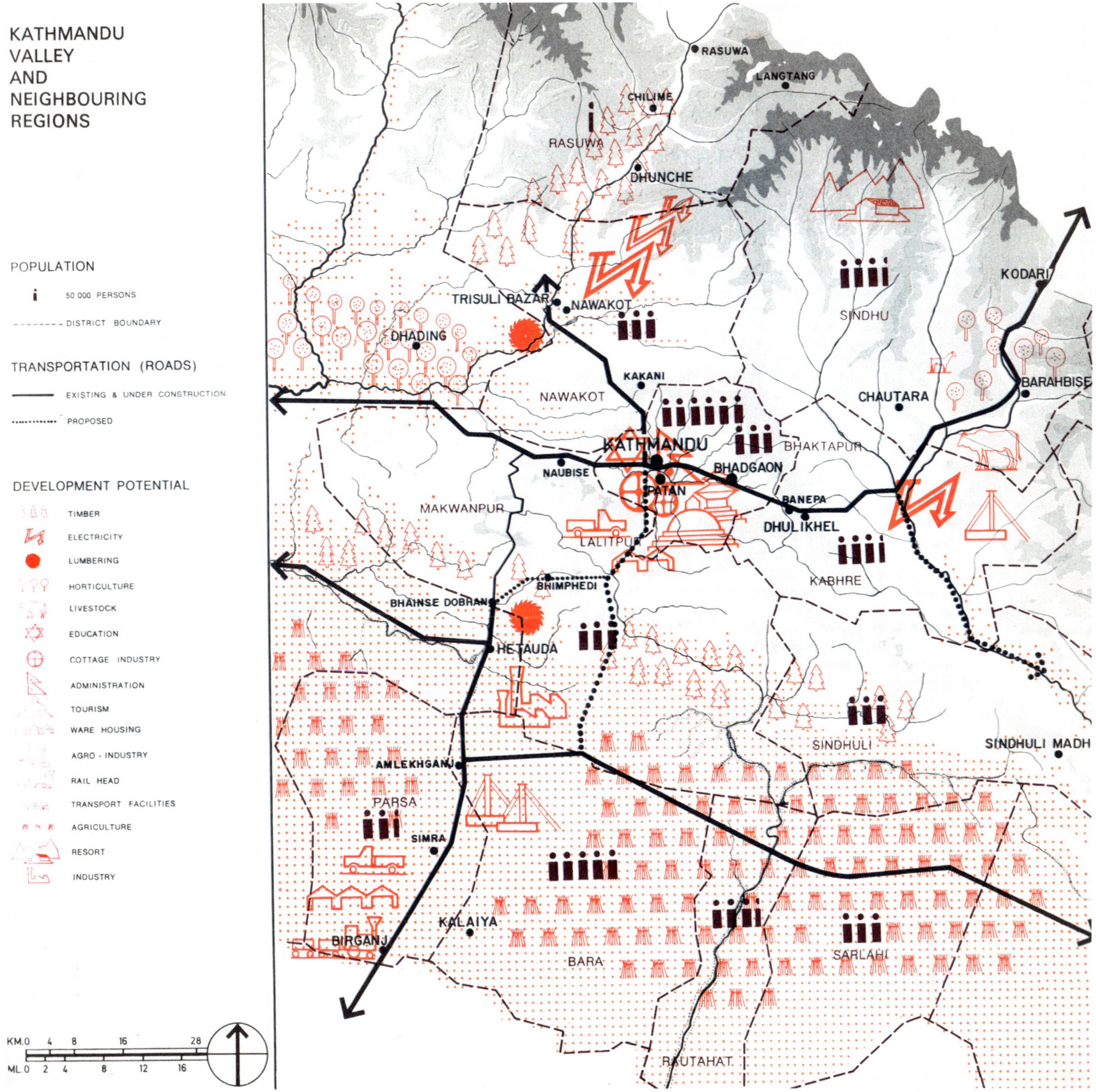

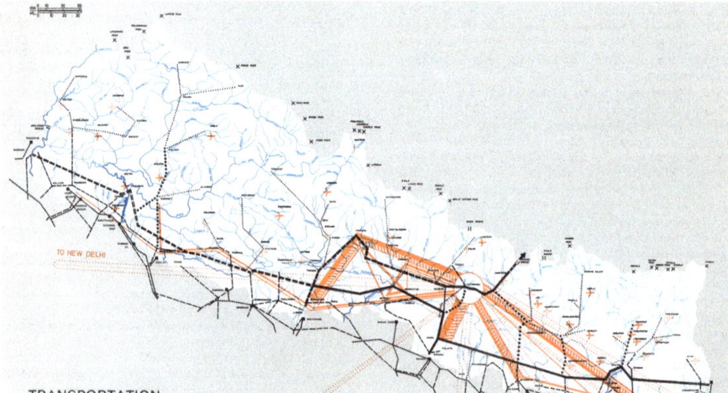

TRANSPORTATION
SURFACE AND AIR

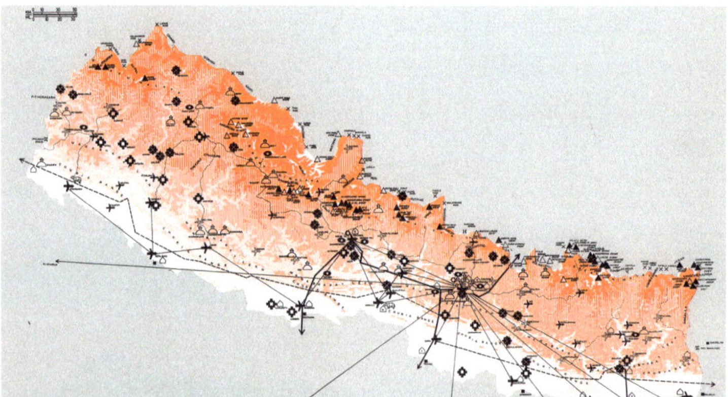

POTENTIALS FOR TOURISM

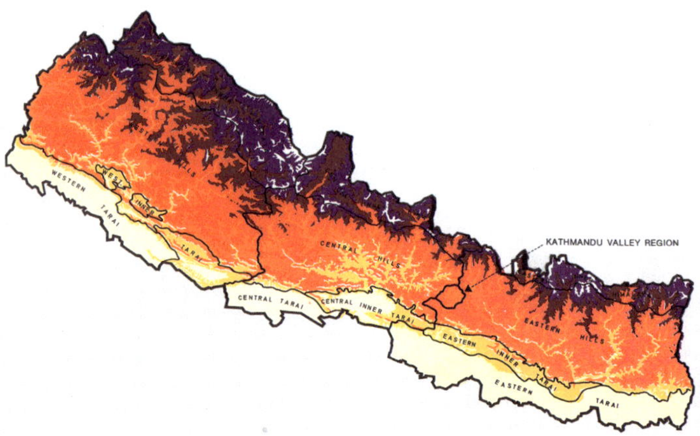

(d) Kathmandu-Pokhara Road: The mineral potentials of this area are still unknown. Mapping work is being carried out.

Apart from these, special mention must be made regarding slate occurrences. It occurs at numerous localities and is of varying qualities.

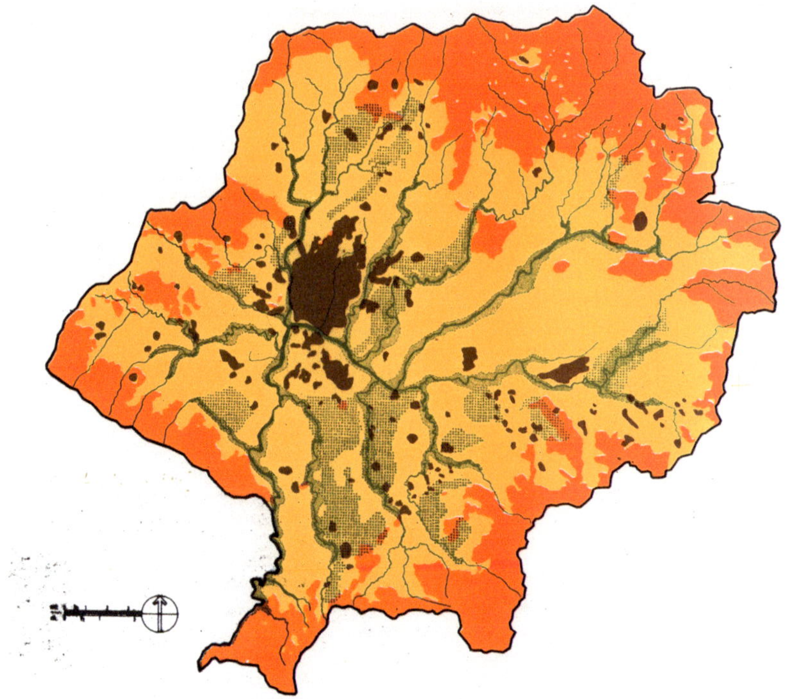

GENERALISED LAND USE

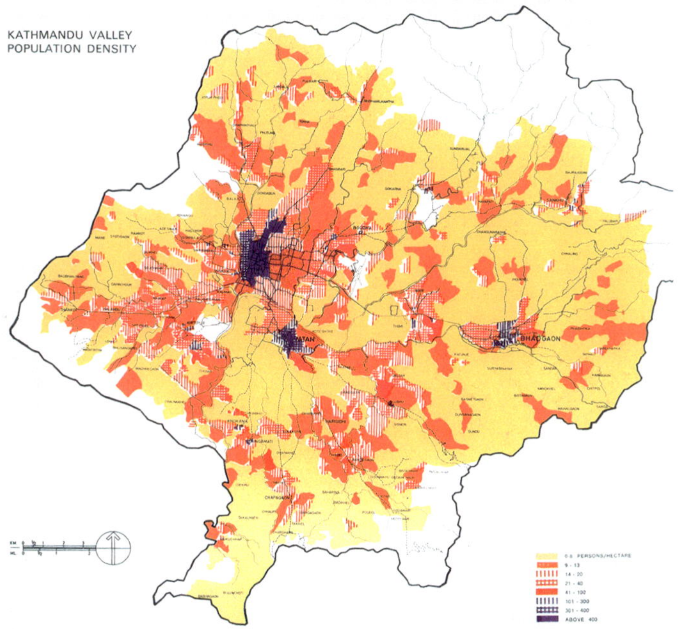
KATHMANDU VALLEY
POPULATION DENSITY
PATAN
BHADGAON
0-8 PERSONS/HECTARE
9 - 13
14 - 20
21 - 40
41 - 100
101 - 300
301 - 400
ABOVE 400

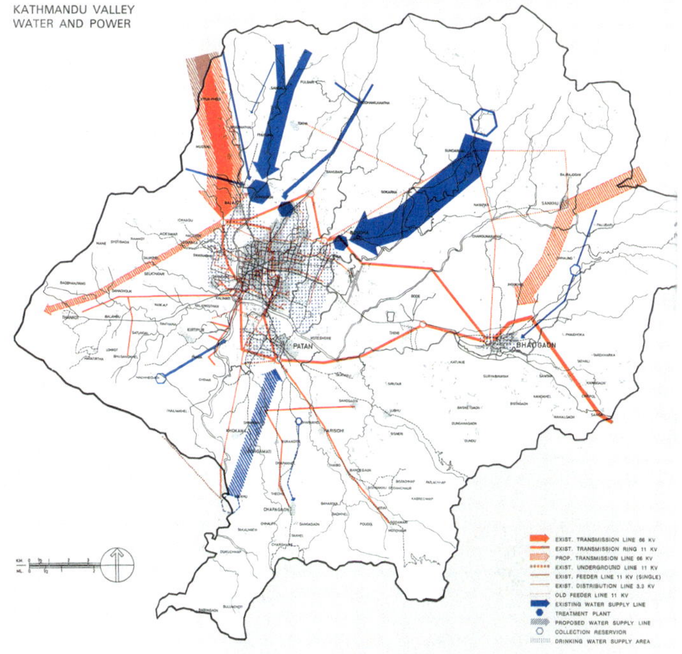
KATHMANDU VALLEY
WATER AND POWER
PATAN
BHADGAON
EXIST. TRANSMISSION LINE 66 KV
EXIST. TRANSMISSION RING 11 KV
PROP. TRANSMISSION LINE 66 KV
EXIST. UNDERGROUND LINE 11 KV
EXIST. FEEDER LINE 11 KV (SINGLE)
EXIST. DISTRIBUTION LINE 3.3 KV
OLD FEEDER LINE 11 KV
EXISTING WATER SUPPLY LINE
TREATMENT PLANT
PROPOSED WATER SUPPLY LINE
COLLECTION RESERVIOR
DRINKING WATER SUPPLY AREA

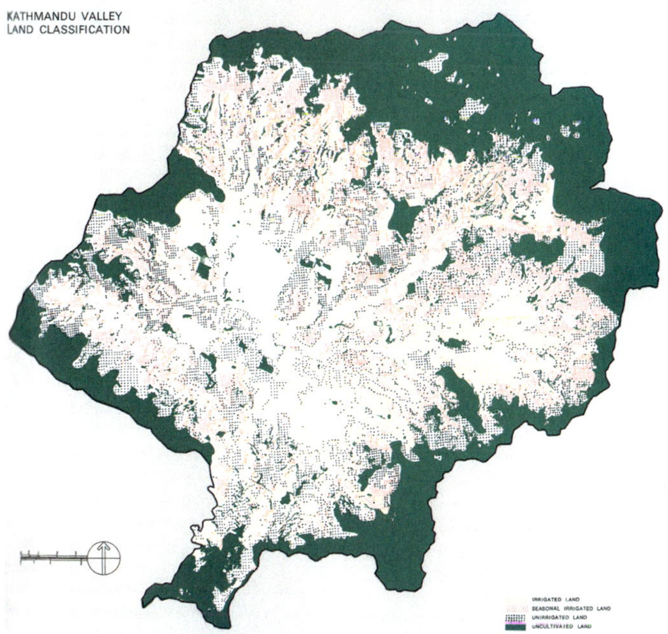
KATHMANDU VALLEY
LAND CLASSIFICATION
IRRIGATED LAND
SEASONAL IRRIGATED LAND
UNIRRIGATED LAND
UNCULTIVATED LAND

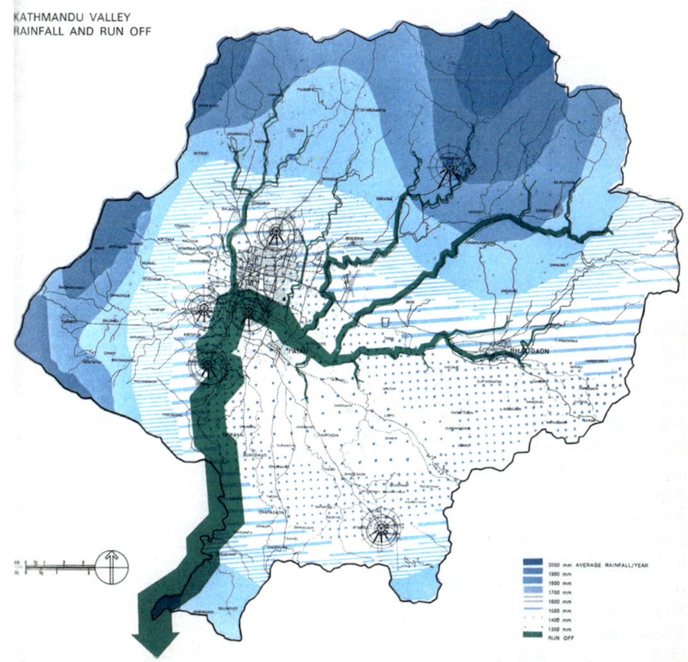
KATHMANDU VALLEY
RAINFALL AND RUN OFF
BHADGAON
2000 mm AVERAGE RAINFALL/YEAR
1900 mm
1800 mm
1700 mm
1600 mm
1500 mm
1400 mm
1300 mm
RUN OFF

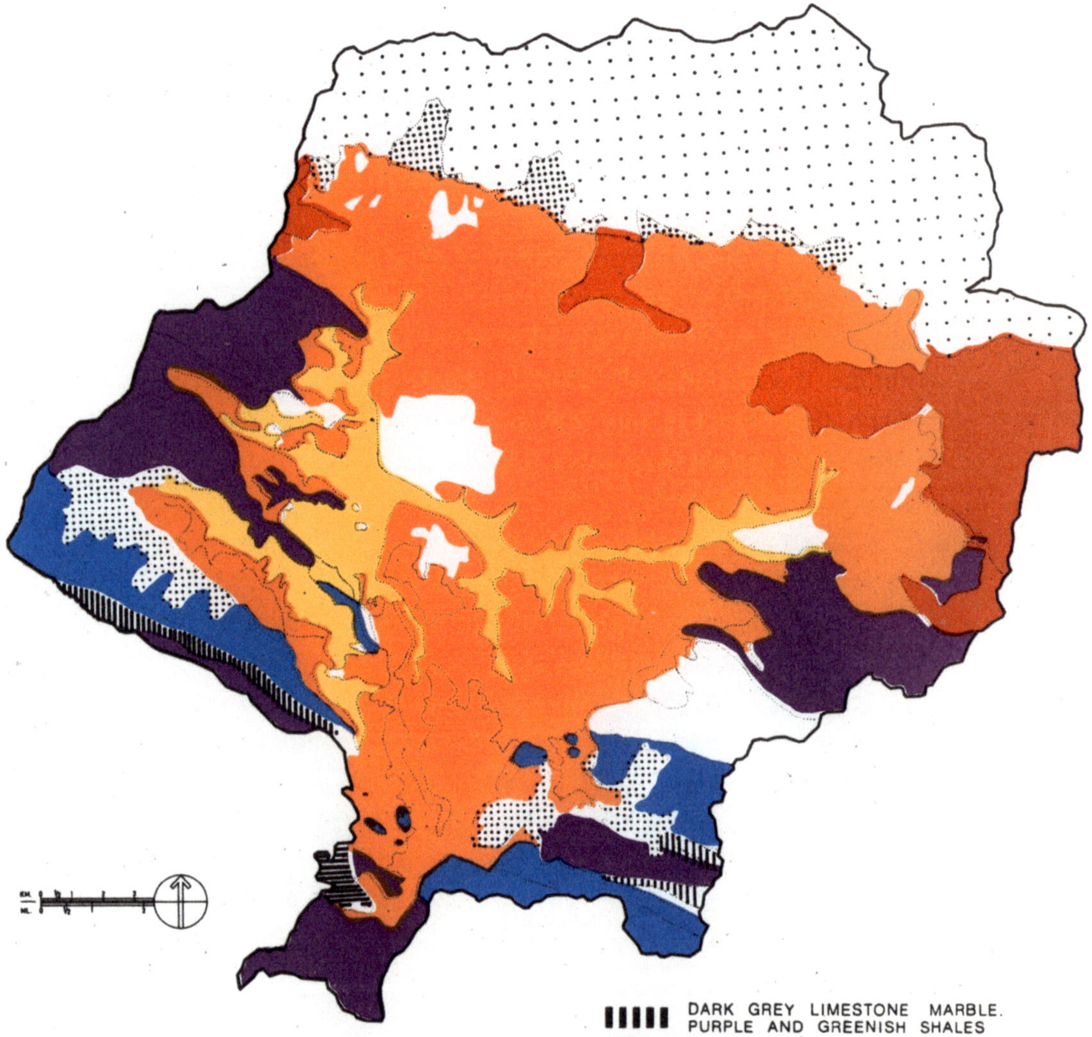

GEOLOGICAL CHARACTERISTICS

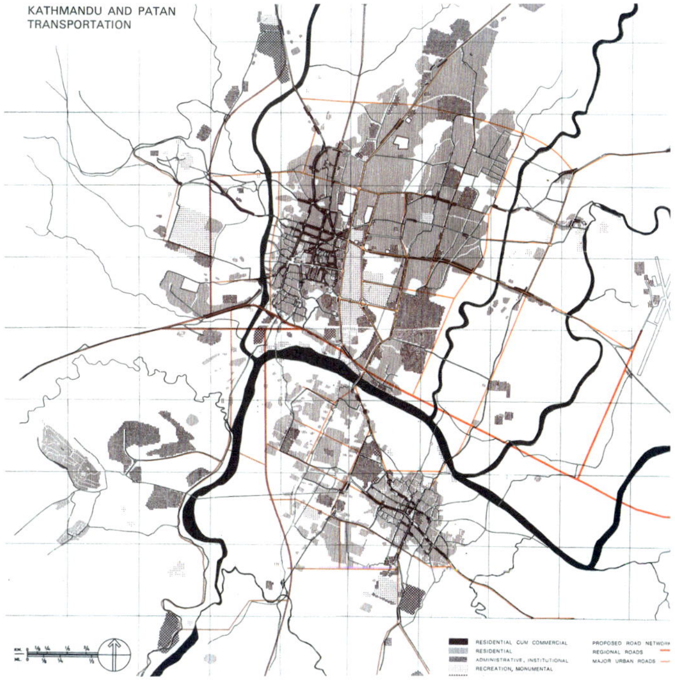
KATHMANDU AND PATAN
TRANSPORTATION
RESIDENTIAL CUM COMMERCIAL
RESIDENTIAL
ADMINISTRATIVE, INSTITUTIONAL
RECREATION, MONUMENTAL
PROPOSED ROAD NETWOR
REGIONAL ROADS
MAJOR URBAN ROADS

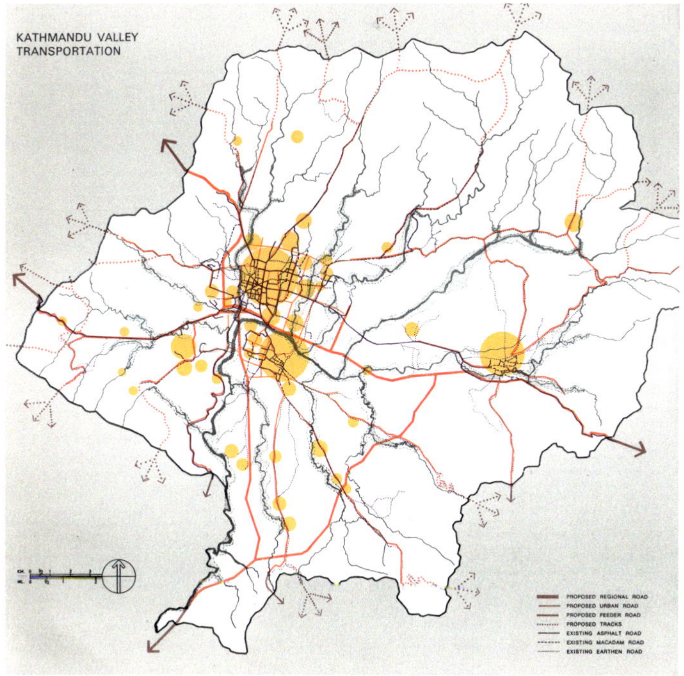
KATHMANDU VALLEY
TRANSPORTATION
PROPOSED REGIONAL ROAD
PROPOSED URBAN ROAD
PROPOSED FEEDER ROAD
PROPOSED TRACKS
EXISTING ASPHALT ROAD
EXISTING MACADAM ROAD
EXISTING EARTHEN ROAD

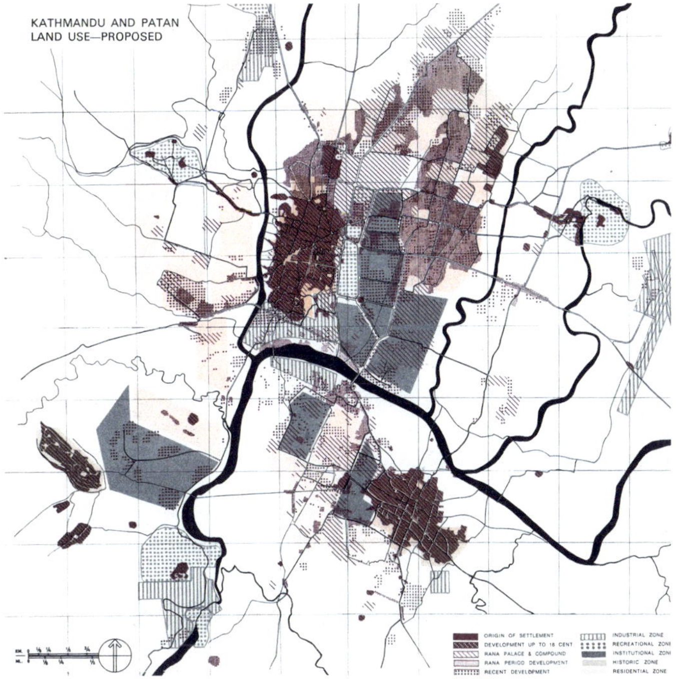
KATHMANDU AND PATAN
LAND USE—PROPOSED
ORIGIN OF SETTLEMENT
DEVELOPMENT UP TO 18 CENT
RANA PALACE & COMPOUND
RANA PERIOD DEVELOPMENT
RECENT DEVELOPMENT
INDUSTRIAL ZONE
RECREATIONAL ZON
INSTITUTIONAL ZON
HISTORIC ZONE
RESIDENTIAL ZONE

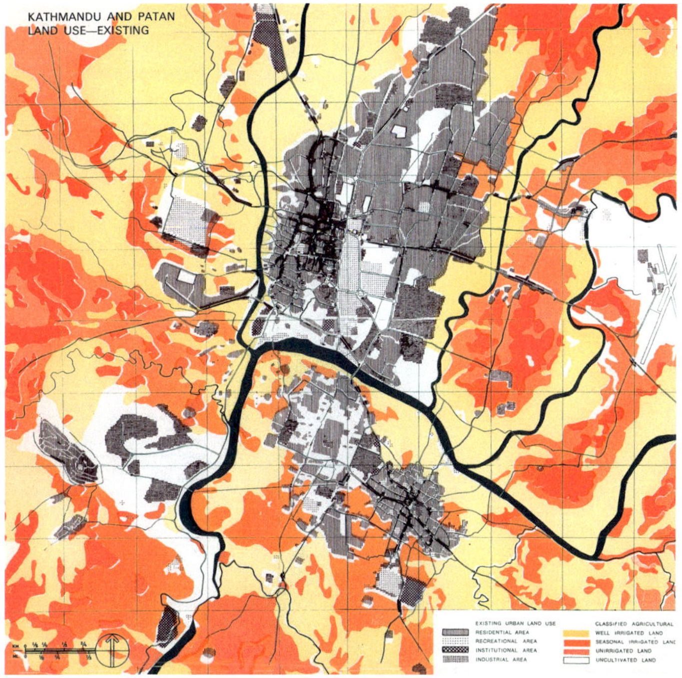
KATHMANDU AND PATAN
LAND USE—EXISTING
EXISTING URBAN LAND USE
RESIDENTIAL AREA
RECREATIONAL AREA
INSTITUTIONAL AREA
INDUSTRIAL AREA
CLASSIFIED AGRICULTURAL
WELL IRRIGATED LAND
SEASONAL IRRIGATED LAN
UNIRRIGATED LAND
UNCULTIVATED LAND

To assemble a team for the inventory project, Pruscha and Chief Engineer Krishna Raj Pandey recruited three draftsmen—A. Tuladhar, R. R .Bajracharya, and K. K. Joshi—from the Department of Housing and Planning, and two more staff from the Department of Archaeology: H. R. Sakya and K. Lamichane. The dean of the Institute for Nepal Studies at Tribhuvan University, Dr. Prayag Raj Sharma, was placed in charge of interpreting individual monuments. To find other international experts, Pruscha turned to René Maheu, director general of UNESCO. Maheu was impressed by the project and agreed to send two advisers to impress upon Nepal's government the importance of the inventory. The British archaeologist Raymond Allchin was working in India with his wife and partner, Bridget Allchin. UNESCO dispatched him to Kathmandu to join the team. UNESCO also added Eduard Sekler, Pruscha's architecture professor at Harvard, to the team.

The documentation work that had gone into *The Physical Development Plan for the Kathmandu Valley* had demonstrated that hand-measuring all of the valley's monuments and monument zones would be too time-consuming. The inventory project instead asked a Swiss pilot to fly a Pilatus Turbo Porter with the Austrian mountaineer and cartographer Erwin Schneider. The photographer Fernando Grifoni then plotted their photographs at Aermap in Florence. The final team members were two photographers—Ganesh Man Chitrakar, who had opened Nepal's first photography studio, and S. D. Manandhar—and three editorial and clerical assistants: J. Oates, B. P. Shrestha, and D. Durkee Miller. After obtaining government permission, the team started to work on the inventory.

Pruscha also created several new examples of modern Nepali architecture as bold alternatives to the "service station architecture" that he so disdained. Nepal had no architecture school then; it still does not have one today. Most of its few architects were in fact engineers by training. Only one or two had trained abroad as architects. Across the border in India, things were very different. With Independence, the country began to seek out a truly modern Indian architectural aesthetic. Private patrons had invited Le Corbusier to design the town of Chandigarh and four buildings in Ahmedabad in the 1950s. B. V. Doshi, who had studied under Le Corbusier in Paris, had opened a firm in Ahmedabad. He had designed the campus for the Centre for Environmental Planning and Technology in Ahmedabad, which trained generations of new Indian architects. The nearby campus of the Indian Institute of Management had been designed by Louis Kahn, whose building also served as models for the students. Charles Correa, a leading post-Independence urban designer and architect, was also blazing new trails. There was a creative ferment surrounding architecture in India.

Nepal had none of this. In its absence, Pruscha began to design a few modern Nepali buildings, beginning with one for the newly established Centre for Economic Development and Administration on the Tribhuvan University campus. In a way, CEDA was born out of the research that Pruscha, Harka Bahadur Gurung, and Arie Beenhakker conducted in Pruscha's first year in Nepal. Going from *panchayat* to *panchayat,* the team had observed how little the local government knew about the central government in Kathmandu. Gurung was able to act on this observation when he was appointed vice-chairman of the National Planning Commission in 1968. CEDA was established on May 15, 1969, with the collaboration of the government, the university, and the Ford Foundation. It was intended as a center for dialogue and learning for *panchayat*-level officials.

The Ford Foundation pledged US$100,000 for CEDA's building and asked Pruscha to design it. He would not, of course, be paid; it would be part of his work for the UN. Pruscha no longer thought of himself as a practicing architect, and was of a mind to refuse. By this time he had let go of Futurism, and yet—despite having designed his own house in Kathmandu—he had not fully crystallized his vision of the modern vernacular, a creative fusion of the local and the global. But the site, in Kirtipur, was very alluring, amid an expanse of terraced fields looking onto the Kathmandu Valley. Pruscha knew of the growing body of modern architecture that was coming up in the rest of South Asia. He decided to add to it, and set to conceptualizing a building for CEDA.

The process for approval was very bureaucratic because the government was involved. King Mahendra himself had to approve of the design. On the day when he was scheduled to conduct a site inspection, Pruscha and others, including Mr. Pandey and several ministry officials, showed up early to wait for the king. There was not much to the site: set apart from the Newar town of Kirtipur, the Tribhuvan University campus housed only a few buildings. The group waited at the side of the road. Pruscha had never before had occasion to meet the king. The group spotted a small car racing toward them. Pruscha recognized it as an Infiniti, a Japanese sports car. The driver, a military assistant, hopped out and opened the door. Out stepped King Mahendra. Everyone bowed, bending deeply in a kowtowing gesture. Pruscha followed suit. As was his habit, the king wore sunglasses, which made his expression impossible to discern. He ignored Pruscha completely as the military assistant asked him, in English, about his plan. Pruscha showed the king a model of the building and explained his design. The military assistant translated everything he said into Nepali for the king's benefit. No one else said a single word. King Mahendra seemed to take an interest in what he was saying, and afterward, to Pruscha's relief, finally acknowledged him. He turned to him and said, in English, "I think you've chosen a good place; go ahead."

The earth at the construction site was dense and black, and rich with alluvial deposits. It felt sacred to Pruscha. When workers began to dig, he felt that he was causing great harm by erecting such a large building. This made him take his responsibility all the more seriously. His intention had been to create a building with a strong relationship to the nature, geography, and history of the Kathmandu Valley. He had designed it to sit in the midst of the terraced fields, and had given it prominent horizontal lines to echo the shape of the fields, as well as a sweeping diagonal silhouette to echo the hills of the valley wall. The semicircular core faced away from Kirtipur to open toward the Swayambhu Temple, which was visible on a hill in the distance. By legend, the Swayambhu Temple predated the valley: Pruscha wanted the building to receive its blessings. The interior of the building was laid out to meet CEDA's multiple goals. At the top were guest quarters for visiting *panchayat* officials, with private rooms and a kitchen and dining room. There were office rooms and seminar halls on the other levels, all of which were connected with a plain wide concrete-and-brick stairway that was as austere and minimalist as it was grand and imposing.

Constructing such a large building posed serious practical challenges. Pursuing his vision of a modern vernacular aesthetics, Pruscha had chosen traditional materials in his design: mainly brick and wood. But all of the timber in Kathmandu had to come from the Tarai-Madhes, and there was simply not enough of it available. It would also be extremely time-consuming to produce the large number of bricks required. Seeking a solution, Pruscha turned to Zenon Zielinski, who had recently designed prefabricated houses in Calcutta for the Ford Foundation. At the start, the two clashed, as Zielinski's solution required altering the building design. On the design, Pruscha was adamant: he would not compromise. They reached an amicable solution only after Zielinski adapted one of his innovations from Calcutta to Kathmandu, designing a hollowed-out concrete element of 3 × 1 meters. This was stronger than either brick or wood and, though it was large, it was light enough to be carried by four men. Pruscha used these concrete elements on the building's roof.

As construction neared completion, he entrusted Jörgen Thomsen to prepare final measured drawings of the building. Thomsen was one of the group of Danish architect students who had, in the mid-sixties, surveyed the small town of Bungamati in the valley upon Pruscha's advice. There was a lot of excitement when the CEDA building was inaugurated. Whether or not they fully understood the concepts behind its design, people grasped that it was special, somehow, that it was a thoroughly modern building that was nevertheless distinctly Nepali. They came from all parts of the valley to see it.

For Pruscha it was a creative breakthrough: he had articulated, with complete clarity, the modern vernacular aesthetic that would mark all of his future architectural projects. It pleased him deeply to have played a role in imagining the possibilities of modern Nepali architecture. He also liked the work that CEDA initiated in the building, inviting people from the *panchayats* to Kathmandu. This level of decentralization was unusual in the Panchayat system, which was so heavily centralized that it kept the king directly involved in governance. The gesture toward decentralization did not last. The royal palace quickly learned that there was no advantage in training *panchayat*-level officials in governance, and transformed CEDA into an administrative center, one that went on to craft staunchly nationalistic policies on education and governance.

Among many visitors from the West as well as from India, one group was most memorable: a team of architecture students from Ahmedabad with their teacher, Charles Correa, came and were quite exited about Pruscha's activities. A lifelong friendship with

Correa started from here, a deep understanding from both sides of the intentions and architecture of the other. Some of Correa's students asked to work for Pruscha, and since the construction of the CEDA building quite interested him as an architect, two more interesting commissions appeared, giving Pruscha the opportunity to hire three of them—Vinod Vijas, N. Kanade, and B. Chatterjee—for his small office.

The first project to be taken on by this team was a private building for Jagadish Sumsher Jung Bahadur Rana, the chief of protocol at the royal palace, who was given to living in style. He had a house in the Lainchaur neighborhood, by the Tukucha stream, which flowed into the grounds of the royal palace. But it lacked accommodation for foreign guests. He asked Pruscha to design him a guesthouse that would have modern amenities yet retain the distinct feeling of a Nepali home. Pruscha agreed to do so in his free time, in a purely private capacity. There was an old *sal* tree that towered over the property. Pruscha designed the guesthouse around it, with the tree at the center. The structure was built of traditional materials—brick and wood—with large, sunny windows, with stacked terraces that looked out over the surroundings. The building was finely crafted and costly, but the chief of protocol could afford it. When he went on to become the foreign secretary, and afterward, when he rented the building out to foreign embassies, it served as a unique showcase for modern Nepali architecture.

With three of his buildings constructed in Kathmandu, Pruscha felt a sense of accomplishment that he had not previously felt, not even as a practicing architect in New York. All three buildings forwarded a unified vision, responding to Lewis Mumford's call for organic humanism with a modern vernacular aesthetic. Pruscha's designs drew inspiration from the common architectural traditions of their surroundings, but were also part of the contemporary global moment. This marked an intellectual breakthrough for him. This was when he let go of his Futurist past and embraced his role first as a practitioner, and later as a conceptualizer, of modern vernacular architecture.

At work, as per the recommendation of *The Physical Development Plan for the Kathmandu Valley,* the Town Planning Office was placed in the newly established Department of Housing, Building, and Physical Planning. Pruscha spent a couple of days there each week, devoting the rest of his time to field work with the project to inventory the Kathmandu Valley's monuments and monument zones. Nepal's young crown prince, Birendra, got married to much fanfare in 1970. Pruscha went to observe the official celebrations but did not get caught up in the spectacle. He was more focused on work.

In the meantime, Kathmandu was transforming into a hippie paradise around him. Overland buses from Europe kept rolling into the valley, and the streets were filling with wide-eyed foreigners on the lookout for cheap hashish and free love. A part of Pruscha's life was in tune with the hippie spirit, given his family's lifestyle, with their Nepali home and local-style clothes that he, Edda, and their daughters wore. Pruscha had taken to smoking

Carl Pruscha with the wife of Vinod Vijas, 1968

Vinod Vijas, 1968

clove-flavored joints openly, even at diplomatic parties. He enjoyed being teased as the UN's "marijuana advisor." Once, at a party that he threw for a UN official, he offered a joint to an unsuspecting female guest, who mistook it for a clove-flavored cigarette and inhaled far too deeply. Another time, when Edda was in Europe on holiday, Pruscha returned from the office to find an overland bus parked in front of their house. Inside, the dazed household staff were hosting an idiosyncratic cohort of hippies. They introduced themselves as the organizers of Woodstock, which had taken place the previous year. They had rolled into Kathmandu a few days before, and after asking around, had heard that Pruscha was a like-minded soul. They asked him to help screen a film about Woodstock. They also asked to stay with him. They had picked up high-quality hash in Afghanistan and were happy to share it around.

Pruscha found this amusing and agreed. He did not realize that the cohort would stay on for weeks, drinking and smoking hash all day, causing a constant uproar in his house. At any given time, he could walk into his bedroom and find a threesome going on. The scandalized cook abandoned his job and ran away. Pruscha himself began to come home late from work to avoid his guests. Their film screening, which took place at his home, didn't attract much of a crowd. No one outside of a small circle of expatriates cared about Woodstock. Pruscha finally asked the cohort to leave once the screening was done. Only after they scattered to other houses in Kathmandu did he regain control of his home.

By comparison with Western hippies, Nepalis were proper and even socially conservative, with lives structured around festivals, or around life-cycle ceremonies involving birth, coming-of-age, weddings, and funerals. Many passed strict moral judgment on hippies especially, but more generally on all foreigners, whom they saw as uncouth, even impure.

The next building that Pruscha designed with his private office was for a group of very concerned Nepalis. One day, Ambica Shrestha, the head of the Nepal Women's Association, came to Pruscha's house with Annemarie Spahr, a Swiss aid worker who had worked in Nepal from 1962 on. Ambica Shrestha would go on to become a leading figure in tourism and heritage conservation in Nepal. She had heard about Pruscha's house from Spahr and wanted to see it for herself. She told Pruscha that the Nepal Women's Association was worried about the moral corrosion that Western visitors were causing in Kathmandu, particularly among the youth. The organization wanted to build guest accommodation where visiting scholars, artists, and thinkers could stay long-term without intermingling too much with Nepalis. Their vision was to recreate a Newar village with modern homes as well as a public square that also housed a library. Shrestha asked whether Pruscha might design it. Despite the positive response that the CEDA building had received, the UN preferred that Pruscha worked on a larger scale as a planner, rather than as an architect designing individual buildings. Pruscha decided to take on the Nepal Women's Association's project in a private capacity, through the small office that he had set up with Vinod Vijas and the other two students of Charles Correa.

Charles Correa

While designing the Nepal Women's Association's project, Pruscha replaced the original plan—to re-create a Newar town—with a thoroughly modern barrel-vaulted complex of brick-and-glass that stands in Kathmandu today as the Taragaon Museum.

Vaulted structures were rare in Kathmandu, but Pruscha had seen an example of such in the *patis,* or pilgrim rest houses, which were also called *dharmshalas.* He took inspiration for his design from this vernacular structure.

The rest of his inspiration came from a deep respect for the cultural history of the valley. In his own explanation of the design, he references Kathmandu's high philosophical traditions: "Located along the main route between India and Tibet, the valley accommodated all those holy men, philosophers and teachers who brought the teachings of early Buddhism and later of Tantrism to the north. This tradition of putting up wayfarers caused specific types of buildings to evolve which were often located near important sanctuaries and at scenic points. These lodges or *dharmshalas* are ground-floor vaulted rooms, open to at least one side, large enough to provide shelter for a few wayfarers.

"The Kathmandu Valley faces a growing influx of visitors. Many come and go without getting into any real contact with the exceptional civilization, in harmony with nature. Few want to remain for a longer period, devoted to meditation which is still practiced by the descendants of those wise men.

"For wayfarers of our time, who seek contact to this world, the Taragaon village [*Sterndorf,* or 'star village' in English] was created as a hostel or shelter on the periphery of the Buddhist sanctuary of Boudhanath, east of Kathmandu. While Tibetan and Buddhist pilgrims find accommodation in the houses surrounding the stupendous stupa, a separate realm was created at Taragaon for visitors from other cultural realms."

Pruscha was particularly interested in the vaulted structure: "Following the principle of the barrel vault, the buildings could be completed in a short time with moving segmental shuttering, supported by bamboo poles. The barrel vaults are made up of one brick on edge; a second layer follows after isolation with locally available bitumen. The result was the creation of a homogenous mass of bricks which had a considerable cooling effect. Penetrating rainwater evaporates at the level of the bitumen and is thus a cooling factor. The openness of the rooms at both ends allows ideal transverse ventilation."

The first phase saw the construction of fourteen small rooms and two larger common buildings that formed the core of the complex. Even more than in Pruscha's earlier buildings, brick was the dominant construction material: all of the walls, floors, and vaulted ceilings were made of bricks. The rooms were austere, recalling monastic cells, with only a bed or, in the larger rooms, a bunk bed, a table, and an built-in brick bench. There were cooking and washing facilities in an annex outside. The structure fitted harmoniously into its surroundings, with the rooms standing on staggered platforms that echoed the shape of the terraced fields. A series of brick stairs and pathways connected all of the structures to a brick-paved common space that resembled a public square.

External views of the Taragaon village under construction and after completion, 1971–1972

The Taragaon Hostel opened in 1973. Annemarie Spahr oversaw its management at the start. Much later, it fell into disrepair, being used variously as staff quarters and even a storage facility during the construction of the nearby Hyatt Hotel, with a few quick additions and repairs along the way. It was restored to its original form in 2010 by the Saraf Foundation, and now houses the Taragaon Museum.

Over time, without quite meaning to, Pruscha slipped into practicing as an architect. For several years more, he used the staff of his small private office to conduct research for his UN work and to draw up his designs. They also worked on a few private commissions, including a government minister's house on a hill near Thimi and a private home renovation.

Pruscha and Zenon Zielinski advised the National Industrial Development company to innovate new construction systems such as the concrete elements they had used for the CEDA building. NID was able to mass-produce these and other new products to replace costly and increasingly rare timber and handmade bricks. It was satisfying to Pruscha not just to design buildings but also to be involved in the technical aspects of their construction, which could be equally creative.

Pruscha's next bold move to promote modern architecture in Nepal can be evidenced by proxy at the Buddha's birthplace, Lumbini. *The Physical Development Plan for the Kathmandu Valley* had recommended that Lumbini be developed as a global pilgrimage and tourism site. This idea had long been cherished by Nepal's government as well as by top officials at the UN. UN Secretary-General Dag Hammarskjold had visited Lumbini in 1959 and written a poem about it in his personal diary. The succeeding secretary-general, U Thant, had visited Lumbini in April 1967. A Buddhist, he had described this visit as "one of the most important days in my life."

There was little to mark the site then: only a modest shrine to the Buddha's mother, Mayadevi, by a tree at the birthplace. Nearby stood a pillar erected by the Buddhist Emperor Ashoka in the third century BC. All around was open agricultural land.

The UN had since established the International Committee for the Development of Lumbini, with members from nations with Buddhism in their present or past cultural life. When the Nepal government's plans began to firm up, U Thant praised them and committed UN support toward them. Pruscha was then able to accomplish something that Nepal has been proud of ever since: to convince the UN to involve Kenzo Tange in the Lumbini Master Plan. Tange had established himself as postwar Japan's most influential architect and urban planner. Inspired early on by Le Corbusier, he had reconstructed Hiroshima and reshaped modern Tokyo with his 1960 Plan for Tokyo. His focus was on creating modern Japanese forms. By the 1970s he was working on projects worldwide, and his love of new materials had earned him a name as the father of Brutalism.

The Lumbini International Research Institute by Kenzo Tange, 2017

Pruscha had followed Tange's work ever since visiting Tokyo en route to Nepal in 1965. His thoughts returned to him when officials at the Ministry of Public Works asked him to help plan Lumbini. Exciting as that prospect was, he knew that the government wanted to build up the site heavily, constructing monasteries and hotels on agricultural land. He worried about being part of a project that he could not control, which would ultimately dilute his vision. These worries were renewed when he visited Lumbini with ministry officials. This was when he decided to involve higher officials at the UN, and to also inform the UNESCO about these plans. He recommended, and both the UN and Nepal's government agreed, that the project was important enough to merit a high-caliber Asian architect: Kenzo Tange.

Tange came to Kathmandu at the start of the project in 1972 with his wife, Takako Iwata. They stayed at the Soaltee Hotel, owned by the king's brother, Prince Himalaya. Pruscha took them to Lumbini, briefing Tange on Nepal's culture and history, as well as on the practicalities of planning and construction in the Tarai-Madhes. He expressed his concern that the agricultural land not be built on too much, and shared how his own modern vernacular aesthetic had emerged in Nepal. By the time they returned to Kathmandu, they had struck up a friendship, as had their wives. Edda took the stylish Iwata jewelry shopping, while Pruscha showed Tange the CEDA building and the Taragaon Hostel. Tange admired the Taragaon Hostel enough to incorporate its unique barrel-vaulted structure into his design for the Lumbini Master Plan. When planning got under way, Tange invited Pruscha to Tokyo for consultation. Pruscha's three months there felt like a magical spell. Tange put him up in an affluent neighborhood, in a residential building inhabited by expatriates. His apartment was elegant, but more than that, he liked the hall on the ground floor where residents would congregate in the evenings to listen to a beautiful Japanese woman playing the piano. Everyone would sit around a small table or wander, talking to one another over a glass of whiskey.

Every morning, Pruscha was chauffeured to Tange's firm near Tokyo's old municipal headquarters. Tange was himself occupied with other projects. Pruscha worked mainly with his staff on preparing a master plan for Lumbini. It fell to him to explain to them Lumbini's background and the ground realities of working in Nepal. Pruscha saw Tange only at a few key events, during which Tange's behavior differed markedly depending on the setting. One very formal setting was a master of tea ceremony symbolizing the accomplishment of the samurai. Being of lower stature, Pruscha was not even allowed to witness the ceremony from close up. He was seated in the lower seats with Takako Iwata, while Tange, for whose benefit the ceremony was held, sat at the very center.

At the end of Pruscha's three months' stay, Tange invited him with two other men to his private club. It was in a skyscraper, with floors and walls upholstered with fur. The club had women for hire who came to sit on their laps. They all seemed eerily similar, and it took Pruscha a while to realize that all of them were Catherine Deneuve look-alikes. The other men told him that they had had plastic surgery to achieve that look. After Pruscha returned to

LIRI—THE LUMBINI INTERNATIONAL RESEARCH INSTITUTE, 1978–1992
Architect: Kenzo Tange

When U Thant, the secretary-general of the United Nations, visited Nepal in 1967, he proposed turning Lumbini, the birthplace of Buddha, into a cultural center. On Carl Pruscha's initiative, the Nepali government invited architect Kenzo Tange to Nepal in order to visit Lumbini together with Pruscha. Tange had been impressed by Pruscha's round Taragaon houses (1970–1972) and invited him to Tokyo to develop the planning principles with his team. The Lumbini complex extends over an area measuring eight by eight kilometers and comprises, among other facilities, a museum, a monastery complex, and a centrally located Holy Garden.
See pp. 18, 50–53

Zenon Zielinski's precast concrete-panel construction, 1970

Nepal, he did not involve himself further in Kenzo Tange's plans for the Buddha's birthplace. The Lumbini Master Plan was completed long after it began, in 1989. Pruscha never saw the changes it brought about in Lumbini. His contribution had been to bring Kenzo Tange's aesthetic to Nepal.

Upon returning from Tokyo, Pruscha's next architectural project was to design low-cost housing for refugees who were coming to Nepal from across the Tibetan border. This project began with a journey with the United Nations High Commissioner for Refugees (UNHCR) representative up the Kali Gandaki Valley and north of the Himalayas to the culturally Tibetan town of Lo Monthang, Mustang.

This was the closest Pruscha got to Tibet, where he had once dreamed of working. Few foreigners had ever been to Mustang: in Pruscha's estimate, he was only the seventh European to visit. At the time, Mustang was the base of the Khampa Rebellion against China's occupation of Tibet. From 1960 onward, the CIA had supported rebels from the Kham region, who fought under the leadership of General Wangdu. The CIA had built Mustang's main airport in Jomsom to air-drop weapons to the rebels, some of whom they had trained in camps in Colorado. Trekking north from there, the UNHCR representative and Pruscha came upon the rebels' base halfway to Lo Monthang. All of the villages in the area were under rebel control, and the tension was palpable. Though their visit was taking place with the permission of Nepal's government, it felt unsafe to be there.

By this time, Pruscha had come to appreciate the great variety of architectural styles and techniques in Nepal, depending on the geography, available materials, and culture of each locale. Even among the northern communities, there was significant variation. The stone houses of Tamang settlements did not resemble the multilevel settlements in Jumla. Mustang's Tibetan-style houses were also unique: adobe-style structures of mud and wood, with open, multipurpose balconies that were accessed by a log with notches that served as steps. Pruscha studied these houses so as to design housing suitable for Tibetan refugees. In Lo Monthang, they met the Raja of Mustang, who held administrative power over the area, as well as the rani. Studying their grand multistory palace, Pruscha found the toilet quaintly familiar: in Tyrol, people used to throw moss over the excreta. Here, they threw ash. They also visited the cave homes in Chhoser village, beyond which stretched the vast plains of the Tibetan Plateau.

Upon returning to Kathmandu, Pruscha drew inspiration from Mustang's local architecture to design a modern, low-cost housing complex for the UNHCR. He used low-cost panels that Zenon Zielinski designed at NID for its construction. The complex sat low to the ground and, as did his earlier designs, echoed the horizontal lines of the surrounding terraced fields. It mattered to Pruscha that his designs fitted into their environment. It also mattered that this complex be suitable for the Tibetan lifestyle. Each house was topped by an open, multipurpose balcony. As was the case with his very first building—the house he lived in—there were no

railings on any of the stairs. This was also in keeping with the notched logs of Mustang.

When King Mahendra died of a heart attack in January 1972, his son, Birendra, ascended to the throne. There was fresh hope that the new king, who had studied in India and attended classes at Eton and Harvard, would prove more liberal. King Birendra summoned Pruscha to the Narayanhiti Palace soon afterward. Edda and Carl Pruscha had repeatedly met royal family member Prince Basundhara, an uncle of the king, a bon vivant with two wives and several mistresses, including the American expatriate Barbara Adams. He hosted glamorous poolside parties. Pruscha went to the palace eager to share his vision of the Kathmandu Valley as a precious artwork urgently in need of protection. He also wanted to talk to the new king about modern Nepali architecture. But the meeting quickly turned into a farce. King Birendra walked Pruscha through the palace grounds, talking about the landscaping of the garden, and showing him some new garden lights that he had installed. Pruscha was then allowed to greet Queen Aishwarya, though they did not talk. The meeting was pleasant but completely vacuous. He left realizing that he could not have any meaningful communication with either the king or queen.

Meanwhile, Kathmandu was changing in ways that would alarm any urban planner. Land prices were rising dramatically, and the profitability of real-estate transactions was leading to a boom in construction. In defiance of *The Physical Development Plan for the Kathmandu Valley*'s recommendations for limited road construction and multinucleated settlements, the city was undergoing ad hoc growth, transforming into an octopus-shaped city with an overcrowded, centralized core that subsumed all of the traditional towns, monument zones, and agricultural lands. This was exactly what Pruscha had wanted to avoid.

He became increasingly convinced that Nepal's government could not stop the destruction of the Kathmandu Valley. He even began to suspect that it would abet the destruction. The drive to develop was simply too pressing. When his former colleague at the Town Planning Office, Shankar Man Pradhan, returned from studying with Louis Kahn in Philadelphia and then promptly cemented over his ancestral home in Patan, Pruscha was ready to give up. He did not see how modern Nepal would honor the vision of *The Physical Development Plan for the Kathmandu Valley*.

At work, he kept receiving futile assignments that did not adhere to his principles. He was loath to become involved in projects he could not fully control. He was asked, at one point, to help adopt European building codes to Nepal. As an architect, he did not believe in standardized staircase widths, wall heights, or room sizes. His own creativity was sparked by the contrast of scales: the narrow staircase of the Newar house, the wide-open porch of the Parbate houses. People had to feel comfortable in their homes; this couldn't be prescribed by a code. He tried to explain the value of vernacular architecture to his colleagues, but

Visiting the Mustang region, 1970

Carl Pruscha together with the king of Mustang, 1970

Louis Kahn

Family Planning Center by Louis Kahn, 1974 and in its present state, 2017

they dismissed his interests as archaic. They believed that the modern era demanded concrete-block homes, which in turn required European-style codes.

Avoiding such assignments, Pruscha focused more and more of his energies on what he began to see as the single most urgent task ahead: to complete the inventory project. He devoted two or three days every week to the project, working closely with the rest of the team. For reasons he could not quite articulate, his instinct was to keep the inventory project quiet. It felt important, for some reason, to get the work done without drawing any attention—or opposition.

In the rest of his time, Pruscha continued to help the government implement the other recommendations of *The Physical Development Plan for the Kathmandu Valley*. Among these was the development of a government center. Singha Durbar, a Rana-era palace, could no longer house all of the offices of the growing state machinery. The government had set aside a nearby plot for expansion. On this plot, the Ministry of Health was going to get an office for its newly established Family Planning and Maternal Child Welfare Program. Because USAID was funding the project, the Ministry of Public Works was obliged to hire an American architectural firm. The minister of public works and construction asked Pruscha to choose from a list. The United States had been commissioning military and industrial buildings all over the world from most of the firms on the list. Pruscha crossed out every name and wrote in his choice by hand: "Louis Kahn, Philadelphia." USAID's director was not amused when the minister handed back the list, but the minister defended Pruscha's choice. The decision passed.

Kahn was at the pinnacle of his career, having designed renowned buildings worldwide, including for the Shaheed Suhrawardy Medical College and the National Institute of Cardiovascular Diseases in Dhaka. He had also designed the campus of the Indian Institute of Management in Ahmedabad, and was working on Bangladesh's ambitious new National Assembly building. Much of his work bore the hallmarks of his style: careful brickwork, monumental spaces, and a contrast between light and shadow. His fee merely for designing the building in Nepal was high, equal to what had been spent on the construction of the CEDA building. When Kahn flew over from Dhaka to Kathmandu, Pruscha met him at the Ministry of Public Works, and showed him around the proposed site, sharing his vision for the government center.

They hit it off. Kahn came to Pruscha's house for dinner with two assistants from Bangladesh. He examined Pruscha's house with a critical eye, as one architect examining the work of another, and declared that it had one step too many. Pruscha explained that he had built it atop an existing foundation. "I would have altered the foundation," Kahn replied. He was warm and funny. Born in Estonia, he was fond of the Polish vodka Wyborowa, which Pruscha had managed to procure through diplomat friends. They had a glass after dinner. Pruscha had planned to give a short lecture on Nepal, but Kahn nodded off. After he woke up, everyone had more vodka.

The building that Kahn designed for the Family Planning and Maternal Child Welfare Program went up in 1974. It was not, by Pruscha's estimate, Kahn's finest work, but it stood out as a novelty, with imposing columns of exposed brick rising up to an open rooftop. There, exposed brick frames ringed the parapet, creating an unexpected lightness and transparency to the top of an otherwise dense, heavy structure. Years later, the building still stands in Kathmandu, even though the Ministry of Health covered its open rooftop in the mid-1990s with unsightly corrugated tin, citing the need for more space.

There was no direct benefit to Pruscha in bringing Kahn's work to Nepal but, as with Kenzo Tange, there was some indirect benefit. He was hoping that by introducing modern Asian architecture to Nepal, he could convince his Nepali colleagues to embrace his own vision for what modern Nepali architecture might look like. It was more advantageous, in that sense, to expose them to heavyweights like Tange and Kahn than to design everything himself. Tange, Kahn, and he spoke the same language. Pruscha dreamed of having that language understood in Nepal.

Traveling to every part of Kathmandu with the inventory project, Pruscha got to know the valley intimately. His appreciation deepened as he grew to know each area's specialized role in the larger Newar society. The settlement of Bulu, for example, was known for producing metal pots for the accurate measurement of grains, while Khokana was known for its skill in oil pressing. The artfulness of each settlement and of the valley's agricultural land always made him marvel. Kathmandu was still magical for him. But the darker sides of Nepal began to reveal themselves as the project progressed.

Out of an instinctive sense of caution, he continued to keep the project quiet, not involving anyone in it outside of the original team. UNESCO had dispatched the British conservation architect John Sanday to work on the renovation of the Hanuman Dhoka Palace complex in Kathmandu. Though their professional interests overlapped, Pruscha maintained some distance from him. Keeping the inventory out of the public eye seemed sensible, as its contents—an exhaustive documentation of the Kathmandu Valley's cultural riches—clashed with the interests of some very powerful circles.

One such circle consisted of the land mafia, who were destroying any possibility for multinucleated development in the valley. The government seemed unable or unwilling to prevent the development of a centralized, octopus-shaped sprawl. Pruscha was also discovering a disturbing shrinkage of the landholdings of the temples of the valley. It was his view that Nepalis, and not Western organizations, should take responsibility for the preservation of their culture. By tradition, the earnings from cooperative landholdings called *guthi*s funded the temples' upkeep and paid for the rituals and ceremonies that took place in their grounds. Pruscha had observed that with the growing profitability of real-estate dealings, *guthi* landholdings were disappearing from the public record. He also kept hearing about the escalation of artifact theft. It was widely rumored that even members of the royal family were involved in smuggling rings. Pruscha understood that an inventory of the Kathmandu Valley's cultural riches would expose exactly what had been stolen, and from where. He knew that smuggling rings would oppose it if they could.

But it surprised him to find his own colleagues expressing skepticism about the inventory. He could not tell exactly who objected to the project, or why they did so, but he could feel a growing sense of rejection. In particular, a colleague with close ties to the royal palace, who showed outward friendliness, exuded a deep envy toward him.

So cautious did this make Pruscha that he began to bring all of the inventory project's documentation home with him at the end of each day. Leaving any of the data, sketchbooks, photographs, maps and notes in the office felt insecure. They contained so much valuable information. Over two years, the inventory team had documented seven ensembles: the Kathmandu palace complex, with sixty buildings of historic value; the Patan palace complex, with nineteen buildings; the Bhaktapur palace complex, with twelve buildings; the Swayambu stupa; the Boudha stupa; the Pashupati temple; and the Changu Narayan temple, one of the Kathmandu Valley's oldest settlement sites. The inventory was not limited, however, to monument zones. In keeping with *The Physical Development Plan for the Kathmandu Valley*'s recommendation to view the valley in its entirety, the inventory also mapped out the valley's natural preservation districts. This was consistent with UNESCO's 1972 convention, which posited that cultural and natural heritage be seen as a single entity.

The final result was going to consist of two volumes containing exhaustive information about 32 preservation districts, 34 monument zones, 29 natural preservation districts, and 888 individual monuments and monument sites. The inventory would be as thorough as it was exact, and serve as a resource for conservationists, scholars, architects, and ordinary residents of the Kathmandu Valley. In the future, it would show the cultural riches the valley retained—and exactly how many of them had been lost.

The closer the inventory project drew to completion, the more hostile the atmosphere grew around Pruscha. Some of this was coming from within the UN. In all of his years in Nepal, Pruscha had continually renegotiated his contract for one- or two-year extensions. This time, he was told that an extension was unlikely. He would have to leave at the end of the inventory project. This troubled him, as did his growing sense that the UN might not actually publish the inventory after his departure. Some of his colleagues wanted control over the research, and he began to suspect that they would suppress it. Right until the end, he made sure to bring all of the documentation home every day. He asked the UN to additionally send experts—his old Harvard teacher and researcher, Eduard Sekler, and Mr. Allchin—to oversee the material he was working on.

Then, one evening, at a party, he was approached by a casual acquaintance, a high-ranking police officer. Pruscha never found out how the man knew that the inventory was almost complete, or that he stored the documentation at home, but the man shared

 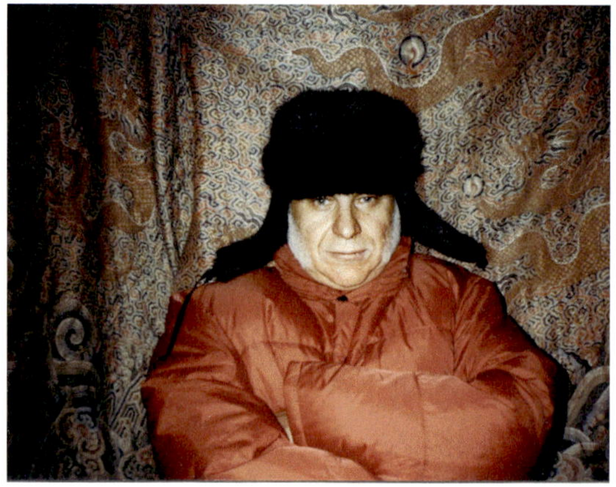

Carl Pruscha in the Everest region, 1972 and 1990

what seemed like a sincere, well-meant tip: the secret police, he said, were preparing to search Pruscha's home and confiscate the research. Pruscha immediately returned home and gathered all of the documents, which fit handily into four wooden boxes. He drove them straight over to the American Embassy and entrusted them to Ambassador Carol Laise, asking her to send them via diplomatic pouch to the Director General of UNESCO, René Maheu. It was imperative, he said, that the boxes reach Maheu himself, and did not get lost in UNESCO's office. It was vital that they not be returned to government officials in Nepal. The following day, three policemen arrived at Pruscha's home, but found nothing after searching the premises. Pruscha told them that he stored everything at the Town Planning Office. The police went and searched the Town Planning Office, but found nothing there. They returned a few more times to search Pruscha's home before giving up.

Pruscha was facing some unexpected difficulties at home, too. Edda had been driving an American guest from their home to his hotel one night when she had met with an accident, hitting a gray cow on a gray asphalt road with their Austin-Healey. Cows were held sacred by the law. The punishment for killing one was the same as for murdering a high-caste priest: a life sentence, or twenty years in prison. The cow Edda hit was injured, but alive, if only barely. It would have to survive a full thirty days for Edda to escape imprisonment. There were no veterinary hospitals to take the cow to for treatment. Friends advised the couple to build a shed by their house so that they could tend to the cow. They did so in the desperate hope that the cow would not die. Their predicament was as absurd as it was grave. The police cordoned off their house for the entire month. Rumors began to circulate in the neighborhood that the couple were cow killers. The atmosphere around them chilled. Despite their best efforts, the cow died on the twenty-ninth day. Under great duress, Pruscha convinced a doctor to write the date for the following day when they went to obtain a death certificate to present to the police.

That had been Pruscha's first experience with insecurity in Nepal. The police searches of his home were the second. Pruscha still felt very attached to Nepal; indeed, he still had the private firm run by Vinod Vijas and remained involved in National Industrial Development. He still dreamed of living in Kathmandu and practicing as an architect while working to preserve the valley. Nonetheless, he and Edda left Nepal as abruptly as they had left New York ten years earlier, storing some belongings at a friend's home and flying to Vienna the day after Pruscha's contract with the UN expired.

In Vienna, Pruscha began to look for a way back to Nepal, and also for a way to get the inventory published. He was able to do the latter when René Maheu visited Vienna. Maheu happened to sit with Minister of Culture Hertha Firnberg at a gathering. They discussed the inventory, and Maheu asked Firnberg if the Austrian government could finance its publication. Firnberg was a friend of Chancellor Bruno Kreisky, who, in turn, was friends with the socialist politician Olof Palme. Palme knew Nepal's deposed prime minister, B. P. Koirala, and had helped to pressure Nepal's government to free him from jail in 1968. These connections to Nepal resonated with Firnberg. After she agreed to fund the publication of the inventory, Maheu, who had held on to the four wooden boxes that Pruscha had sent via diplomatic pouch from Kathmandu, forwarded them to her. Pruscha found Firnberg very collegial when they met. She told him that she had the wooden boxes, and offered to dispatch a staff member to help Pruscha put its documents into book form. Pruscha went on to painstakingly draft the mock-up of the two-volume inventory, *Kathmandu Valley, the Preservation of Physical Environment and Cultural Heritage: Protective Inventory,* which was published by Anton Schroll & Co. in Vienna in 1975. This should have been cause for celebration in Nepal.

The Austrian government asked that the ambassador to Nepal, who was based in New Delhi, India, come to present the two-volume *Kathmandu Valley* to the royal palace. The Nepal government replied that the inventory could be presented to the royal palace only if the names of all foreign nationals were deleted. Only Nepali names could remain. This meant erasing the names of two of the editorial and clerical assistants, J. Oates and D. Durkee Miller, and of Eduard Sekler and Raymond Allchin, as well as of Erwin Schneider and Fernando Grifoni, not to mention of the man who had directed the inventory project: Carl Pruscha. The ambassador flatly refused this strange request, but in the copies that it circulated, Nepal's government did erase Pruscha's name.

Pruscha never learned how many copies of *Kathmandu Valley*'s two volumes were distributed in Nepal. He made sure that organizations and individuals involved in heritage conservation received copies. A few copies were also sold in Austria. Beyond that, he could not tell what impact, if any, the inventory might have.

Indeed, *Kathmandu Valley* might have been lost to time had circumstances not led to its republishing almost forty years later. Around 2013, ruscha visited the model workshop of his friends Coop Himmelb(l)au in the basement of the former publishers, Anton Schroll & Co. There he found by coincidence a huge pile of printed matter, containing loose, unbound pages of both volumes of *Kathmandu Valley* that were slated for the garbage dump. Pruscha was unsure about what to do with it. He tried to contact Nepal's ambassador in Berlin to see if the Nepali government might want it, but received no reply. Then he got in touch with the Austrian ministry dealing with UNESCO, who agreed to pay for 1,000 copies to be bound. But the Ministry's financial agreement with the press fell through, and even Eduard Sekler, who knew the ministry staff, couldn't convince them to work something out. When the press went out of business, all of the printed matter was at risk of being lost once again. Pruscha went to meet the minister for Arts and Culture, and finally obtained approval for a second publication of the inventory through a joint undertaking of the UNESCO commissions of Austria and Nepal.

A fellow Austrian, Thomas Schrom, was working in Nepal with another Austrian conservation architect, Götz Hagmüller, on the restoration of the Patan palace complex. Schrom took charge of

Carl Pruscha with his wife Edda Velim and his daughters Alexandra and Czeslavia in front of their future summer residence in Austria, 1975

the publication in Kathmandu. *Kathmandu Valley, the Preservation of Physical Environment and Cultural Heritage: Protective Inventory* volumes 1 and 2 were reprinted by Vajra Books in Kathmandu in 2015. This is when the inventory turned into the public resource that it had originally been intended as, accessible to all.

By this time, Pruscha was firmly part of Vienna's cultural establishment, having launched into an academic career in 1976. But when he left Nepal a year earlier, he fully intended to return, if only to work through his private firm there. He also wanted to continue working for the UN—if not in Nepal, then elsewhere. But Edda was keen to develop her own career in art restoration. The couple separated soon after returning to Vienna.

Then events took over. Pruscha applied for a full professorship at the Academy of Fine Arts in Vienna, where he had himself studied. He was too much of an outsider at the time. His application was rejected. But Roland Rainer, whose research on Burgenland's architecture Pruscha had participated in as a student, put him in touch with Hubert Hoffmann, a Bauhaus architect and city planner and professor emeritus at the Technical University in Graz. Impressed by Pruscha's work in Nepal, Hoffmann accepted him on a one-year Ph.D. program. A year later, Dr. Carl Pruscha was appointed professor for planning and architecture at the Academy of Fine Arts in Vienna.

In the meanwhile, Pruscha visited Kathmandu briefly to close down his private firm even though it had received new commissions; the thought of living in Nepal alone, without his family, struck Pruscha as unrealistic. He returned via Thailand after persuading a Thai Air stewardess to transport a dog that he and Edda had left behind, an ill-tempered Lhasa Apso that was always biting people.

Pruscha and Edda remarried after he took up teaching. They set up in Gattendorf, in a building that Pruscha remodeled, showing off his prowess as a practitioner and theorist of modern vernacular architecture. Edda pursued her own path. Pruscha had always longed for a simple family life, but it was not to be. Edda's sudden death from a heart attack in June 1992 put an end to such hopeful endeavors.

Once Pruscha entered academia, it became obvious that his orientation had always been conceptual, more suited to teaching than to practicing as an architect. He continued to follow Nepal from afar, and to stay in touch with those working there, including Eduard Sekler, who was involved in several restoration projects, and a new generation of conservation architects who arrived after his departure: fellow Austrians Thomas Schrom and Götz Hagmüller. Pruscha advised them when they reached out, but was not consulted often, especially not by government officials in Nepal.

He consoled himself with the thought that later architects harbored a more conventional approach to conservation than his approach. His abiding love was for modern vernacular architecture, after all, and this he had pursued while remodeling his home in Gattendorf and later, after marrying the artist Eva Schlegel, in a beachside bungalow that they built in Sri Lanka.

Yet he did return, around the turn of the millennium, traveling with a group of students from the Academy of Art through Tibet and Bhutan. There was a brief stopover in Kathmandu. For someone who had seen the valley in 1965, it was painful to see it as it was by now, built up into a dense, centralized octopus-shaped sprawl, with hardly any open agricultural land left. Several monument sites had been restored since his departure, but Pruscha found being in Kathmandu personally very painful.

Even though Pruscha stayed away physically after that, he kept returning to Nepal in his mind. All of his earlier research in Nepal bore fruition in his 2004 book, *Himalayan Vernacular,* an examination of the local materials and construction techniques of the Himalayan region, written at the Getty Research Institute in Los Angeles. The book includes the architecture of Tibet, Bhutan, and Nepal. Pruscha's earlier travels through the Kathmandu Valley and the remote parts of rural Nepal informed much of the book. Then, after the earthquake of 2015, Pruscha helped to design a prototype house based on Tamang architecture for the worst-affected areas, to which he had trekked in his first few months in Nepal in 1965. This, too, returned his thoughts to Nepal. And his very aesthetic connected him to the land where he had arrived as a young Futurist and left as a mature architect of the modern vernacular.

Today, Pruscha's house in Lajtakatta is a daily reminder of all he attained in Nepal. In that house, on a pedestal by his desk, sits a mask of the fierce protector-god Bhairava. It, too, transports him to Nepal every day.

KATHMANDU VALLEY, THE PRESERVATION OF PHYSICAL ENVIRONMENT AND CULTURAL HERITAGE, 1975

When he drew up the *Physical Development Plan for the Kathmandu Valley* in 1969, Pruscha was already aware of the extraordinary significance of its cultural heritage. He saw the ultimate form of its special landscape features as the greatest potential for its future development. As Nepal's cultural heritage was highly endangered, Pruscha saw as his most urgent task the creation of an inventory of all cultural assets in the region. After several years of field work the concept was developed of structuring it into preservation districts, monumental zones, and landscape or nature conservation districts. To this end, 888 individual objects were documented and included in the inventory. Unfortunately, the preservation order Pruscha envisioned for the entire region never became a reality. Thus, this project remains a utopian dream laid out in the recently released second edition of his publication.

See pp. 35–43, 54–60, 129–138, 185

KATHMANDU VALLEY

THE PRESERVATION OF PHYSICAL ENVIRONMENT AND CULTURAL HERITAGE

A PROTECTIVE INVENTORY

PREPARED BY HIS MAJESTY'S GOVERNMENT OF NEPAL IN COLLABORATION WITH THE UNITED NATIONS AND UNESCO
THE PUBLICATION WAS SUPPORTED BY GRANTS FROM UNESCO, THE AUSTRIAN FEDERAL GOVERNMENT AND THE JDR 3RD FUND

2nd Edition 2015 VAJRA PUBLICATIONS, KATHMANDU
1st Edition 1975 ANTON SCHROLL & CO, PUBLISHERS, VIENNA

PAST SITUATION:
Towns and settlements in harmony with environment

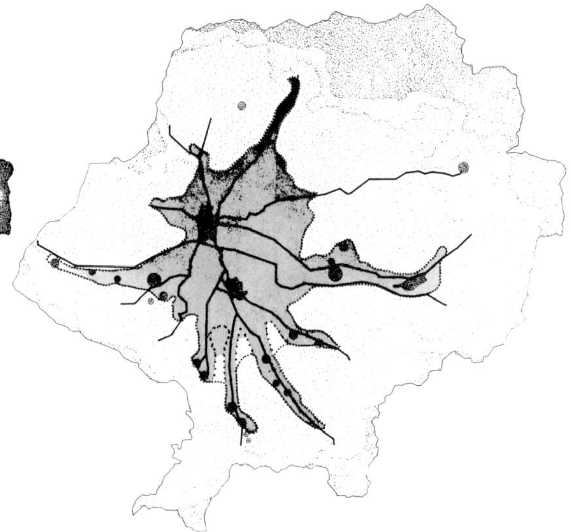

PRESENT TREND:
Fingers of a central urban octopus growing to endanger agricultural land and historic settlements

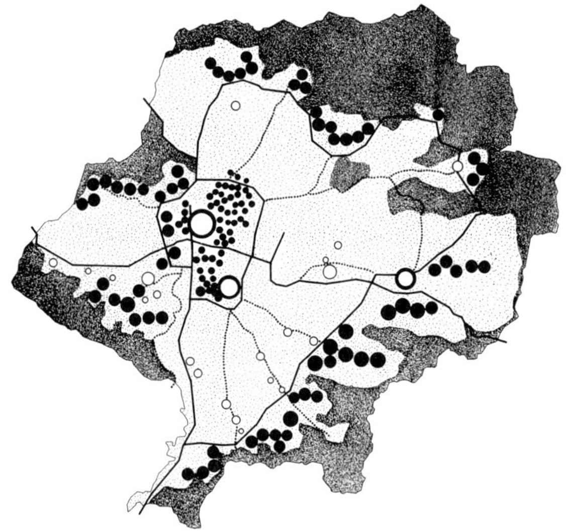

FUTURE ALTERNATIVE:
Multi-nucleated growth pattern. Historic settlements and proposed new settlements in harmony with natural environment

Extracts of the publication *Kathmandu Valley*, vol. 1 (2nd edition, 2015)

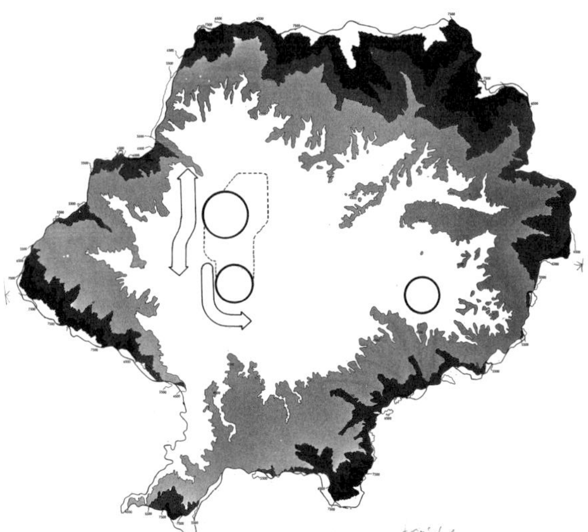

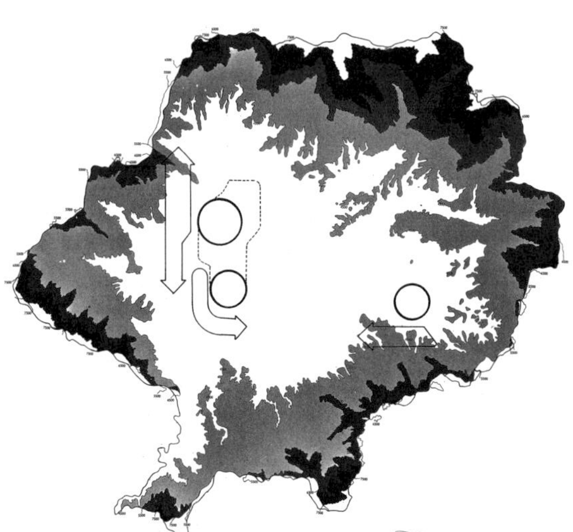

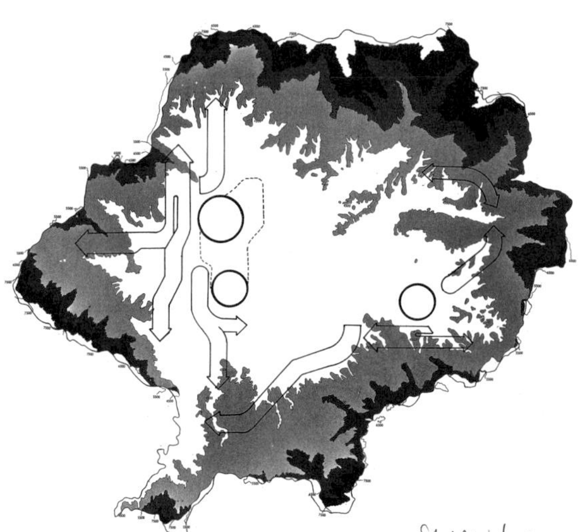

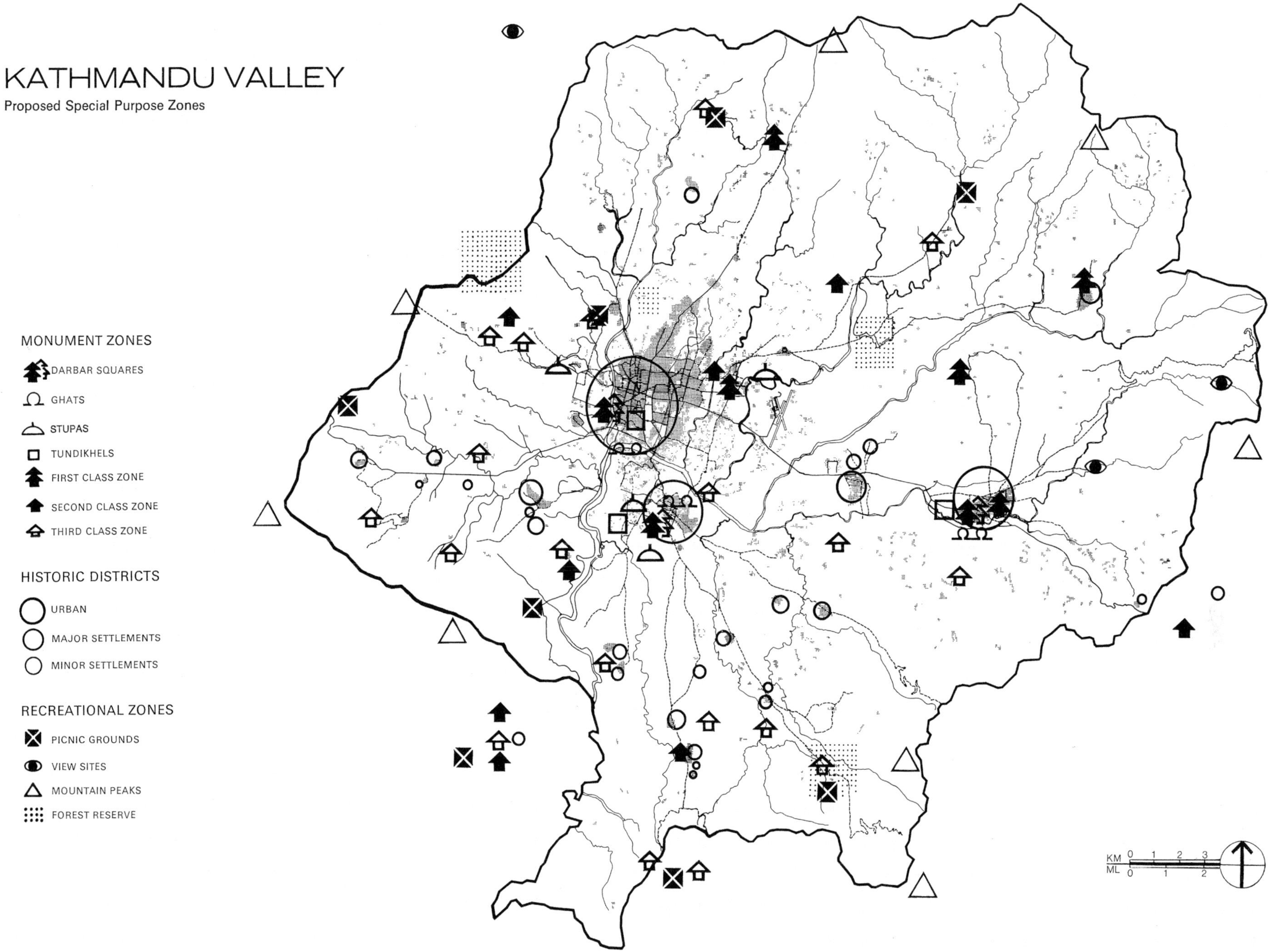

KATHMANDU VALLEY
Proposed Special Purpose Zones
MONUMENT ZONES
DARBAR SQUARES
GHATS
STUPAS
TUNDIKHELS
FIRST CLASS ZONE
SECOND CLASS ZONE
THIRD CLASS ZONE
HISTORIC DISTRICTS
URBAN
MAJOR SETTLEMENTS
MINOR SETTLEMENTS
RECREATIONAL ZONES
PICNIC GROUNDS
VIEW SITES
MOUNTAIN PEAKS
FOREST RESERVE
KM 0 1 2 3
ML 0 1 2

PRESERVATION DISTRICTS

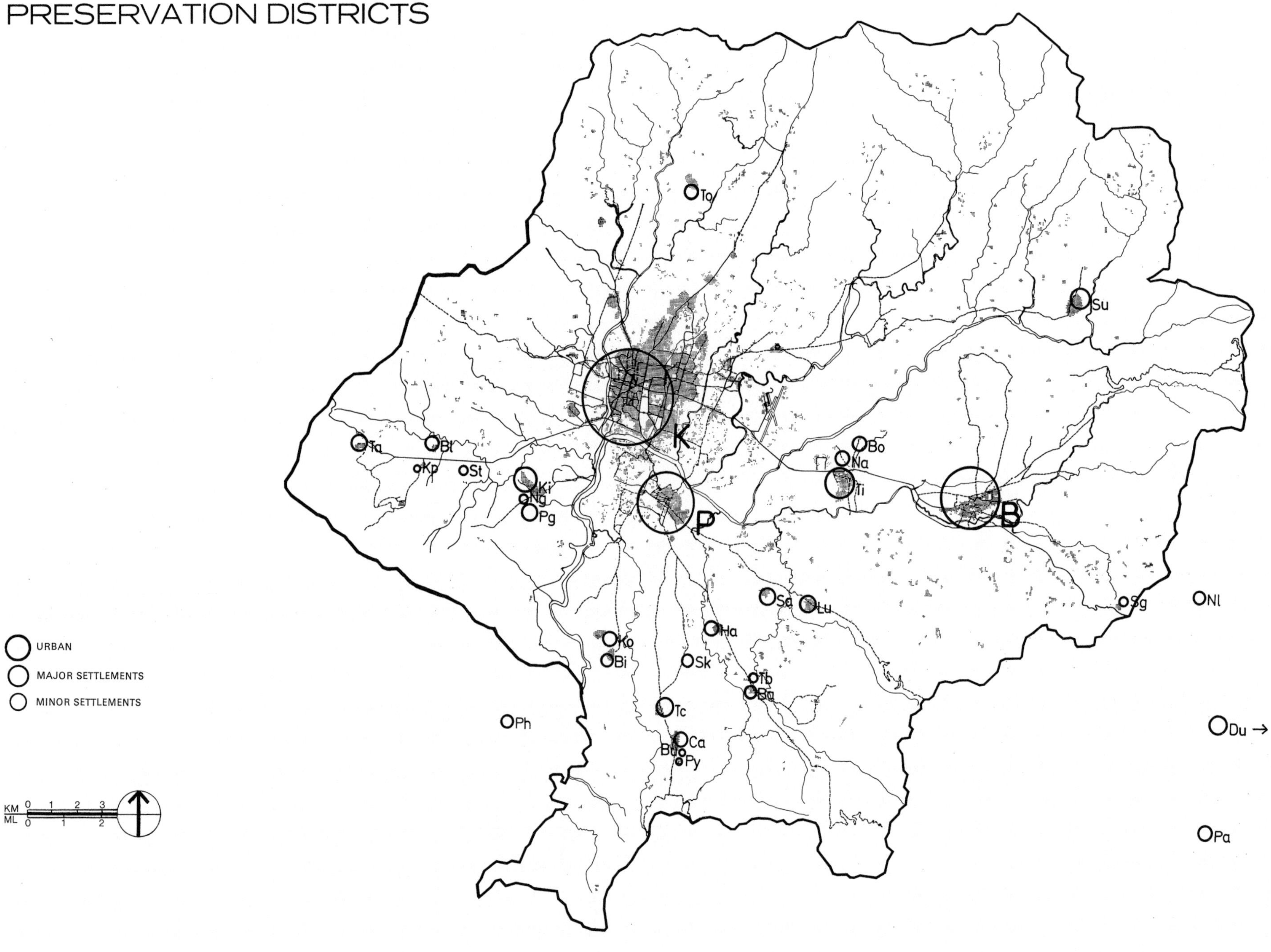

MONUMENT ZONES WITHIN AND ADJACENT TO THE KATHMANDU VALLEY

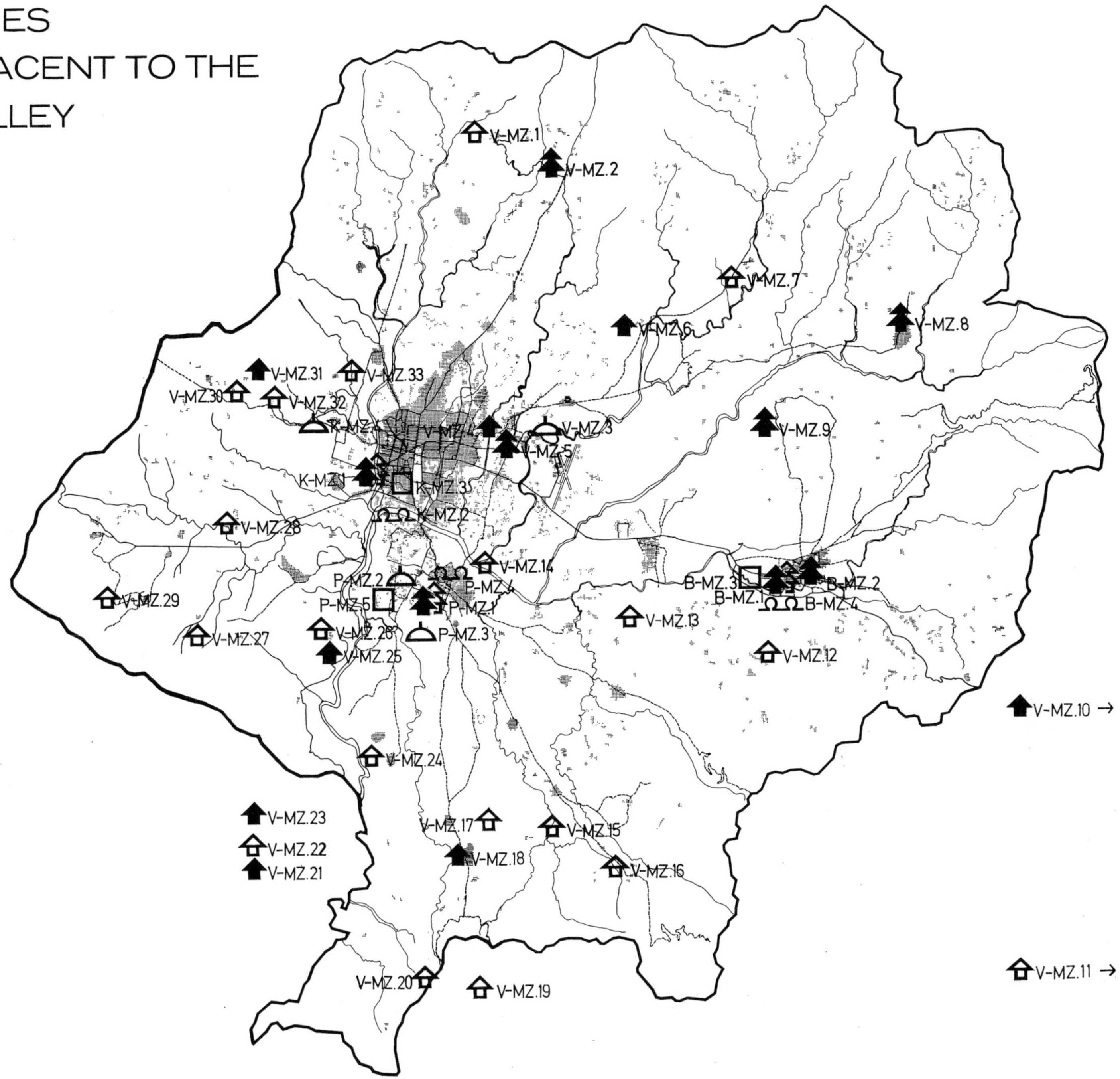

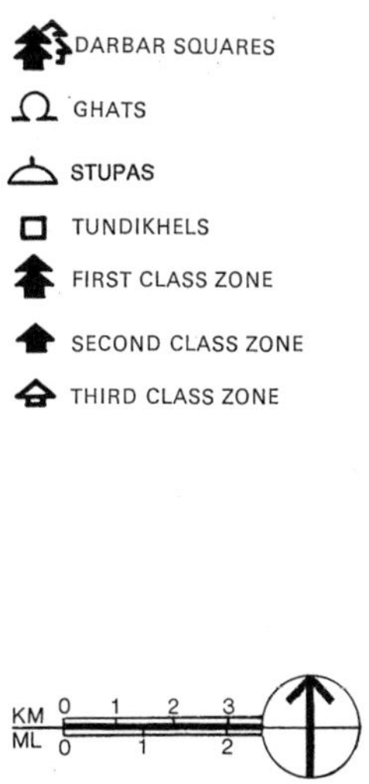

URBAN PRESERVATION DISTRICT: PATAN

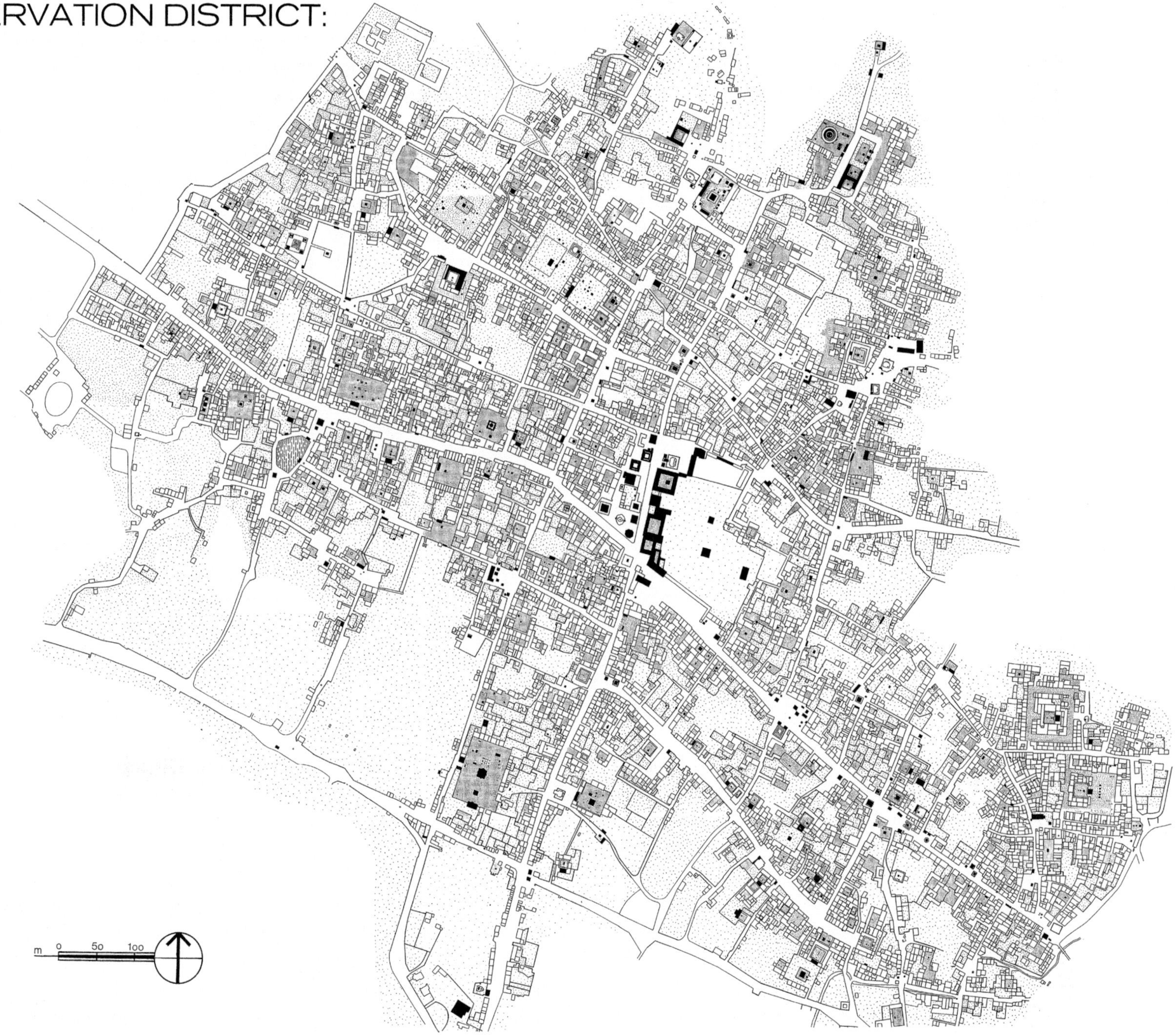

P-MZ 1

DARBAR SQUARE

Darbār Square

Settlement PATAN

Panchayat LALITPUR NAGAR

Boundaries SEE ATTACHED LOCATION-INDEX MAP

RURAL PRESERVATION DISTRICTS

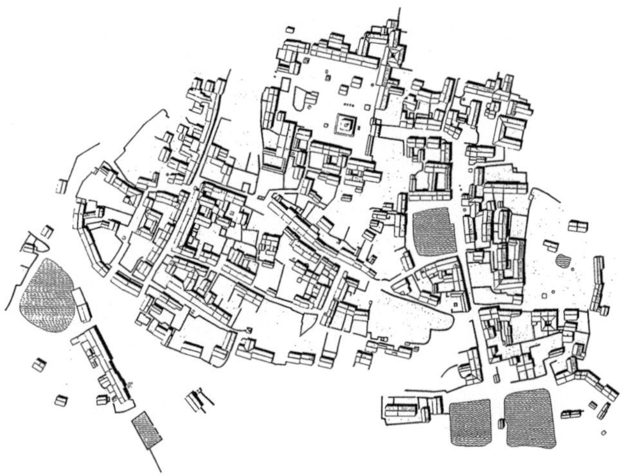

BUNGAMATI

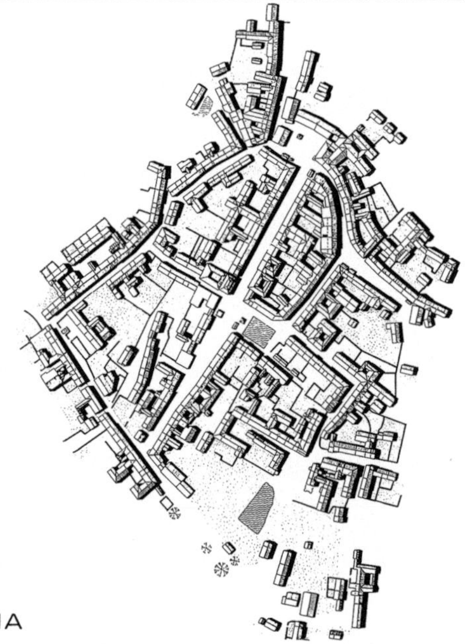

KHOKANA

SANKHU

THANKOT

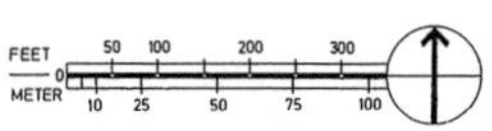

Ti

THIMI, Madhyapur

Ṭhimi

Settlement	THIMI VILLAGE
Panchayat	BHAKTAPUR DISTRICT
Boundaries	ENTIRE SETTLEMENT AND GREENBELT

URBAN MONUMENT ZONES

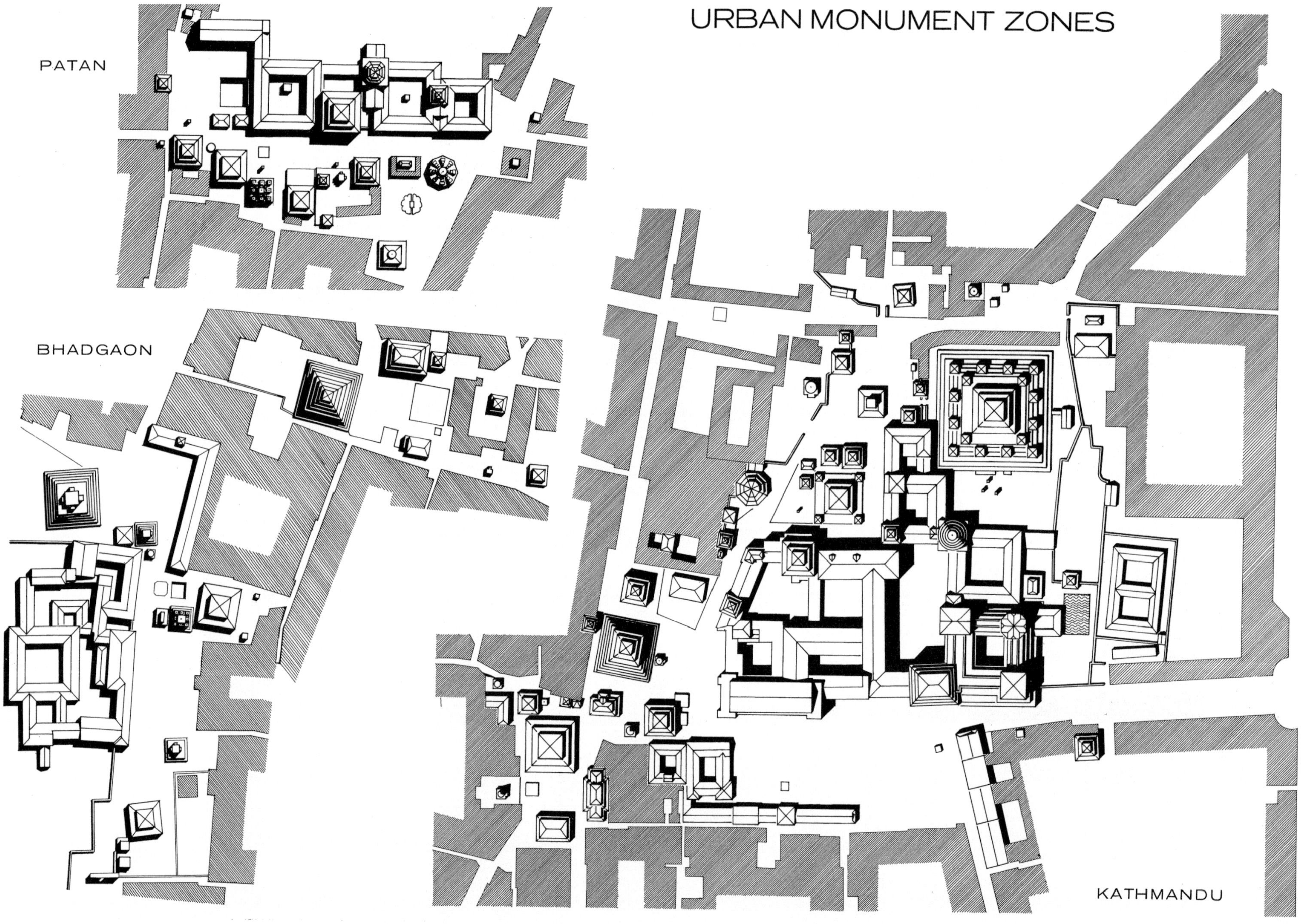

K-MZ 1

DARBAR SQUARE

Darbar Square

Settlement KATHMANDU

Panchayat KATHMANDU NAGAR

Boundaries SEE ATTACHED LOCATION-INDEX MAP

RURAL MONUMENT ZONES:

GOKARNA
BAJRAJOGINI
CHANGUNARAYAN

DAKSHINKALI
CHOBAR-ADINATH
GODAVARI

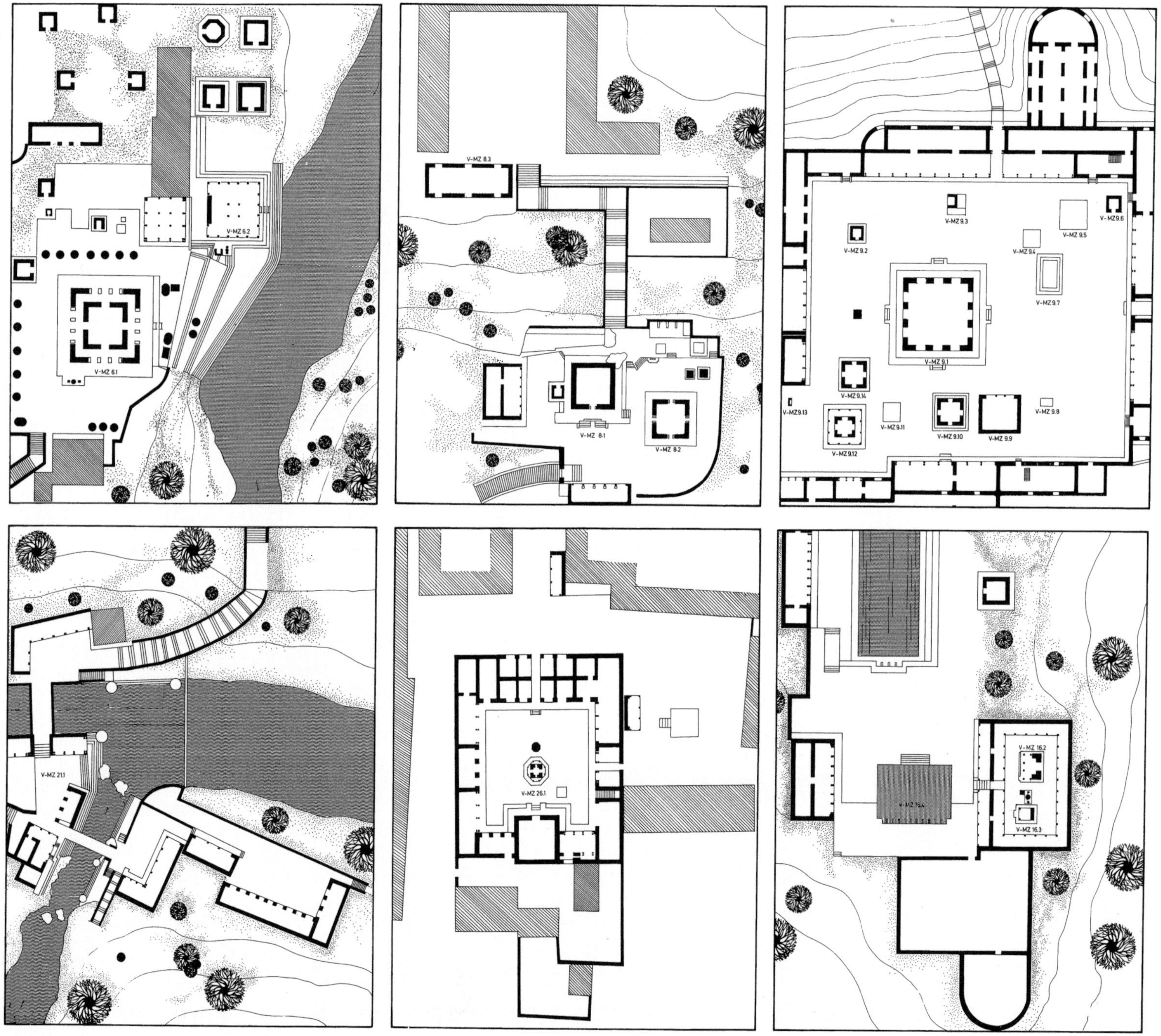

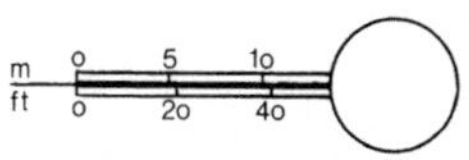

V-MZ 4

CHABAHIL

Cābahil

Settlement	CHABAHIL
Panchayat	KATHMANDU DISTRICT, CHABAHIL
Boundaries	THAT PART OF CHABAHIL VILLAGE CONTAINING THE TWO SITES

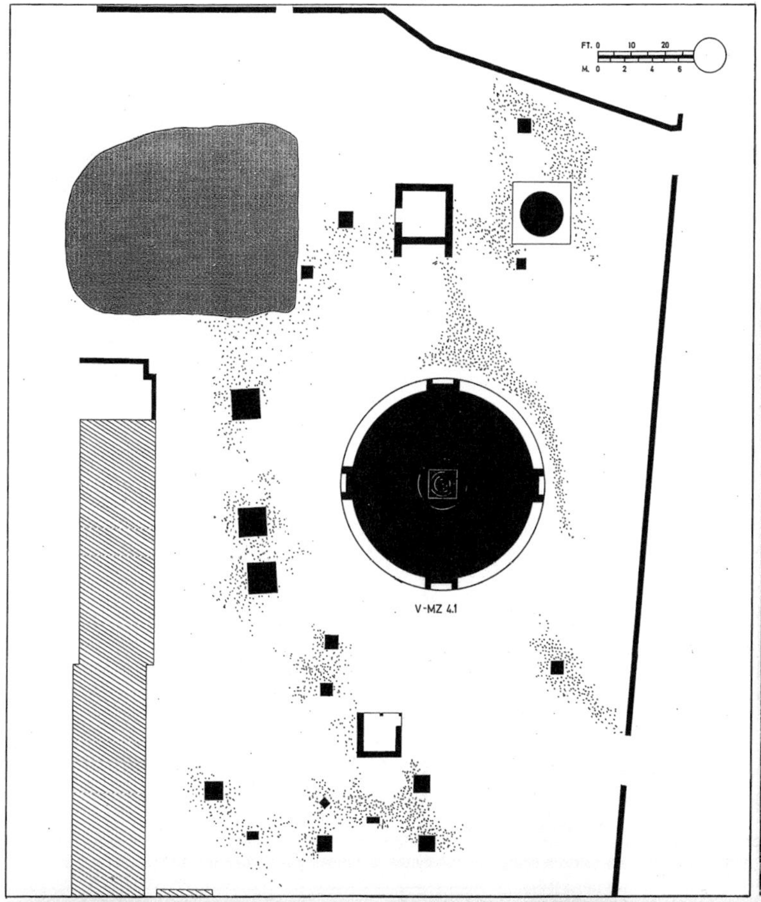

PROTOTYPICAL MONUMENTS

SINGLE STOREYED TEMPLE

MORE STOREYED TEMPLE

AGAM HOUSE, DYOCHEN

BAHAL

BAHIL

PROTOTYPICAL MONUMENTS

GRANTHAKUT

STUPA and CHAITYAS

ENCLOSED SHRINE

SHIKHARA

WATERFOUNTAIN

OPEN SHRINE

INDEX SUMMARY CHART

	Symbol	Kathmandu and Vicinity	Patan and Vicinity	Bhadgaon	Monument Zones	Preser-vation Districts	Total
TYPE							
Temples:							
a — More storeyed	1	82	55	19	24	41	221
b — Single storeyed	2	35	20	6	7	10	78
Chaityas:							
a — Stupas	3	2	4	—	2	—	8
b — Chaityas	4	5	7	—	1	—	13
Bahals, Bahils, Nanis	5	102	136	14	3	11	266
Shikharas, Granthakuts	6	14	12	5	8	5	44
Enclosed shrines	7	42	19	4	12	1	79
Open shrines	8	14	11	4	17	5	51
Agam houses, Dyochhen	9	30	7	6	1	8	52
Water tanks, Wells and Fountains	10	6	11	—	6	—	23
Historic Palace Estates	HP	26	14	—	—	—	40
Others	0	4	2	4	4	—	14
Total		362	298	62	85	81	888
CLASSIFICATION							
First Category	A	31	24	13	11	15	94
Second Category	B	60	52	18	21	9	159
Third Category	C	199	154	31	53	57	496
Additional Category	D	46	54	—	—	—	100
Historic Palace Estates	HP	26	14	—	—	—	40
Total		362	298	62	85	81	888
TIME OF ORIGIN (Period)							
Before 1350	*****	7	14	2	14	—	37
1350—1500	****	9	10	4	4	1	28
1500—1750	***	161	177	35	35	51	459
1750—1900	**	117	53	14	31	23	238
1900—on	*	68	44	7	1	6	126
Total		362	298	62	85	81	888

NATURAL PRESERVATION DISTRICTS

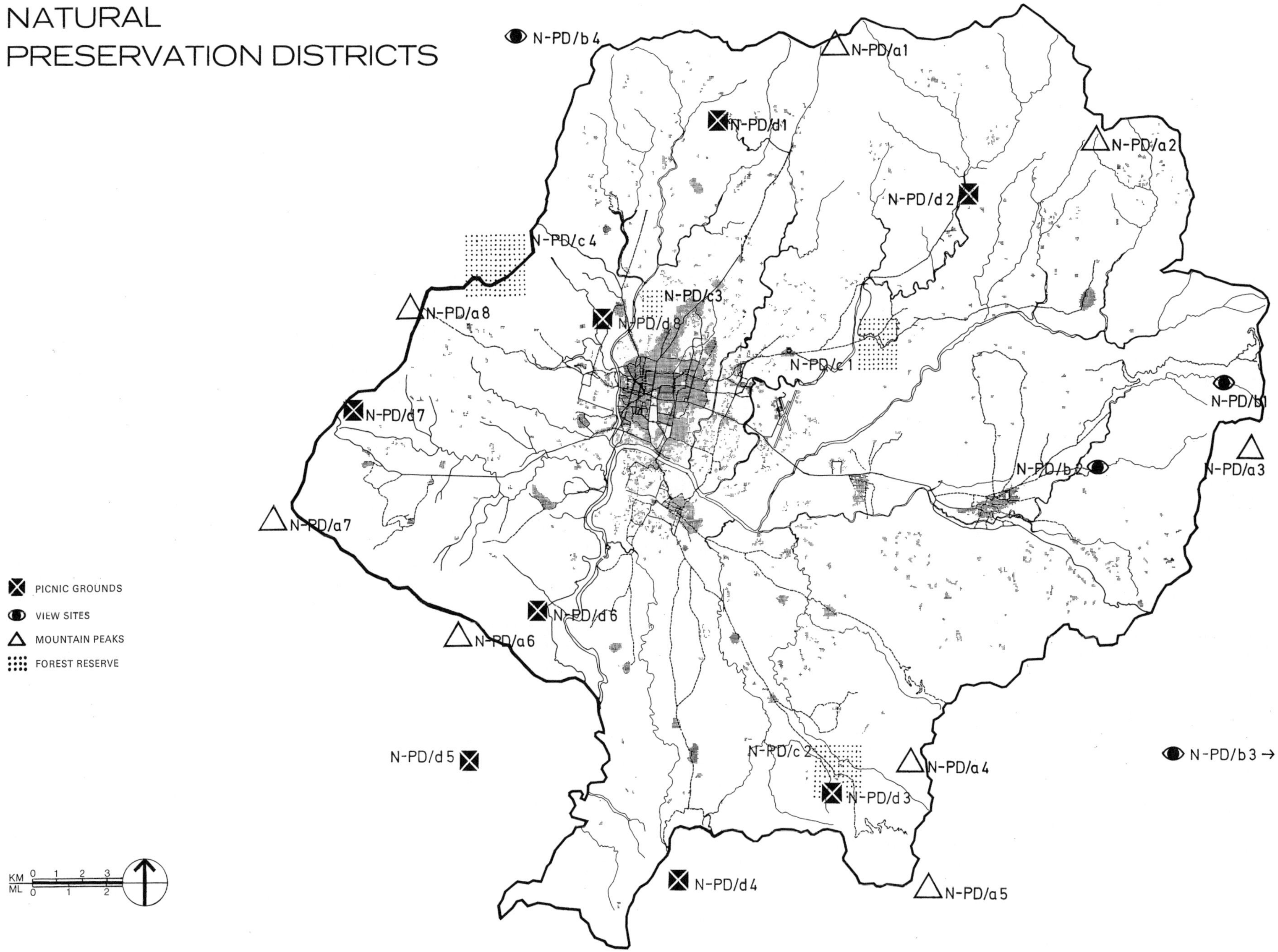

PATAN — MONUMENTS AND MONUMENT SITES

The eighteenth century temple of Vishnu, flanked by Lakshmi and Garuda, is located inside the Patan palace. Because of royal patronage it was richly endowed. In the same courtyard there are an inscription of the Lichchhavi King Narendradeba, dated 643, a broken image of Krishna, and a mandala.

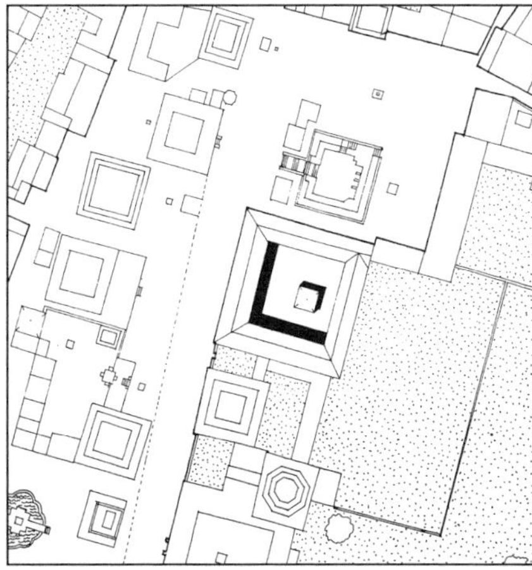

A/P-133

MANI KESHAV NARAYAN CHOK

Maṇi kesav Nārāyaṇ cok

Location	DARBAR SQUARE
Style	STONE TEMPLE WITHIN PALACE
Deity	NARAYAN
Sect	VAISHNAVA
Records	1761 AN 1799

This is the most remarkable building in stone ever made in the Valley. It is basically in the Shikhara style, but there is a blending of other styles as well. The temple is built on a stepped platform. There is a columned porch all around the ground floor. The first and second storeys are made up of a line of pavilions. The slender Shikhara tower emerges from the second floor. The shrine is located on the first floor. Along the horizontal beams the two epics, the Ramayana and the Mahabharata, are narrated on a panel with explainations in Newari. The temple reflects something of the storeyed style seen in the local architecture, and the pavilions are reminiscent of the Moghul style found in India. Every slab used here was polished which gives it a smooth appearance. The temple took about six and a half years to build. It was built by Siddhinarasingh Malla. The main divinity was installed in 1637 with the performance of a kotyahuti.

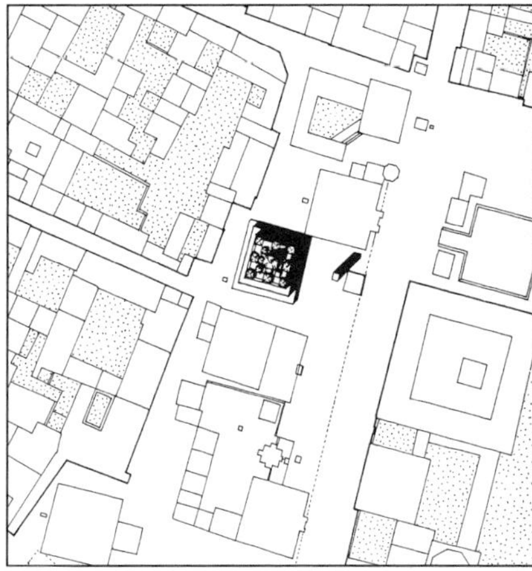

A/P-134

KRISHNA MANDIR

Kṛṣṇa Mandir

Location	DARBAR SQUARE
Style	SHIKHARA STYLE TEMPLE
Constructed	1637
Deity	KRISHNA, RADHA, SATYABHAMA
Sect	VAISHNAVA
Records	1637

This two-storey brick temple is built on a square base of brick and stone. Two mounted elephants guard the door. Each one ot the arches, formed by the colonnade on the ground floor, has a carved torana depicting various divinities, or aspects of Shiva. The roofs are supported by figure struts of Surya, Ganesh, Annapurna, Shiva and Parvati. The temple was built by King Siddhinarasingh Malla. The priest is a Brahman.

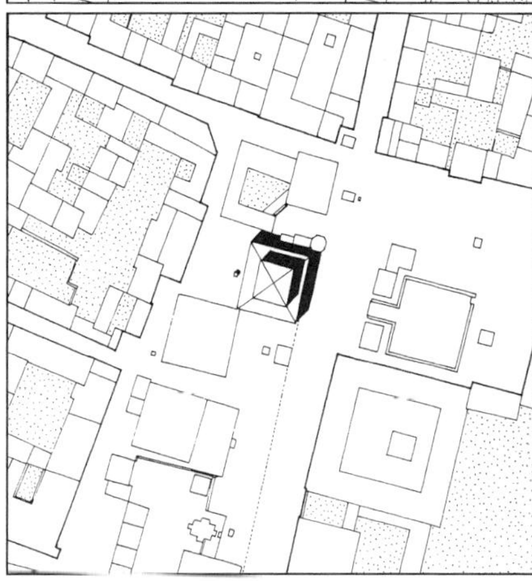

A/P-135

BISHWA NATH MANDIR

Visvanāth Temple

Location	DARBAR SQUARE
Style	TWO-STOREY TEMPLE
Constructed	1626
Deity	VISVANATH, SHIVA-LINGA
Sect	SHAIVA
Records	1626

KATHMANDU CITY — MONUMENTS AND MONUMENT SITES

S.-No.	*Name*	*Transliteration*	*Location*
K-173	HANUMAN	Hanumān	HANUMAN DHOKA
K-174	JAGANNATH	Jagannāth	HANUMAN DHOKA
K-175	GOPI NATH	Gopināth	HANUMAN DHOKA
K-176	MAHADEV	Mahādev	HANUMAN DHOKA
K-177	KAL BHAIRAB	Kāl Bhairav	HANUMAN DHOKA
K-178	LAKSHMI NARAYAN	Laksmi Nārāyan	HANUMAN DHOKA
K-179	DEGU TALLE MANDIR	Degu Talle Temple	HANUMAN DHOKA
K-180	SWETA BHAIRAB	Śveta Bhairav	HANUMAN DHOKA
K-181	CHASIN DEGA	Cāsī Dega	HANUMAN DHOKA
K-182	SARASWATI	Saraśvati	HANUMAN DHOKA
K-183	KRISHNA	Krisna	HANUMAN DHOKA
K-184	TAGA GAN	Taga Gā	MARU TOLE
K-185	LAYAKU BAHI	Lāyaku Bahil	MARU TOLE
K-186	NAVA JOGINI	Nava Yogini	MARU TOLE
K-187	BHAGVATI	Bhagvati	MARU TOLE
K-188	KUMARI	Kumāri	MARU TOLE
K-189	NARAYAN	Nārāyan	MARU TOLE
K-190	JOSHI AGAN	Jośi Agā	MARU TOLE
K-191	MAJU DEGA	Māju Dega	MARU TOLE
K-192	GARUD NARAYAN	Garud Nārāyan	MARU TOLE
K-193	ASHOK BINAYAK	Aśok Vināyak	MARU TOLE
K-194	DURGA	Durgā	MARU TOLE
K-195	AGAN DYO	Āgā Dyo	MARU TOLE
K-196	SHIVALING	Śivalinga	MARU TOLE
K-197	KASHTHA MANDAP	Kāstha Mandap	MARU TOLE
K-198	MAHADEV	Mahādev	MARU TOLE
K-199	SILYAN SATA	Silyan Sattal	MARU TOLE
K-200	DHANSA	Dhāsa	MARU TOLE
K-201	BIMALESWAR MAHADEV	Vimaleśvar Mahādev	MARU TOLE
K-202	NARAYAN	Nārāyan	MARU TOLE
K-203	SIKHONMU BAHA	Sikhomu Bahāl	MARU TOLE
K-204	KUMARI BAHA	Kumāri Bahāl	BASANTAPUR
K-205	KUMARI DYO CHHEN	Kumāri Dyochē	BASANTAPUR
K-206	BANIA BAHA	Vaniyā Bahāl	BASANTAPUR
K-207	SARASWATI	Saraśvati	BASANTAPUR
K-208	AAGAN DEGA	Āgā Dega	BANSATAPUR
K-209	JHO CHHEN BAHA	Jhochē Bahāl	JHO CHHEN
K-210	NA BAHI	Na Bahil	NA BAHI
K-211	NA BACHA	Na Bācā	NA BAHI
K-212	WATUM BAHA	Watum Bahāl	JORGANESH
K-213	JORGANESH	Jor Ganeś	JORGANESH
K-214	NRITESWAR	Nriteśvar	JORGANESH
K-215	NHUCHHEN BAHA	Nhuchē Bahāl	JORGANESH
K-216	TWAKE BAHA	Twake Bahāl	OM BAHA
K-217	GUVA BAHA	Gubhā Bahāl	OM BAHA
K-218	MIM NANI	Mim Nani	OM BAHA
K-219	BISWAKARMA BAHA	Viśvakarmā Bahāl	OM BAHA
K-220	OM BAHA	Om Bahāl	OM BAHA
K-221	PUNCHHEN BAHA	Pūchē Bahāl	OM BAHA
K-222	RATNAPUR MAHA BIHAR	Ratna Pur Mahā Vihār	GANCHENANI
K-223	BUDDHA KANTI MAHA BIHAR	Buddhakānti Mahāvihār	GANCHENANI
K-224	BHON BAHA	Bhō Bahāl	OM BAHA
K-225	THANA BAHA	Thānā Bahāl	CHIKAN MUGAL
K-226	NARAYAN	Nārāyan	CHIKAN MUGAL
K-227	JORESWAR	Joreśvar	CHIKAN MUGAL
K-228	ADKO NARAYAN	Arko Nārāyan	CHIKAN MUGAL
K-229	HARI SHANKAR	Hariśankar	CHIKAN MUGAL
K-230	BAJRA JOGINI	Vajrayogini	CHIKAN MUGAL
K-231	NHU BAHA	Nhu Bahāl	CHIKAN MUGAL
K-232	LAKHE NANI	Lākhe Nani	MAJIPAT
K-233	MIKHA BAHA	Mikhā Bahāl	MANJESWARI
K-234	JYA BAHA	Jyā Bahāl	JYA BAHA
K-235	MANJESWARI	Manjuśri	MANJESWARI
K-236	SHO BAHA	Śo Bahāl	YANGAL-MANJESWARI
K-237	YANGA HITI	Yāgā Hiti	YANGAL
K-238	IKU BAHA	Iku Bahāl	YANGAL
K-239	CHAITANYA MAHA BIHAR	Caitanya Mahāvihār	JYA BAHA
K-240	KHALACHHEN BAHA	Khālāchē Bahāl	LAGAN
K-241	JOG BAHA	Jog Bahāl	LAGAN
K-242	WANTA BAHA	Wanta Bahāl	LAGAN
K-243	LAGAN BAHA	Lagan Bahāl	LAGAN
K-244	MACHHENDRA NATH	Macchendranāth	LAGAN
K-245	NHAYAKAN BAHI	Nhyakan Bahil	LAGAN
K-246	CHWAKAN BAHI	Chwakā Bahil	LAGAN
K-247	TA BAHA	Ta Bahāl	LAGAN
K-248	YATA BAHA	Yatā Bahāl	GOPHALE
K-249	BHAGWATI	Bhagvati	GOPHALE
K-250	NA BAHA	Na Bahāl	GOPHALE
K-251	PIKHA BAHA	Pikhā Bahāl	BRAHMA TOL
K-252	BARE NANI	Bare Nani	MUSUM BAHA
K-253	BHALA NANI	Bhalā Nani	MUSUM BAHA
K-254	MUSUM BAHA	Musum Bahāl	MUSUM BAHA
K-255	MUSUM BAHA	Musum Bahāl	MUSUM BAHA
K-256	DHAN CHAKRA BAHA	Dhancakra Bahāl	MUSUM BAHA

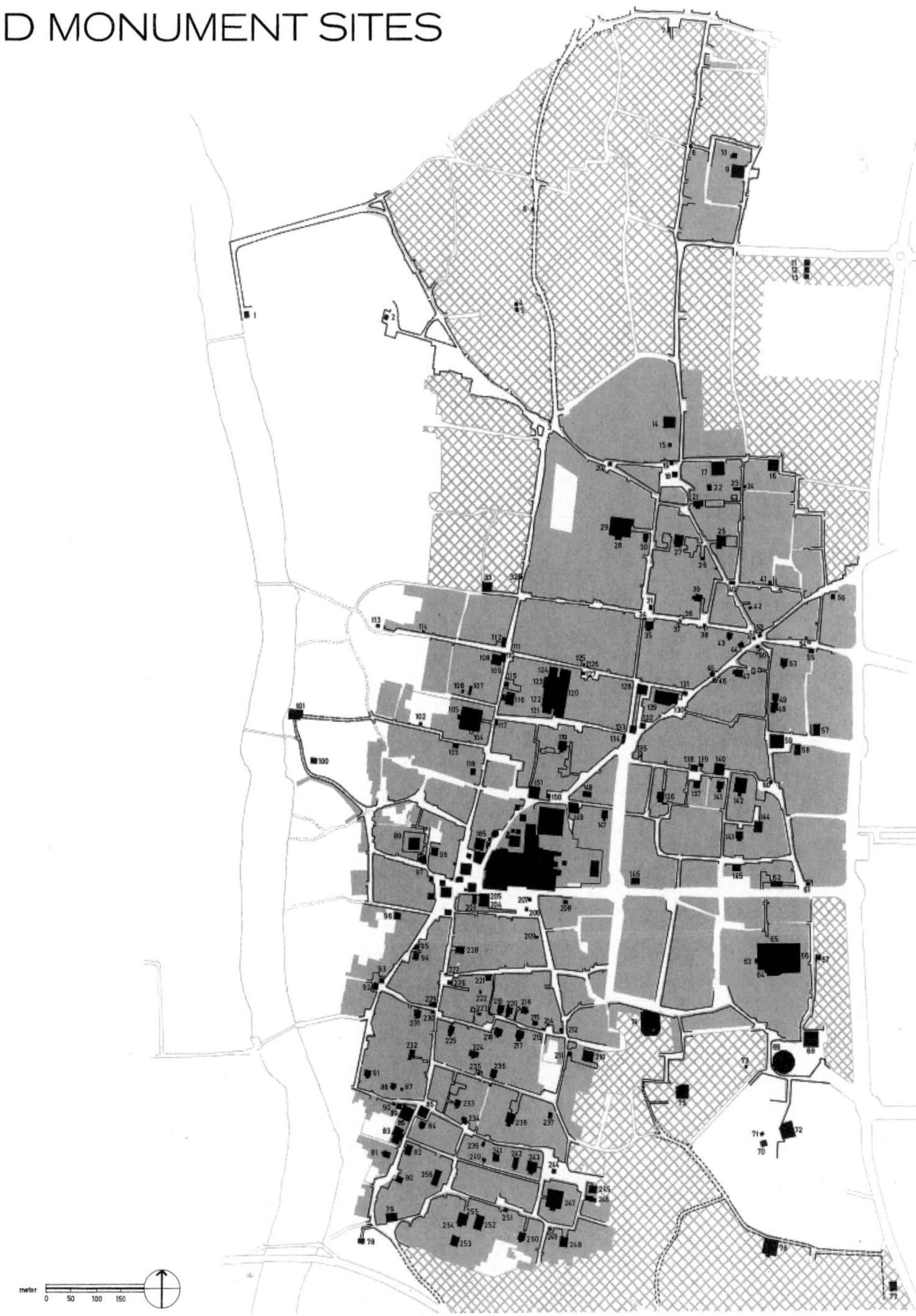

This is one of the three pavilions built on the corners of Lohan Chok. The upper floor is completely made up of carved window-frames, it is topped with a tiled roof. Each of the pavilions is said to have been designed by another carpenter, one coming from Kirtipur, the other from Patan, and the third from Bhadgaon. This one is the Lalitpur Mandir. All three probably served as watchtowers or plaisances for the palace.

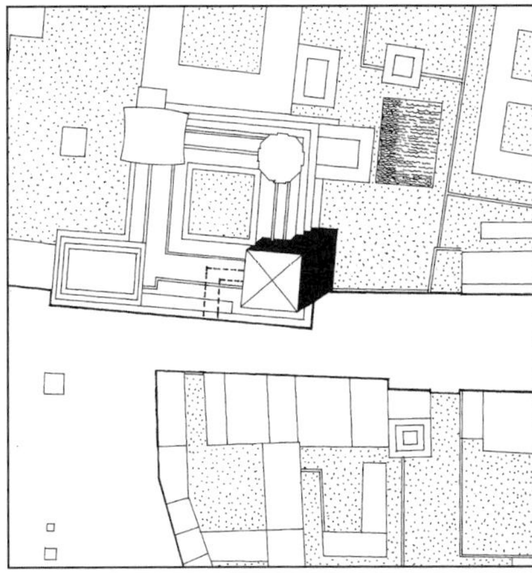

B/K-165

LALITPUR BHAWAN

Lalitpur Bhavan

Location	HANUMAN DHOKA
Style	STOREYED STRUCTURE
Constructed	1769
Deity	SECULAR

This is one of the four crowning features of Lohan Chok in Hanuman Dhoka. It is basically an octagonal timber structure with tiled roof, raised on a brick base which forms part of a fifth storey of the Chok. The tower stands on the north-east corner. The facade consists of a series of carved windows with interesting figures. It was built c. 1769 at the order of Prithvi Narayan Shah, and the craftsmen who executed the work are supposed to have come from Bhaktapur.

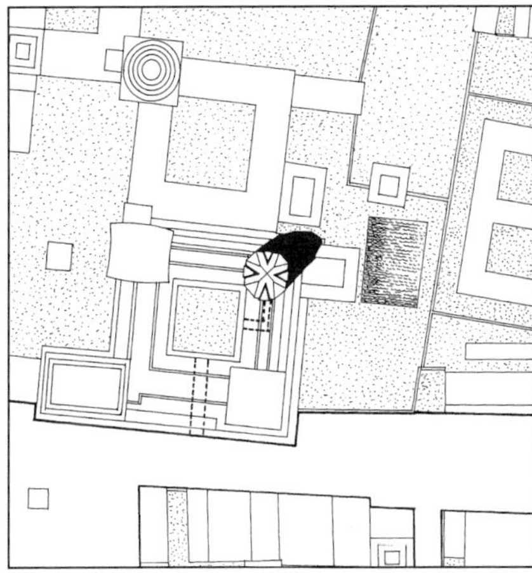

A/K-166

BHAKTAPUR BHAWAN

Bhaktapur Bhavan

Location	HANUMAN DHOKA
Style	STOREYED STRUCTURE
Constructed	SECOND HALF OF THE 18TH CENTURY
Deity	SECULAR

This is one of the crowning features of Lohan Chok in Hanuman Dhoka. It is a timber structure raised on a brick base which forms part of the fifth storey of the Chok. This tower stands at the north-west corner. The roof is covered with metal sheets. Its curvilinear form recalls the Bengal hut style of roof of Bangla Desh. The work was done at the command of Prithvi Narayan Shah in c. 1769, and this pavilion is said to have been the work of craftsmen from Kirtipur.

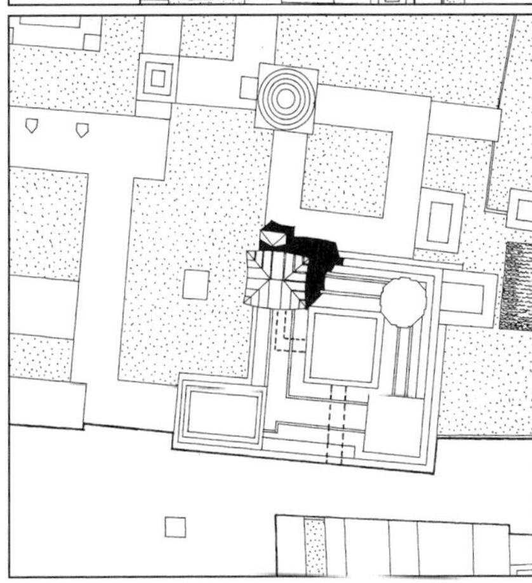

A/K-167

KIRTIPUR BHAWAN

Kirtipur Bhavan

Location	HANUMAN DHOKA
Style	STOREYED STRUCTURE
Constructed	SECOND HALF OF 18TH CENTURY
Deity	SECULAR

HISTORIC PALACE ESTATES OF THE GREATER KATHMANDU AREA

HP/20

BABAR MAHAL

Babar-Mahal

The palace was built under the supervision of Kumar Narshing, after the return of Chandra Shumsher from England in 1909. The design is said to have been based upon Buckingham Palace in London which had greatly impressed him. It took four years to complete the palace with all its elaborate interior decorations all in contemporary European style.
The symmetrical front is three-storeyed with a double-storeyed portico. Built around three spacious courtyards it faced a magnificent garden with fountains and groups of beautiful trees in a 7 hectare compound. Chandra Shumsher, however, never occupied the building which came into the possession of Babar Shumsher, he established his residence there in 1928.
A part of the compound has since been subdivided by Babar Shumsher's heirs while the main palace with front garden was nationalized by the Government in 1957 and is now housing administrative offices.

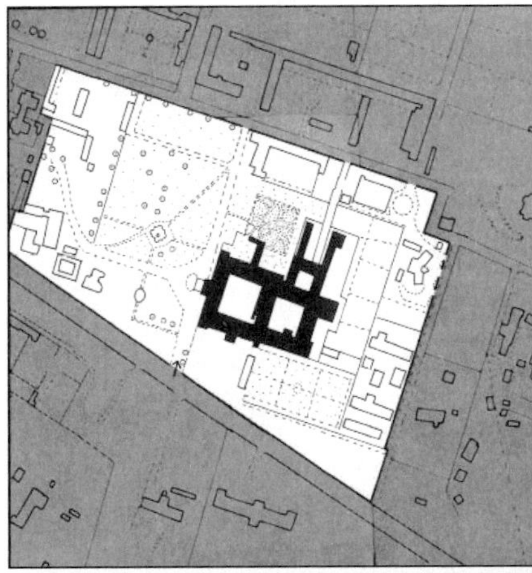

Location	BABAR MAHAL
Constructed	1913 A. D.
Renovated	AFTER 1934
Ownership	HMG
Usage	HMG OFFICES

HP/22

SINGHA MAHAL

Sinha-Mahal

Located near the bridge across the Bagmati River on the way to Patan this palace was constructed in 1919 on a small hillock with a good view of Kathmandu and Patan. It was built by Kishor Narshing for Chandra Shumsher, who then lived there, before he became prime minister and built Singha Darbar.
The palace is built around two courtyards; its front consists of two parts set at an angle to each other. There is a protruding portico on the ground floor. The vertical lines of the lower floors are emphasized by attached wallpillars, while the fourth floor of the main section has an open gallery carried by freestanding columns. The second section carries this open gallery over the third and fourth floors. A unique feature of the compound is its magnificent sunken garden in front of the main entrance.
Chandra made his son Singha Shumsher sole heir of this palace and its compound. This present owner subdivided the original 5 hectares and built a small house for himself at its edge. In 1971, the palace with front garden was acquired by the government, and the banking offices of Nepal's State Bank were installed there.
The general state of the building and garden is good.

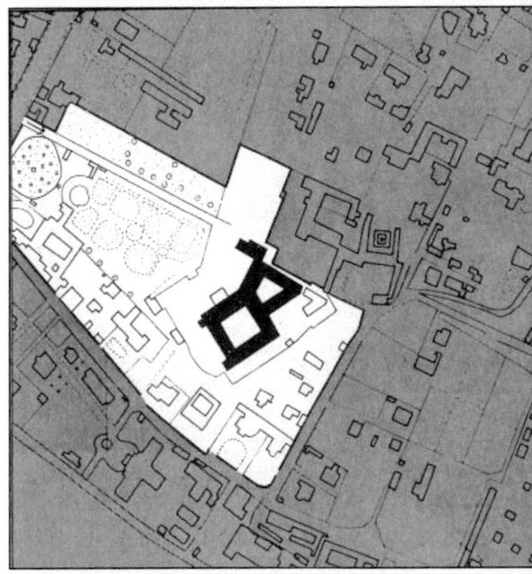

Location	THAPATHALI
Constructed	1919
Renovated	AFTER 1935
Ownership	H. M. GOVERNMENT
Usage	OFFICE OF NEPAL RASTRA BANK

HP/23

HARI BHAWAN

Hari-bhavan

Among the earliest palace estates established in the valley was the one built by Prime Minister Bhimsen Thapa on the southeastern fringe of Kathmandu City. Its appearance reflects the influence of Middle-Eastern Moslem architecture and shows Bhimsen Thapa's great admiration for the Taj Mahal. Originally known as Bagh Darbar, a tiger cage with living tigers in it was kept beside the entrance to the palace. After Bhimsen's death, the palace was nationalized and later made the property of the Shah family. Ram Raja and Laxman Raja Shah expanded and renovated it. Later it was acquired by Juddha Shumsher.
Severely damaged during the earthquake of 1934, it was not used until 1940 when its restoration was completed and it became the residence of Hari Shumsher. Since then it has been known as Hari Bhawan. The changes carried out on both building and gardens were so many that little of the original form and style remainded. The once beautiful large pond within the compound has decayed and many of the old trees have been cut down. Originally occupying 7 hectares, the palace as well as the land have been much subdivided. The palace is now occupied by a foreign aid mission.

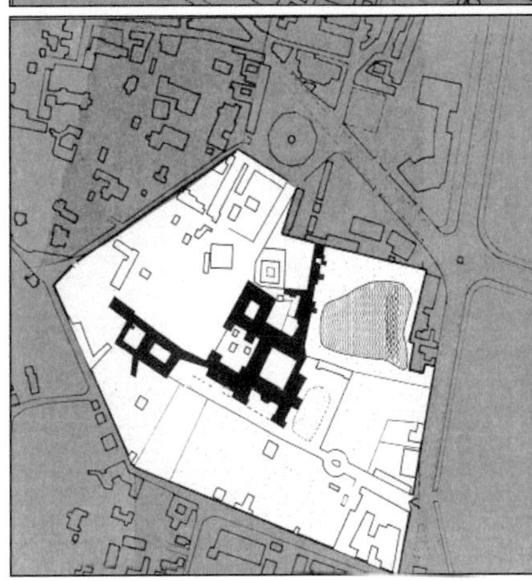

Location	DHARAHARA
Constructed	1805 A. D.
Renovated	1940
Ownership	PRIVATE
Usage	OFFICE, INDIAN MISSION

In 2017, photographer Iwan Baan documented the current condition of Carl Pruscha's structures in Kathmandu. The use of the buildings has partly changed since their construction and their maintenance and upkeep shows significant differences.

PRUSCHA'S PRIVATE RESIDENCE, BANSBARI
Documented 2017
Built to become Pruscha's residence, and after his departure the residence of Barbara Adams from 1975. Later partially demolished and turned into a small suburban restaurant.

RANA GUESTHOUSE, KATHMANDU
Documented 2017
Originally built as the residence for the chief of protocol of Nepal's palace, Jagadish Sumsher Rana. Now rented to foreign embassies as a residence. It was the first assignment to Pruscha's architectural studio with Vinod Vijas and N. Kanade in Kathmandu.

CEDA BUILDING
Documented 2017
Originally conceived as a learning center for *panchayat* members of remote regions, later becoming part of the nearby university.

TARAGAON HOSTEL
Documented 2017
Originally built for the Nepal Women's Association for foreign artists and scientists. Later it became part of the nearby Hyatt Hotel as staff quarters. Recently restored by the Saraf Foundation and turned into an architectural museum and exhibition space for fine arts.

CARL PRUSCHA. BIOGRAPHICAL SKETCHES

Natalie Lettner

Haus Treichl by Lois Welzenbacher, Innsbruck, 1929–1931

I. PROLOGUE

The quality of the spaces
Carl Pruscha creates
is felt even by the blind.
Wolf D. Prix

BABEL, BAUHAUS, FARM

Carl Pruscha is a "cunning, coquettish, sensitive fundamentalist," says his close friend Wolf D. Prix, co-founder and current head of the internationally renowned architectural firm Coop Himmelb(l)au. Of course, Prix isn't sure whether, instead of "fundamentalist," he wouldn't rather call him a "dictator," or "badass." But the crucial point follows in the next sentence: "And that's why he's such a good architect, and the only one who could finish construction on the Tower of Babel."[1] You can hardly pay a greater compliment to an architect than to attest to his ability to complete this utopian and mythical edifice of world literature, which is also considered the epitome of human hubris. On a metaphorical level, Pruscha's architectural ideas really do scrape the sky—by virtue of their being so uncompromisingly involved and innovative. Pruscha is not interested in doing things by halves. The Tower of Babel can be read against the grain, not only as megalomaniacal hubris, but—in a Promethean sense—as the self-determined emancipation of humanity from any form of divine or authoritarian rule, as the enlightened pursuit of freedom.

In purely practical and physical terms, however, Pruscha's designs, unlike many of those by Coop Himmelb(l)au, don't reach for the clouds in any way. They are less intended as conspicuous statements in their scenic or urban environment, but rather enter into meaningful communication with them. In short, Pruscha doesn't build high-rises. Nevertheless, the Tower of Babel is a perfect fit for him. Not so much because towers have played a recurring role in his career, such as his utopian linear-city infrastructure towers, his tower studio at the Academy, or Vienna's Narrenturm ("Fools' Tower"). The reason is that this mythical building embodies the idealization of precisely what has fascinated him all his life: the ruin and the incomplete. The Babylonian tower incarnates both at the same time.

There are two further cornerstones of Pruscha's approach to architecture. Once when he was three or four, little Carl and his mother were walking from the cemetery down to the university in his hometown of Innsbruck and a radiant white house with huge glass windows filled the boy with awe. He had never seen anything like it; that was not what houses in Innsbruck normally looked like. He never forgot this building. He was going to find out much later that he had admired a multi-family house by Tyrolean architect Lois Welzenbacher that no longer exists. At the time, it was one of the few Bauhaus-style buildings in Innsbruck, namely Haus Treichl, built between 1929 and 1931 and destroyed in World War II. "My very first architectural memory,"[2] Pruscha points out, his very own private utopian Tower of Babel, as it were, representing a singular achievement, one that reached far beyond anything Innsbruck's architecture had to offer in those days. It was a formative experience—some fifteen years later, he decided to study architecture under Lois Welzenbacher.

But Bauhaus and international Modernism form only one important anchor point in Pruscha's life as an architect. There is also what he calls "the absolutely primal." This interest is likewise rooted in his childhood, specifically in an old, remote farm.

Carl carving a walking stick, 1943

II. CHILDHOOD AND YOUTH IN TYROL

1936–1955

The structure of the wooden alpine cabin was such that it evoked in a child an understanding of a building, basically as a logical concept.

CP

THE ARCHAIC–FORMATIVE CHILDHOOD YEARS IN A TYROLEAN FARMHOUSE

"I'm not a family man," that is the first sentence Carl Pruscha somewhat reluctantly brought himself to say when asked about his childhood. His middle-class family lived in a civil servant's apartment in Innsbruck. His father, Karl Franz Pruscha, hailed from Vienna and worked as an official in the Directorate-General of the Austrian Federal Railways. His Tyrolean mother, Maria, née Sommer, was a stay-at-home mom. Carl, then still Karl, was the couple's first child and was born on June 10, 1936. Six years later, they welcomed his sister Hannelore.

In March 1938, when Carl was not even two yet, Austria became part of the National Socialist Third Reich. When he entered elementary school, he was confronted with a school system that had been brought into line with the regime. Early on, he had a sense that he loathed any form of coercion. Without actually knowing anything about the political context, he felt the repressive atmosphere that emanated, albeit in ways defying comparison, both from the National Socialist state and the Catholic Church, which was deeply rooted in Tyrolean culture. He hated crossing himself every Sunday in church just as much as having to greet his school teacher with "Heil Hitler" every morning—"Hitler and sweet li'l Jesus, both of them were always no-go areas for me." In church he used to suck at his cap out of sheer boredom—"And the priest came and told me to fold my hands and not suck at my cap."

Neither his birth family nor the family he went on to start himself played a central role in his life. With the clarity of hindsight, he realizes this fact but feels little regret. With his father, especially, young Carl hardly developed any relationship—"To me, my father was an alien being. I had no idea what to do with him." There were reasons for that. As Carl grew up, until about his ninth birthday, his father was absent due to the war. While he was exempted from military service in the Wehrmacht for health reasons, he was tasked with organizing the supply trains the Third Reich ran to Italy and was thus constantly on the move. Even on the weekends he rarely came home, something Carl hardly noticed—"I never missed him."

When the bombs of World War II reached Tyrol in the fall of 1943, Maria Pruscha and her two children moved from Innsbruck to the safe countryside, to Auffach Wildschönau, a highly remote area in the Alpbachtal Valley. His mother's brother-in-law, who was from the valley, arranged for a place in a big farmhouse where the family could stay. Carl spent an hour every day getting to his school in Auffach; in winter he strapped on his skis. At school he had his first experiences with otherness because his classmates rejected him as an outsider. In their eyes, he had a highfalutin way of talking, could not speak their dialect, dressed differently, and was simply a city boy. They broke his pretty colored pencils and beat him up.

In spite of it all, nothing in the world could make Carl trade country life for the city. He loved the remote farm as well as its higher-up mountain pastures. Both not only shaped his under-

Wooden barn, Tyrol, 1943

Farmhouse, Tyrol, ca. 1940

Tyrolean Alp, in front: seven-year-old Carl drinking from a fountain, 1943

standing of architecture, but also his later building projects. In retrospect, he sees the wooden cabin on the alpine pastures particularly as "the origins of architecture," the archetypal, archaic—two of the central notions in which Pruscha's concept of architecture is rooted. In his later life, he became an enthusiast of so-called anonymous architecture.

As a child in the mountains he was in his element; this is where he thrived, felt "incredibly free." He loved the spacious rooms of the farmhouse—a counter model to the "cubbyholes" of the petit-bourgeois civil servant's in Innsbruck. Here, a large front room forms the center where people live, cook, and eat. Just as everyone enjoys meals together, they also spend the night sleeping in a big room with many beds. Even though Carl was a loner and hardly made friends with other kids, he loved these collectivist, down-to-earth ways. He liked the simple life, especially the manner in which everything was taken for granted, and not least the ubiquity of sexuality. It was the most natural thing in the world to watch animals copulating. "On the farm I lived my days like the animals out in the country. And that way I never felt attached to the family." The archaic rituals of cooking, eating, and sleeping—"these basic concepts of life," as Carl Pruscha calls them—always stayed with him.

While he felt indifferent toward his father, he was fascinated with the farmer the family lived with. This was a rough-hewn guy and an alcoholic who made his liquor from berries that Carl enjoyed picking in the woods. His heavy drinking led the farmer to do all sorts of "crazy things" that impressed the boy immensely. To him, this was a free spirit who flaunted all rules, had a blatant disregard for etiquette, and "acted out" when he felt like it. He didn't have any children himself and, in his own way, was happy to take on a bit of a father role for Carl. He let him participate in his work and even made farming equipment for him, for example a "Kraxn," which is to say a miniature wicker pannier carried on the back, which enabled little Carl to carry hay from the field into the barn just like the farmer.

Hannelore, Carl's sister, can still see him sitting on a tree stump or a bench carving wood.[3] Again, he was emulating the farmer who had a huge workshop full of great carving tools and knives—a boy's dream. Carl's greatest pride, of course, was his knife. Being able to produce something on his own gave him a triumphant feeling of autonomy and freedom.

RORSCHACH TEST–PREDESTINED TO BE AN ARCHITECT

On May 3, 1945, Innsbruck was liberated from the Nazi regime. Northern Tyrol now became part of the French occupation zone for the next ten years, until the Austrian State Treaty was signed on May 15, 1955. The Pruschas moved back to Innsbruck, into the cramped spaces of the civil servant's apartment Carl so vehemently disliked. The father now lived with his family again, but Carl, approaching his teen years, still did not develop any relationship with him. With his briefcase, hat, and tie the father set out for his office every day. "For me, that was a nightmare," Pruscha remembers. Again he found a kind of surrogate father in his uncle,

Carl, ten years old, upon return to Innsbruck, 1946

Karl Sommer, an Innsbruck-based graphic designer. During the Nazi regime, Sommer worked for the National Socialists. As early as March 1938, for instance, he designed a poster with a heroically waving swastika flag, which called on the Tyrolese to vote for the *Anschluss* of Austria to the German Reich. After 1945, he worked for the Christian Social ÖVP (Austrian People's Party) and kept on designing political posters—for example, one intended to motivate the population to actively take part in the reconstruction effort. At the time, these political affiliations made no difference to Carl. He was fascinated by his uncle's free life of an artist and especially by his large live-in studio, which was full of pencils and other interesting work material. Living and working formed a unified whole—a model diametrically opposed to the life led by his father who, day in and day out, sat in his office from nine to five and only had a cramped little room for himself at home.

Carl now went to a secondary school emphasizing classical languages in Innsbruck, albeit with little motivation and moderate success. He had a particularly hard time with Latin. After the first four years, his mother decided to take him out of this school. When a team of Swiss researchers was looking for subjects for Rorschach and other psychological tests in Innsbruck, Maria Pruscha signed him on because she thought that it might provide some indication on her son's vocational aptitude. And she was right. After Carl had not only interpreted the famous inkblots, but also assembled and built a few things, the researchers came to the conclusion that he was gifted with excellent spatial intelligence and seemed almost predestined for a career in architecture. The family sent him to a technical college where he entered the building-construction class. One of his teachers was Tyrolean architect Norbert Heltschl, who developed an interest in classic Modernism early on and was one of the first in Tyrol to champion off-shutter exposed concrete as a construction material. Heltschl, too, noticed Carl's talent for spatial thinking and also suggested to his parents that they let the boy study architecture. Carl himself no longer had any doubts, he desperately wanted to become an architect.

At the new school he also, finally, made two important friends, and he was going to stay connected with them over many decades. One was South Tyrol-born artist-to-be Walter Pichler who was in the parallel graphic-design class; the other was Bruno Gironcoli, who hailed from Carinthia, was also of the same age, would go on to become an artist, and was serving an apprenticeship as a goldsmith. Carl would revive his friendship with Pichler not only during his academy years in Vienna but also in the 1960s in New York. Gironcoli and Pruscha would meet again when they were each appointed to a chair at the Vienna Academy of Fine Arts in the 1970s.

In early 1950s' Innsbruck the three teens formed a close-knit trio that defied their narrow-minded, post-Nazi, provincial Austrian environment. Pruscha and Pichler, especially, developed an interest in international fashion and wore duffle coats, jeans, and corduroy slacks, clothing that was bought in Italy and downright avant garde at the time. Carl could relate very little to his father, not to mention his buttoned-down clothing style, but he certainly inherited his sensitivity to his own appearance from him. That, at least, is what his sister Hannelore thinks—"Karli sure is finicky, he's very much concerned with his looks. He got that from dad; he was also like that, all the way into his old age."[4] One of Pruscha's few childhood memories of his father seems to prove her point. Once when Carl was four or five, he went to Vienna with the boy and took him to a tailor to have a snappy children's coat made for him. Perhaps this marked the beginning of Carl's awareness of fashion. All through his life, he put great effort into upholding an exquisite, sometimes even extravagant appearance.

Pichler and Pruscha met during school breaks and discussed everything under the sun, especially art, architecture, fashion, and much-longed-for progress. The teenagers distinguished themselves from their environment through not only their clothing but also their ardent interest in the newest and latest art. During the Nazi era, Austria had remained untouched by any currents of Modernism; in the postwar years, the majority of the population continued to hold on to the aesthetic proclivities of the Nazi regime and rejected anything smacking of Modernism as "degenerate." This Nazi term disappeared from common parlance only gradually, and far too late.

Pruscha was all the more enthused when he saw how avant-garde his friend Bruno Gironcoli's painting technique was. The eyes and nose of a portrait were shown from several angles at the same time, the landscape was dissolved into geometrical elements, the central perspective no longer applied, colors were fragmented. Unbelievable, the sixteen year old Carl thought, Bruno was a genius: he had completely reinvented painting—or, what's more, seeing! Only later did Pruscha realize that Cubism had not originated in a teen's bedroom in Innsbruck in the 1950s but in 1907 Paris, and that the invention of this famed new way of seeing was credited not to Bruno Gironcoli but to Georges Braque and Pablo Picasso.

If young people in the 1950s wanted to follow international currents of contemporary art or read up on classic Modernism, which by then was already historic, their only reliable sources were the cultural institutions of the liberators. These were designed to foster democratic values and advance the denazification of the Austrian population.

For Carl, it was especially the America House on Innsbruck's Anichstrasse that proved a treasure trove. At the time, it was an exceedingly successful institution that attracted over 250,000 visitors in the year 1950 alone—not least because one could borrow popular American whodunits, comics, and paperback western novels for free.[5] But Pruscha was interested in something else. He immersed himself in the architecture magazines and catalogs also available there. It was here that he first discovered for himself the icon of modern American architecture par excellence, Frank Lloyd Wright. He was even more enthralled with buildings by Brazilian architect Oscar Niemeyer, especially the private home in Rio de Janeiro he built in 1953, the Casa das Canoas, with its flowing curves and interpenetrating indoor and outdoor spaces.

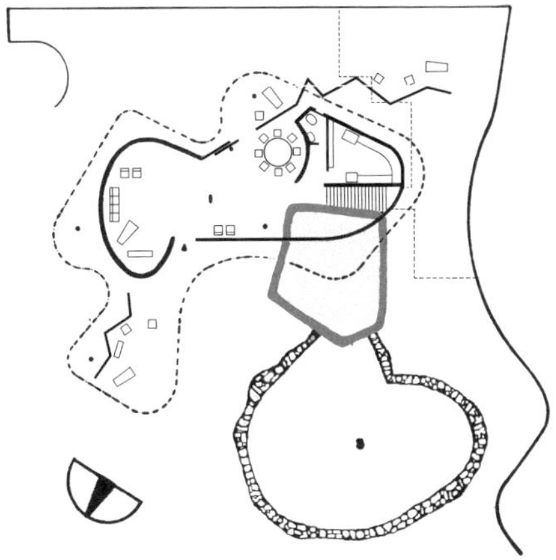

Plan and view of Oscar Niemeyer's country house, Rio de Janeiro, 1954

Oscar Niemeyer

He had never seen anything like it: "To me, Niemeyer seemed as far away as the moon."[6] At the age of seventeen, he didn't know yet what it was that attracted him so strongly. Architectural history later dubbed it critical regionalism. Or, as Pruscha puts it, Niemeyer succeeded in reinterpreting the rigid Bauhaus style "with South American verve." Carl further developed this approach, particularly in his own buildings in Nepal and Sri Lanka.

His favorite reads at the America House included the *arts & architecture* magazine, edited by John Entenza since 1940. Already its outstanding graphic design was striking to him—"I can still clearly remember the beautiful lettering." It was here that he first saw the famous Case Study Houses that were sponsored by *arts & architecture*. The project was aimed at developing simple, affordable residential buildings in accordance with the principles of Modernism. Leafing through the magazine's back runs, he discovered the Case Study homes designed by, among others, Charles and Ray Eames, Ralph Soriano, Richard Neutra, Craig Ellwood, and Eero Saarinen. The magazine also combined architecture with painting and sculpture, and it was here that Pruscha saw works by Joan Miró or Hans Arp for the first time. That the visual arts and architecture speak a common language was an insight that stayed with Pruscha; he was to see himself not only as an architect but also as an artist throughout his life.

He was soon sure which professor he wanted to study architecture with in Vienna. It was Lois Welzenbacher whose radiant, white Haus Treichl had already fascinated him as a child. Welzenbacher was Tyrol's most important exponent of Modernism in the interwar period and the only Austrian architect invited to participate in the 1932 exhibition *The International Style: Architecture since 1922* at MoMA in New York. During the Nazi period, he served as a company architect with the Siebel aircraft factory in Halle an der Saale. That is, like many other proponents of Modernist architecture, which the Third Reich condemned, he worked in industrial and defense construction. Since 1947, he had served as professor of architecture at the Academy of Fine Arts in Vienna.

Pruscha did not want to leave his future to chance. He had long known that Welzenbacher spent his weekends in Absam, Tyrol, and decided to contact him personally. Without knowing what the professor looked like, he lay in wait for him at the nearby Hall train station on a Friday afternoon in the spring of 1955. "And then a little man in a white, hand-woven suit really got off the train and, carrying a little case, began to walk in the direction of Absam." That could only be Welzenbacher. Pruscha followed him, snuck up to him, and blurted out, "Mister professor, I would like to ask, can I study with you?" As a young aspiring architect he was, of course, well prepared and had his portfolio of sketches with him. Welzenbacher replied, "Let me see what you've got there?" And he finally said, "Well, you do seem to be a bit talented." He told Pruscha to get in touch with him in the fall and to come to his class. But it wasn't meant to be. In August of that year, Welzenbacher died at the age of sixty-six.

Carl Pruscha, shortly before finishing high school, 1955

III. ACADEMY YEARS IN VIENNA

1955–1959

Of course, architecture largely has to do with anti-freedom. It forces people into rigid situations. To confront this problem and, on the one hand, meet man's primal desire for space, and, on the other hand, leave them their freedom, that's the goal.
CP

THE TRUTH IN ARCHITECTURE—THE RUIN AND THE INCOMPLETE

In the winter semester of 1955, Carl Pruscha enrolled at the Academy of Fine Arts in Vienna and joined the master class formerly headed by Welzenbacher. In the first semesters, he had to complete courses in preparatory subjects, such as statics, descriptive geometry, materials science, and the like. One of the most inspiring classes all students had to attend was the legendary evening nude with Herbert Boeckl—Pruscha remembers him as "a daredevil."

In the meantime, his image of the late Lois Welzenbacher transformed into an idealized myth. The older students told him the most incredible stories about the oddball professor, as they saw him, who had spent his nights in the assistant's room next to the art room. With regard to his clothing style, Welzenbacher is said to have stated that, as an architect, one had two choices, either go to the best tailor and be superbly dressed, or just be an artist like him. He thus wore suits tailored from fabrics his wife had woven for him, and as a belt he tied a thick piece of string around his waist. Carl would have loved to experience all that for himself.

He admired Markus Prachensky, one of the older students in Welzenbacher's master class who was four years older than him and also hailed from Innsbruck. He cut an impressive figure, "running around in a monk's cowl and designing a monastery as his diploma project." Prachensky was in his last year and also studied painting on the side. From 1956, he was, along with Arnulf Rainer, Josef Mikl, and Wolfgang Hollegha, part of the core avant-garde group of Galerie St. Stephan, which decisively shaped the art scene of 1950s' Vienna.

The first architectural model Pruscha developed all on his own presented a highly original design that, at its core, already contained much of what his work would center on later. He developed a new solution for the war-ravaged Dogana building in Innsbruck, located right near the Hofburg palace, which had been left to fall into further ruin. That was precisely what fascinated Pruscha, he was completely taken with the high, windowless walls of the elongated edifice. He wanted to leave the derelict part as it was and designed a modern extension and superstruction.

It was only ten years later, when Pruscha was already working for UNESCO in Nepal, that the accompanying theory was delivered to him there by the renowned Louis I. Kahn. During a visit with Pruscha, he suggested that already-existing architecture could only be a source of inspiration as a ruin or an incomplete structure. Only in this imperfect state does a building reveal some of its deeper meaning. "What remains of the ruin, is the essential," Pruscha adds, "you are able to make out some of the truth of a building." Something similar is true for the fragment. As long as something is under construction, its interesting aspects are still visible. "Later, when the structure is 'blessed' with accessorics, it loses the truth." Even though as a student, Pruscha did not yet fully formulate these thoughts, the first project he created at the Academy already pointed toward his later approach. Pruscha's work in 1980s' and 1990s' Vienna was to focus intensely on such incomplete projects or ones that presented themselves to him as ruins.

In 1956, finally, the then 46-year-old Roland Rainer succeeded Welzenbacher as head of the School of Architecture. He ranked as one of the foremost architects and urban planners of Austrian postwar Modernism. His most important buildings include the Wiener Stadthalle, which opened in 1958—"a significant building in architectural history."[7] He tirelessly championed humane building designs and, from an ecological perspective, many of his housing concepts are today considered exemplary and visionary. Rainer was on a quest for alternatives, both to the ever taller and bigger mass high-rises and to the sprawl of detached homes in outlying areas. A couple of decades later, Carl Pruscha, too, would aim to counter these trends with the creative and innovative proposal of his Quadrangle Housing project.

In the 1950s, Rainer's Nazi past[8] played no role in public debates—in keeping with the then customary way of dealing with Austria's National Socialist history. It was not an issue either for Carl Pruscha who was now studying under Roland Rainer. To Pruscha, it was something else that stood out. He was initially disappointed and disenchanted about not being able to study under the creative Welzenbacher and having to submit to Rainer's strict regime. The focus was not on free ideas, but on rational argumentation, mathematics, and statics. This was less about architecture as an art form and more about its status as a science. What's more, Rainer used to wear a double-breasted gray flannel suit, "all buttoned-down, like a government official," observed Pruscha, who was reminded of his father. He saw Rainer as rigid, strict, and distant. He completed his projects at the Academy "blindfold, on the side," as "a purely routine job," without great commitment. He would come to appreciate Rainer's qualities at a later point.

A STUDIO, A WIFE, AND A GIRL'S ROOM IN INNSBRUCK

At first, Carl Pruscha stayed with relatives, friends, and acquaintances in Vienna. But he soon found a live-in studio for himself on Osterleitengasse in the 19th district. It was the former studio of painter Anton Velim, whose depictions of workers sometimes earned him the moniker "Egger-Lienz of the proletariat."[9] After Velim's death in 1954, his daughter Edda decided to rent out the studio, and her first tenant was Carl. He renovated and expanded it with dedication and vigor, turning it into a live-in studio with a new wooden ceiling, a kitchen, and a bathroom. It was the first project he actually realized as an architect—"The studio was so beautiful! It's too bad I don't have any pictures." Edda Velim, who was studying restoration at the Academy, occasionally worked at the studio, too. "She had cast an eye on me"—and the two soon became a couple. This relationship just happened to him, Pruscha recounts. He liked the idea that Edda was an artist's daughter and appreciated her unconventional and anti-bourgeois demeanor; to him she was a kind of hippie *avant la lettre*. Their relationship proved difficult from the start. Nevertheless, the two went on to marry in 1961, and this came about when Edda threatened to marry someone else. Carl reacted impulsively and called two fellow students, asking them to come and serve as witnesses at the bureau of vital statistics. A schnapps at Café Hawelka concluded this not very ceremonious wedding. Pruscha was now married, even though he deeply rejected this bourgeois institution. He framed their union, in a somewhat contradictory vein, as an "anti-bourgeois statement of an act of defiance."

His old teenage friendship with Walter Pichler was revived and grew even stronger in Vienna. He and Edda introduced Pruscha to parts of the capital's bohemian scene, which included "two totally crazy women"—namely textile artist Ingrid Schuppan, the wife-to-be of Oswald Wiener, and media and performance artist Waltraut Höllinger, who began calling herself VALIE EXPORT in 1967. Pruscha was impressed with the lifestyle of the art scene and loved, for example, the way goulash soup was cooked in a huge laundry-room tub. "I thought that was cool. That's what I'd always imagined bohemian life to be like." Not least, it reminded him of the big pot in the alpine cabin of his childhood, from which everyone ate soup together.

Carl's sister Hannelore also got a taste of this bohemian scene. She was delighted when her brother invited her to his new studio in Vienna. "He always looked after me. That was something really wonderful."[10] After all, being able to travel from Innsbruck to Vienna was not to be taken for granted in postwar Austria, and there was hardly another girl in her class who had been to the Austrian capital. In Vienna, Carl always bought her new clothes—"pretty extreme stuff, of course," as Hannelore remembers. "In Innsbruck people laughed at me. My god, what a sight you are." But she was proud of her extravagant outfits. Among other things, Carl also bought a "gaudy checkered wool fabric" from which her mother had to sew a coat for her. There was one episode that Hannelore would never forget. Carl came to visit in Innsbruck and their parents were not at home. Without so much as an explanation, he began moving the heavy, high-quality, carpenter-made larch-wood furniture his father was particularly proud of from Hannelore's room to the attic. Everything had to go, even the ugly glass pane in the door. The girl—"Back then, you were still a child at fifteen"—began to cry in desperation, dreading how their parents would react. All his life, Pruscha was certain that his father never understood him, but his sister had quite a different perception. She maintains that while their mother actually suffered under Carl's ideas, their father always took his son's side and firmly believed in his talent. He did everything he could to support his son's passion. From an early stage, he took him on trips, for example to Marseille. There the architecturally inclined teenager marveled for the first time at a building designed by Le Corbusier, the famous Unité d'habitation. In the same vein, he also bankrolled his architectural studies without further ado as well as the refurbishment of Hannelore's room according to Carl's plans. Its floor was covered with made-to-measure corn-stover mats. The walls were painted in three different shades of gray; the windows were adorned with contrasting yellow curtains. The bed, table, stool, and bookshelf were made of square iron tubing. Wire-glass panes were used as a small tabletop and for the new door. When she got over the initial shock, Hannelore was delighted. It was "A beautiful room. Everything he did was sacrosanct for me."

Roland Rainer's first studies of anonymous architecture in northern Burgenland, Austria, 1961

At about the same time, Carl Pruscha began an intense collaboration with young carpenter Grabner in Vienna—on the one hand, because the projects assigned by Roland Rainer were not challenging enough for him; on the other, to make money. He now invested most of his time in designing furniture made of steel, wood, and glass for the carpentry. Among other things, he planned a kitchen for Peter Weck, who was six years his senior and went on to become a Burgtheater and film actor. To this day, Pruscha himself uses the comfortable modern armchairs he designed then, which is to say, he later had replicas made for himself. See pp. 175, 235 He enjoyed drawing furniture and it came easily to him. With the money he made, he was able to buy his first car, an old VW. Cars remained important to him all through his life, and he would later exchange his VW for Porsches, Jaguars, and the like. He relished the independence and financial freedom his work for the carpentry afforded him. But when one day Grabner made him an offer to no longer work as a contractor but join the firm as a partner, that woke him up—"It gave me a shock." By no means did he want to spend his life in a commercial company. He turned down the partnership and decided to focus on his architectural studies again.

ROLAND RAINER AND THE FINAL PROJECT THAT WON THE FIRST PRIZE

Initially, Pruscha saw Professor Roland Rainer as the very antithesis of Vienna's bohemian art scene, the circles he had gained access to, not least, through Edda Velim. But he then discovered something that, while having nothing to do with architecture and art, still softened his image of Rainer as an uptight square. For starters he was one of the first in Vienna to drive a Citroën DS—a dream car. When he and fellow students, "shoe-horned into a small Fiat 600," took a trip to the Cobenzl restaurant on Vienna's scenic Höhenstrasse, he saw Rainer's Citroën and the professor in female company. From that point on, he found him less bourgeois.

And soon Pruscha began to appreciate Rainer's qualities as an architect and architecture theoretician. One of his great passions was his interest in anonymous architecture. Initially, Pruscha, the technology-obsessed student, did not share this fascination to the same degree. But he did catch on to it at this point, and it was to play a central role in his later life. Together with his students, Rainer examined the anonymous architecture of the northern Burgenland region and analyzed the arrangement of the elongated *Streckhof* farm complexes with attached barns. As Pruscha remembers, "There you had rationality and sensuality in juxtaposition, and I really liked that." Rainer's research with his students led to a 1961 publication that is widely recognized to this day.[11] Furthermore, Rainer invited his master-class students to his own studio house in St. Margarethen in the state of Burgenland, which was still under construction. For the walls, he acquired the stones of a nearby abandoned train station. Rainer was able to convey to his students a sense of the value of these old blackened stones from the era of steam engines. Vines formed the "roof" of an extensive pergola. "That was an altogether different Rainer than the one teaching his class at the Academy."

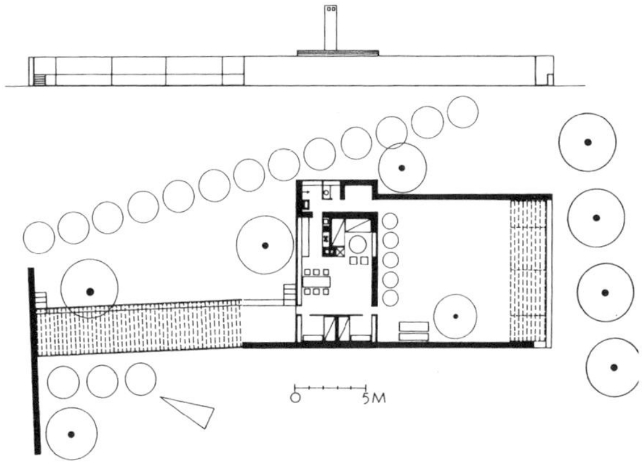

Plan, view and inside of Roland Rainer's summer house in St. Margarethen in Burgenland, 1957

The professor, in turn, became aware of Pruscha's talent at the latest when he turned in his design for a small administration building with a conference hall. It proposed an unusual solution, "A long, geometrically regular strip and, next to it, a circular disk as a conference hall—without any further ado, 'ideas,' or complications," Rainer still remembered more than forty years later.[12]

He was so enamored with Pruscha's final project that he awarded him the so-called State Prize of the Academy, an honor bestowed on the best project of each year. Pruscha had developed a design for a student dormitory that was based on the geometrical forms of circle and square. Reminiscent of the then cutting-edge Airstream trailer, its long aluminum building contained two floors of cube-shaped cells, which served as the student living quarters. An underground passage led to a subterranean common room with a circular layout and a domed roof light—"in Niemeyer's style," as Pruscha recounts.

A colleague three years his senior, whom Pruscha didn't yet know at the time, saw the student-dormitory project at the exhibition of the final projects at the Academy. To Carl's chagrin, he didn't share Rainer's enthusiasm and only wondered, in an arrogant and condescending tone, "What's that supposed to be?" It was exactly the kind of thing Pruscha takes as a challenge. He tries to engage detractors in conversation. As it turned out, he was dealing with later-to-be renowned Austrian architect Raimund Abraham. Despite—or maybe precisely because of—this bumpy start, a lasting friendship developed between them.

After his graduation, Roland Rainer helped his favorite student get several jobs, at first in Salzburg where Pruscha collaborated on an urban-planning project for the Alpenstrasse, which was never realized. Pruscha found Salzburg to be "terrible, stuffy, very conservative." He subsequently relocated to Solingen, where he assisted with a competition for a sports hall. He made so much money that he was able to exchange his VW for a silver-gray Porsche 356—"that had long been my dream!" He subsequently worked for Paul Schneider-Esleben in Düsseldorf who had designed the glazed Haniel Garage, one of the most important buildings of German postwar Modernism.

He had soon made up his mind to set out for the New World. This decision went back to a series of lectures by Austrian architect and architectural historian Eduard F. Sekler in 1959, Pruscha's last year at the Academy. In his guest lectures, Sekler traced an arc from the beginnings of architecture to the Gothic and Renaissance period and all the way to Le Corbusier and Mies van der Rohe. He looked at these historic buildings from the perspective of the present and emphasized, for instance, the continuities between the Classical order of columns and Mies van der Rohe's columns. It had always been important for Pruscha to see himself as a man of Modernism and dissociate himself from the past, and he had never heard anyone approach the matter in this way. He was so taken by his remarks that, after his lecture, he approached Sekler, who was delighted with the enthusiastic student and invited him for lunch. Sekler told him about his upcoming

Carl with his first car, the famous Porsche 356, 1960

Graduation at the Academy, 1959

professorship at Harvard and the new urban-design class. Pruscha had already caught the bug and, when projects in Europe seemed less and less gratifying to him, he decided to apply for a post-graduate course at Harvard. He was actually accepted. Austrian patron of the arts Manfred Mautner-Markhof, Sen., who had supported Arnulf Rainer, Friedensreich Hundertwasser, and others in the past, also provided a grant to Carl Pruscha. Pruscha's father also jumped in to help with the sizable tuition fees. His sister Hannelore remembers that "Dad had to act as guarantor for Harvard. It was 100,000 Austrian schilling, I remember that well." And finally, nothing stood in the way of his departure for the New World.

Carl in New York, 1962

Carl as a postgraduate student on Harvard Yard, 1962

IV. NEW YORK AND HARVARD

1962–1964

The basic idea was transport. And for me, transport was a linear system, from which—translated into the vertical—the infrastructure develops. This means there are recurring vertical elements, which contain everything, water, power, etc. For me, an urban design system was actually not about the volume, but about providing all necessary services.
CP

A BUMPY ARRIVAL

Carl Pruscha had no intention of presenting himself as a poor student at Harvard. Before setting out on his journey, he purchased elegant leather bags and filled them with new custom-tailored suits, shirts, coats, and other fine accessories. He packed all his belongings into his silver-gray Porsche and with it he embarked on the SS *Rotterdam.*

In the course of the long crossing he played chess and became friends with a young New Yorker who invited him to spend the first night at his and his uncle's place on the Upper West Side at Central Park. Pruscha was happy to accept. What he didn't know was that, back then, the Upper West Side was still a dangerous place. He followed his friend up a high-rise to greet his uncle. When he went to get his luggage a little later, the windows of his Porsche had been smashed and everything was gone. It was quite a rough welcome to the New World, because, in his words, "things like precision, nice suits, nice bags, and so on are really important to me. It was such a shock to have lost everything…"

The next day, however, his reaction was already one of defiant initiative. He went to what was then the most renowned menswear store, Brooks Brothers, famous for its classic and Ivy-League style clothes. He bought a new suit and a couple of shirts. "That way I'd become Americanized over night."

For the first time, Pruscha saw skyscrapers in real life, first and foremost Mies van der Rohe's bronze-colored cuboid on Park Avenue, the famous and influential Seagram Building, which had been completed just a few years earlier in 1958. "Seeing that on the ground was breathtaking. Simply magical!" He was fascinated with the PanAm (now MetLife) Building, not so much the structure itself, but more its urban-planning function—"How the long Park Avenue is suddenly blocked by this building and the street is thus given a destination!" And finally he stood in front of Frank Lloyd Wright's Guggenheim Museum, which had only opened in 1959. But as much as he was interested in these individual monumental edifices, he never sought to design anything of this kind himself. He understood buildings as part of a network, as elements of a comprehensive infrastructure. He had come to the US to gain a deeper understanding of this subject matter.

When all the paperwork relating to the theft was done, he was finally able to take up his postgraduate urban-design course at Harvard. He only joined the class in the summer semester, because a hepatitis infection had forced him to stay in Europe a few months longer than initially planned. That made his integration into the class more difficult, as everyone already knew each other and hierarchies and alliances had been established. For the first time, he experienced serious competition. Up until that point, everything had come easy for him, and he now found himself in a tougher environment: "The competition was there from the very start, and it was interesting for me to have to stand my ground for the first time." He took on an outsider role, remained "a colorful figure that could not be pigeonholed," as former fellow students would later recount. He made few real friends there, but has remained in contact with Japan-born Koichi Nagashima to this day.

Josep Lluís Sert's realization of Le Corbusier's design for the Carpenter Center for the Visual Arts, Harvard, 1963

Josep Lluís Sert's Holyoke Center, Cambridge, Massachusetts, 1965

Josep Lluís Sert, architect and dean of the Harvard University Graduate School of Design

Studying at Harvard was intense. People only showed up in class around ten or eleven in the morning but then work continued until the evening, often until late at night. What surprised Pruscha was the relaxed manner in which professors dealt with their students. After a long workday, they often even dove into the Boston nightlife together, something unthinkable in 1950s' and 1960s' Vienna, one of the reasons being that many of the teachers were visiting professors who had no access to social networks and were thus more sociable toward their students. That was also what made this postgraduate course so special and set it apart from the master-school principle at the Vienna Academy where students spent years with a single teacher. Here, classes were taught by a varied group of high-caliber visiting professors from around the world, and Pruscha was exposed to widely different trends in the international architectural scene—many of which would keep inspiring him decades later.

GREAT TEACHERS—FROM SERT TO MUMFORD

To start with, there was Catalan architect Josep Lluís Sert, who had succeeded Walter Gropius as the faculty dean of the Graduate School of Design in 1953. Sert wowed his students by being a "living history book" of sorts, as Pruscha remembers. Sert had worked closely with Le Corbusier and had already taken part in the 4th Congrès internationaux d'architecture moderne (CIAM) in 1933 where the Charter of Athens redefined the principles of urban design. Sert was also the one in charge of providing Le Corbusier with an opportunity to design a building for Harvard, his only one in the US. Sert built the famous Carpenter Center for the Visual Arts in accordance with Le Corbusier's plans. A *béton brut* structure, it presented itself as a radical break in the midst of campus buildings that had been constructed from red bricks for 300 years straight. Young Carl Pruscha was enthralled, he considered it "probably the most beautiful building Le Corbusier ever built, as far as its perfect execution and the precision in its details goes. You know, other Corbusier buildings were often built in a really wild and sloppy manner." Modernism aficionado Pruscha also saw the H-shaped Holyoke Center, a hospital that Sert built on the campus in the 1960s, as revolutionary architecture—"a concrete box, but highly elegant!" Not least, he was impressed with the way people in the US were quick to make room for new buildings. When needed, old structures were, "Bang bang, knocked down with the wrecking ball."

Sometimes, octogenarian and gray eminence Walter Gropius would also stop by Sert's classes. Pruscha cherished that, but he attached greater importance to other things, for example the crucial role theory played at Harvard, something he had not been exposed to in Vienna at all. He not only valued Eduard Sekler greatly, but also the classes with British architecture theoretician Jacqueline Tyrwhitt. In the decades after 1945, she had made significant contributions to connecting city planning and social issues in a new way. She was working with the UN and trying to figure out what cities in developing countries could look like in the future—a subject that was not on Pruscha's radar yet, but which would already be at the top of his mind a few years later.

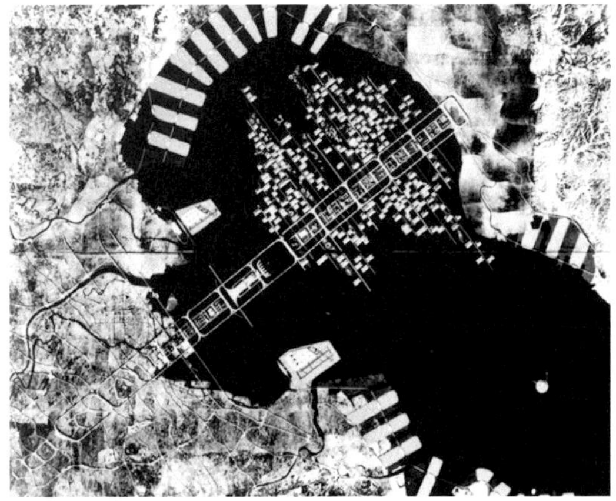

One of Kyonori Kikutake's floating cities: *Marine City*, model, 1962–1963

Kenzo Tange's model for the urban expansion accross the Tokyo Bay, 1960

Kenzo Tange

Tyrwhitt worked in close cooperation with Greek architect Constantinos Doxiadis, the chief planner of Pakistan's capital Islamabad. The professor once even took a select group of students on an excursion to Mykonos and Delos, where Pruscha got to know not only Doxiadis but also luminaries in fields far removed from architecture, such as cultural anthropologist Margaret Mead and philosopher Bertrand Russell. Doxiadis and Tyrwhitt were among the early advocates of an interdisciplinary approach—twenty-five years later when he helmed the Academy of Fine Arts, Pruscha, too, would try to advance such an approach and thus to phase out the antiquated master-school principle in Vienna. The Harvard lecturers who impressed Pruscha included Greek-French architect Georges Candilis, who had also collaborated with Le Corbusier but was later, as a member of the influential Team X, critical of him for being too dogmatic. Candilis wanted to connect the language of the Bauhaus with local building traditions in the so-called Third World—another idea that Pruscha would pick up on and develop further. At the time, Team X, a group of young rebel architects who linked architecture and social concerns, was well represented at Harvard. Pruscha's teachers thus included, for instance, Aldo van Eyck, the founder of Structuralism.

At Boston's Massachusetts Institute of Technology (MIT) Pruscha learned from Kevin Lynch about the psychology of space, which Lynch applied not only to individual spaces but also to entire structures of cities. His research showed that people create mental maps of their environments, their five essential elements being paths, edges, districts, nodes, and landmarks. These were interesting impulses that prompted Pruscha to become a master of the psychology of space himself. Grozny-born Serge Chermayeff somewhat reminded Pruscha of Roland Rainer, as he also designed low, carpet-style housing-development structures, from which protruded only a few mega-shapes containing common spaces. Pruscha would soon take this concept a few steps further to a futuristic and utopian level.

The exchange of ideas at Harvard was intense; occasionally professors from Yale also presented their concepts there. Louis I. Kahn, for example, gave a talk on his then red-hot revitalization plan for central Philadelphia, from which he wanted to ban cars—a downright heretical idea in the 1960s. Pruscha was fascinated with Kahn's thoughts on traffic and transport in urban areas, one of his own primary fields of interest. A few years later, Pruscha got to know Kahn personally in Nepal and owes one of his important insights to him: only as a fragment or as a ruin does architecture reveal some of its truth. Occasionally, the students drove to Yale in New Haven themselves to attend lectures, for instance by Richard Buckminster Fuller or Lewis Mumford. A pattern emerged of Pruscha listening to all kinds of ideas and finding them quite interesting, but not relevant to him at the moment. Only years later did he realize how important these impulses had been for him, what effects they had had on him in the long run—for instance Mumford's notion of a new, progressive, critical regionalism. Or the ideas developed by Fumihiko Maki, a proponent of Japanese Metabolism who taught at Harvard. At first, Pruscha saw Maki as the most boring exponent of this Japanese current. Maki advocated

Frederick Kiesler

Kiesler's *Endless House*, model, 1958

Kiesler's *Endless House*, drawing, 1959

the *Group Form,* small flexible groups of buildings in a loosely interconnected structure without monumental high points. He was looking for a middle ground, but young Pruscha who wanted to change the world called it a "a rotten compromise." He was a lot more enthusiastic about the utopian megalomaniac ideas of other Metabolists, such as Kiyonori Kikutake with his *Ocean City;* Kisho Kurokawa with his *Helix City Project;* and, above all, Kenzo Tange with his *Plan for Tokyo,* a swimming megastructure in the Gulf of Tokyo. "A huge city in the ocean with huge skyscrapers," raptures Pruscha.

In retrospect, he takes a more critical view of these utopian, never realized plans of the Metabolists. "Now that I've grown old, I do look at these things with different eyes. It does give me the creeps, a little bit." As much as he still sympathizes with the utopian imagination and enthusiasm of his youthful self, he can now reflect critically on the megalomaniac projects that, back then, he "developed with such ease." Today he realizes how important the more moderate voices at Harvard had been for him, for example Maki, who had been in search of a humanist approach to architecture, or Mumford, who took regional conditions into consideration. But for now, Pruscha wanted to revolutionize the cities with radical plans.

UTOPIAS FOR THE NEW WORLD

In the summer of 1962, Pruscha's wife Edda was not the only one to come visit him in New York; his old friend Walter Pichler and his wife, Elisabeth, came, too. Together, the four of them rented a studio on 8th Street in the East Village. Raimund Abraham was also in town. "Abraham, Pichler, and I—that was a think tank," and their discussions frequently dragged on into the wee hours. Pruscha was fascinated by the way Pichler could turn architecture into sculptures, and Pichler was enthusiastic about Pruscha's utopian technological projects.

That same summer, Pruscha, at the recommendation of Josep Lluís Sert, did an internship with Paul Lester Wiener, a Leipzig-born architect who had studied, among others, at Adolf Loos' School of Building in Vienna and had emigrated to the US as early as 1913. Sert, Le Corbusier, and Wiener ran a studio together where comprehensive master plans were developed for South America, for example for Bogotá and other Colombian cities, for city expansions in Brazil, and for Havana. Wiener was looking for an assistant and Sert recommended one of his most talented students—"He's got great ideas." Wiener hired Pruscha to conduct a study for the ski-resort town of Aspen, Colorado, which is located 2,400 meters above sea level. Pruscha was impressed by Wiener's appearance. He was "A bon vivant, always elegantly dressed, with a hat and a rose in his buttonhole, a man of the world!" The two hit it off right away, and the young architect was fascinated by the project, as well.

He dug up old historic maps of the former mining village, which prospered in the nineteenth century following a silver-mining boom. However, the depression of 1893 had put an end to this heyday. The town only began to recover after 1945 when it redefined itself as a ski resort, especially after the World Ski Championships had been staged there in 1950. Now a master plan was to be drawn

Yona Friedman's town study, 1962

Carl Pruscha's proposal for Boston's Prudential Center, 1962

up for the town's further development. Pruscha came up with a radical idea. The city map would remain intact, but all future buildings as well as streets would be constructed underground, not least on account of the harsh climatic conditions. "That means, you actually couldn't see anything of Aspen, the entire town was underground." A huge machine formed the center, which supplied infrastructure services and served as a communal space. It provided power and water, as well as community heating, and it housed all public facilities, from theater and sports hall to shopping center and assembly halls. From this machine, tubes with inclined elevators led up to circular traffic islands in the mountains and the skiing areas. Years later, Pruscha took his students on a field trip to the Chilean port town of Valparaíso, where over thirty funicular lifts connect the port with parts of the town that are built on steep hillsides. Stopping at several stations, they deliver people and goods to different elevations. He was thrilled to discover this transport system and saw parallels to his onetime Aspen utopia. To this day, he is convinced of its high quality and sustainability. See pp. 123, 225

Paul L. Wiener liked his assistant's idea, too. He had a model built and presented it in Aspen. There, however, people only shook their heads and laughed at him and his crazy idea. Wiener lost the commission and Pruscha his job. But this did not compromise the friendship that had long developed between the two. What's more, Wiener welcomed Pruscha into his family. Wiener's wife, Ingeborg, clicked with Edda right away and they became friends. The Wieners had a summer house in Amagansett on Long Island, right in the middle of the artists' colony, and "[t]hat was a really wild clique." Edda and Carl turned Wiener's garage into a vacation home of their own and spent two great summers there, enjoying parties and wonderful encounters. "Life there was surreal, utopian."[13] Among the luminaries living there were Arthur Miller and Marilyn Monroe; artist Willem de Kooning; architect Costantino Nivola; cartoonist Saul Steinberg; and, crucially for Pruscha, Frederick Kiesler.

Kiesler was a close friend of Wiener's, and thus Pruscha came into contact with the visionary and exceptional artist from Vienna who can't be pigeonholed to any one discipline. He staged exhibitions such as the legendary 1924 *Internationale Ausstellung neuer Theatertechnik* (International Exhibition of New Theater Technique) in Vienna; created stage sets; styled store windows for Saks, 5th Avenue in New York; designed furniture; and developed radical single-family homes, such as his legendary *Endless House*. Pruscha loved the high-flying discussions with Kiesler, which never revolved around architecture but around visions for the future. And he loved his little whims. When they went for walks on the beach together, for instance, he had to hold a white parasol over his head as he was sensitive to the sun. Since 1957, Kiesler had worked on the famous Shrine of the Book in Jerusalem, the only one of his large-scale projects that was actually built. Kiesler used to complain to Pruscha about all the difficulties he was up against, including not only the constraints of the construction industry, but also those of building in general. Pruscha was impressed by Kiesler's intransigence, a character trait they had in common.

Carl as apprentice at Paul Wiener's office in New York

Paul Wiener's country cottage at Amagansett, 1963

Inside view of Wiener's country cottage

The older he got, the more he was able to identify with Kiesler's reluctance to have to actually build something he had planned. He was enthralled with the Shrine of the Book, "This building fascinated me immensely with its precision, its complex system of thought, the black wall and the white body of the dome."[14]

After the summer of 1963 came Pruscha's last semester at Harvard, and he started working on his final project. He had no interest in architecture detached from its cultural, social, and discursive context. Marshall McLuhan's theories on communication and media, hotly discussed issues in the early 1960s, were an intriguing inspiration. With his exemplary *Plan for a Linear City between Boston and New York,* Pruscha attempted to illustrate the way communication, transport, and environmental protection work in times of increasing population density, and which urban forms are apt to facilitate them. It provided an alternative to traditional cities and their radial expansion. The goal was to shorten transport and commuter routes, enabling the provision of services along a narrow, elongated area, and at the same time guarantee residents' proximity to recreational landscaped areas. Pruscha wanted to leave behind the big city of Modernism that Baron Haussmann had designed in Paris and Otto Wagner in Vienna, where everything was governed by land law. In its vertical population centers, the new big city would operate in accordance with air laws. The bottom level, comprising the ground and lower floors, would not be given into private hands, but serve communal, social, and cultural needs. The next-higher level would be reserved for scientific developments, laboratories, and research, and only the top zone would be designated as a residential area. These structures would not only grow vertically but would also be connected with each other on a horizontal level. To many of his more practically minded fellow students, Pruscha's projects appeared strange—"Why don't you design something reasonable and realistic for a change?" Some professors also thought Pruscha took it "a bridge too far," but Josep Lluís Sert liked his concepts and encouraged him to further explore his utopian approach—"Let your ideas flow freely, it only needs to be consistent. It has to be an idea, but not everything needs to be real."[15] Pruscha didn't have to be told twice, and developed his diploma project into a *Vision for Global Urbanization*. "My idea was that networks and structures cover the entire globe, as it were. I drew world maps, world population accumulations, focus areas, loose connections."[16] Infrastructure towers provided densely populated areas with energy and water. Further volumes were connected to them. Between these towers a linear and ribbon-shaped city encircled the globe. Underground tubes provided for the high-speed transport of people and goods. These densely populated areas and linear urban fields were surrounded by unspoiled open countryside with traditional rural structures. They ensured local supply to the urban areas. Transport routes would thus become shorter and goods would never be shipped back and forth between continents. See p. 126

In retrospect, Pruscha is ambivalent about his global vision: "What I envisioned was not very reasonable, it was almost a communist idea to build interconnected state structures."

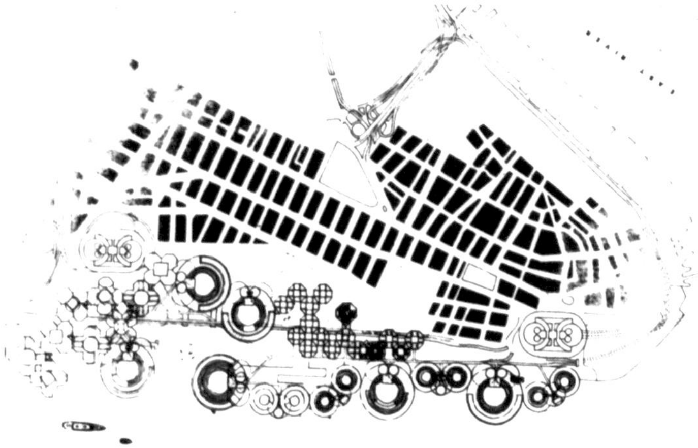

Sketch of the Manhattan development study, 1963

FOUNDERING ON WESTERN REALITY

After graduating from Harvard, Pruscha embarked on his professional career. His plan was to work together with big architectural firms or corporations and carry out large-scale projects for them. One of the most exciting and topical issues of the 1960s was space travel, and the race between the US and the Soviet Union for the moon landing. Pruscha was fascinated with the entirely new spaces and forms that it necessitated, and he would have loved to design innovative space capsules and stations. With a portfolio and first ideas he interviewed with the Martin Marietta Cooperation, a multi-industry company primarily active in the space-travel and defense sector. But it all came to nothing as the company deemed Pruscha's ideas too utopian and not sufficiently functional.

In the meantime, Paul Lester Wiener had arranged for an apartment for the Pruschas on the sixteenth floor of a housing complex he had built near Washington Square—Wiener's most significant commission in the US: two Unités inspired by Le Corbusier, which are now part of New York University. The apartment was beautiful, but small. It had one room, a kitchen, and a bathroom; the combined living and bedroom also serving as Edda's studio, where she restored pictures. Pruscha kept looking for a job, and Wiener suggested he apply to the renowned architect Wallace K. Harrison. Harrison had served as director of planning on the Headquarters of the United Nations in New York, his most important buildings included the Exxon Building on 6th Avenue and, later, the Metropolitan Opera. His office was located at Rockefeller Center in Midtown Manhattan, which he had also helped build. Pruscha saw the Rockefeller Center as one of the most fascinating urban building complexes in New York, as it did not consist of a single high-rise, but of "an interplay of buildings that share a common language" and are connected underground. "That's the beginning of what I imagine urban development to look like."

Harrison was the house architect of Nelson A. Rockefeller, the governor of New York, who commissioned him to come up with an idea for the development of the areas created by landfill in today's Battery Park in Lower Manhattan. At the time, Harrison was already about seventy, "a dignified old man, a gray eminence."[17] For this project, he hired a young international team of graduates from American elite universities, including Pruscha, who, at interview, presented his final project from Harvard, which was met with approval. This made Pruscha feel confident that Harrison might take visionary projects into consideration. As he had done for Aspen, Colorado, he again dug up old maps. They showed Manhattan Island still undeveloped with an intact rocky shore. That was exactly what Pruscha wanted to return to. His idea was to "throw all the areas that were later created by landfill into the water, including the piers." In their place, a new part of town would rise on the ocean. Following the template of the Japanese Metabolists, Pruscha designed floating, bowl-shaped concrete tubs with funnel-shaped residential quarters terraced inward, which were connected to the Manhattan subway system via tubes crossing the Hudson River.

The other young architects—"a Chinese, an Englishman, an Argentinian, and another European"—also endeavored to draw up extravagant proposals. Finally, the big day came. Harrison

Windcatchers on the roofs of Hyderabad, in *Architecture without Architects*

Cover of Bernard Rudofsky's publication *Architecture without Architects*, 1964

Bernard Rudofsky

presented the models and plans to Nelson Rockefeller, who flatly rejected all five projects, threw a tantrum, and smashed Pruscha's model. The team was disbanded, the young people were fired. However, Harrison's partner, Max Abramovitz, thought Pruscha's projects were intriguing and made him an offer to recruit him. Staying inside the Rockefeller Center, Pruscha moved to a small cubicle in a drawing hall with about one hundred employees. Here, the name of the game was divided labor, something that hardly appealed to Pruscha. He felt like a "drawing hand" and grew increasingly desperate. His wishes had not come true. Even in the New World, his ideas were considered too utopian. "I didn't have a chance. So, what to do?"[18]

He felt stuck in an unsatisfying job. The only respite from his dull workdays was his lunch break at the cafeteria of the nearby Museum of Modern Art. And it was there that his life reached a turning point. Starting in November 1964, the museum ran the exhibition *Architecture Without Architects* by architect and cultural theorist Bernard Rudofsky. No star architects were presented, just so-called anonymous architecture from all corners of the earth. "It struck me like lightning," Pruscha remembers. He suddenly knew exactly what he had to do. He had to go "back to the roots." He remembered that Roland Rainer had showed him and the other students anonymous building designs in the Burgenland region. At the time, the subject had seemed a little boring to him and, in any case, at odds with his technology-happy utopian futures. Yet not just Europe but the American world, too, had failed to give him what he had hoped for.

In order to get closer to his goal, he made plans to tackle the subject in a doctoral thesis. Josep Lluís Sert and Eduard F. Sekler recommended him to Ernest Weissmann, head of the UN Center for Housing, Building, and Planning. This department had an extensive archive, and Pruscha was told to start his research there. But when he didn't make much headway and Weissmann teased him, saying that a young man wasn't supposed to go to pot in cellars but should venture out into the world, he remembered his infatuation during his teenage years with the reports of Swedish Tibet explorer Sven Hedin. He asked if he could go to Tibet on assignment for the UN. Weissmann dismissed the idea. He said that Tibet was out of the question; the People's Republic of China would never grant permission for such a thing. Sadly, starting in 1966 during the Cultural Revolution, the Red Guards then actually destroyed several thousand monasteries and other cultural sites in Tibet. But Nepal was an option. Pruscha knew nothing about the country and asked for time to consider. When he told Eduard Sekler, he replied ecstatically, "You definitely have to do that!" Sekler had already been to Nepal; he said the country was "a treasure trove for architects," and the main square in Patan was one of the most fascinating places he had ever seen. Sekler's enthusiasm was infectious and Pruscha decided to take up the offer.

And soon Edda and Carl embarked on a new adventure, again setting out for an entirely new world. Pruscha couldn't wait to immerse himself in his new task.

ASPEN, COLORADO, 1962

Architect Paul Lester Wiener was invited by his friend and former Bauhaus teacher Herbert Bayer to develop a master plan for Aspen. During the summer break, Carl Pruscha joined the project team as a young architect and proposed installing an “energy machine” in the center of town as well as decentralized city-expansion areas, which would be linked to the city by funicular elevators. The project was deemed unfeasible. Years later, on a trip to Chile, Pruscha discovered similar funicular elevators connecting different districts of Valparaíso.

See pp. 118–119, 225

DOWNTOWN PROJECT, MANHATTAN, NEW YORK, 1963
After completing his postgraduate studies, Pruscha joined the New York office of Wallace Harrison, which had been commissioned by Nelson Rockefeller to devise a city-planning framework for the development of the Hudson riverside areas between Battery Park and the World Trade Center. An international team of graduates from eminent architectural schools drew up different concepts for the development of the former shipping piers. Pruscha's plan proposed uncovering the original coast down to the cliffs of Lower Manhattan and floating concrete islands with residential quarters on the Hudson River in the sense of the Japanese Metabolists. They would be connected to Manhattan's existing subway network via tube-like tunnels beneath the Hudson River.

See pp. 121, 258

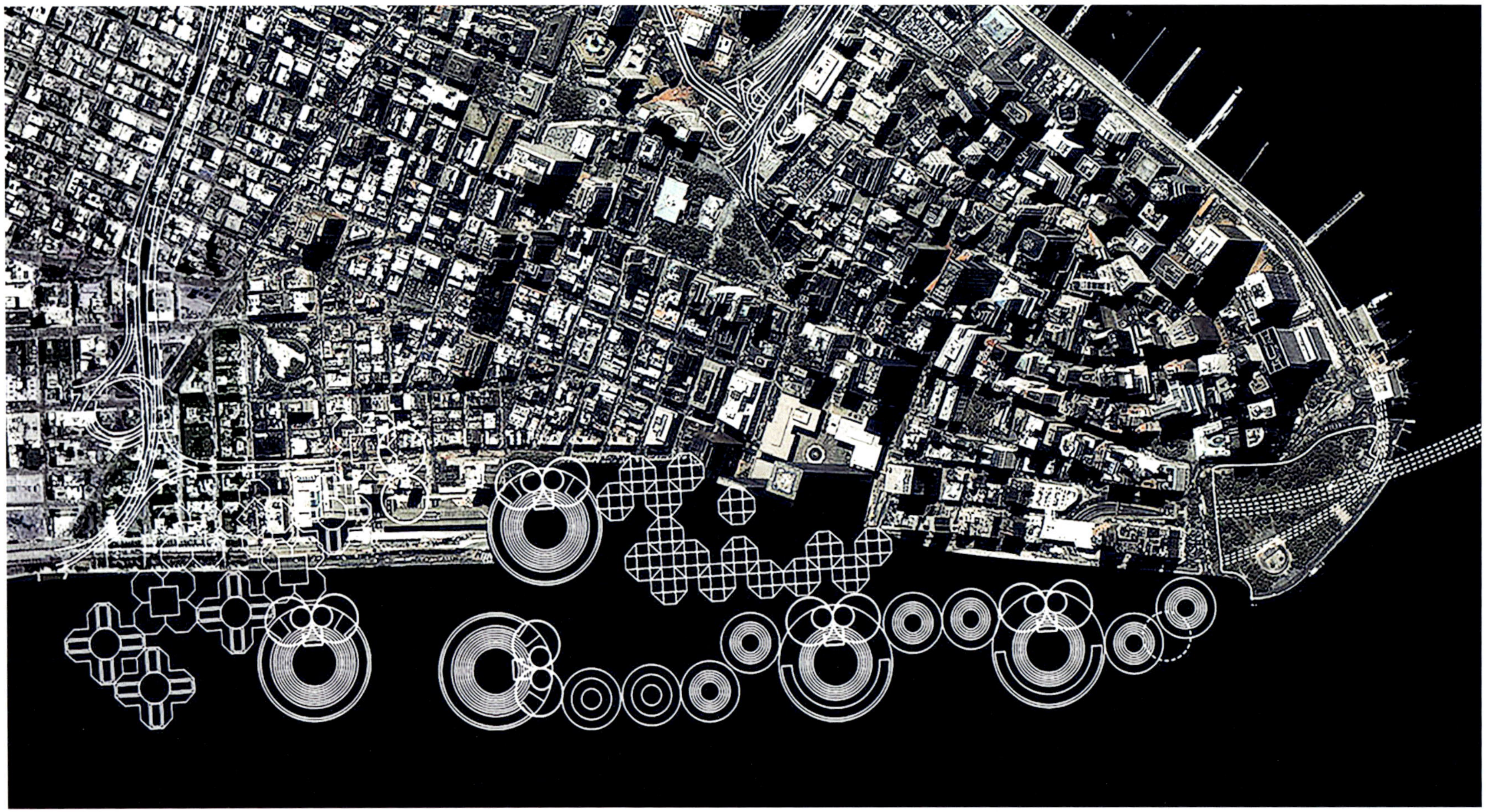

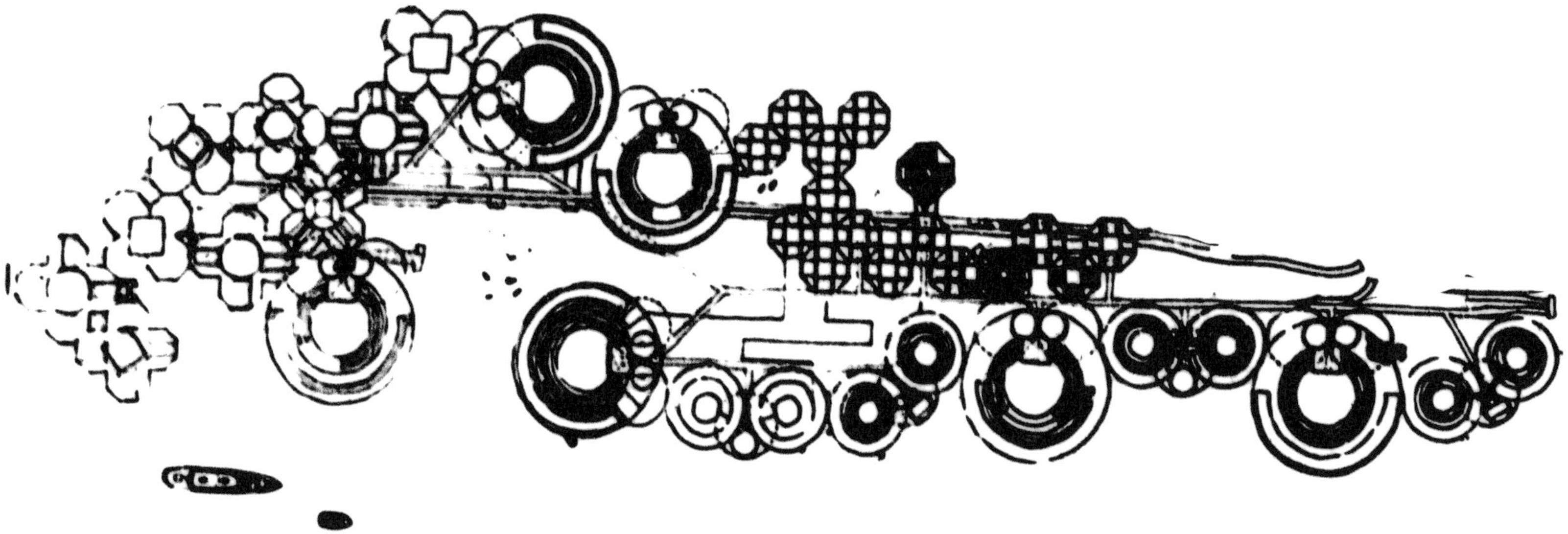

LOWER MANHATTAN
EAST RIVER
HUDSON RIVER

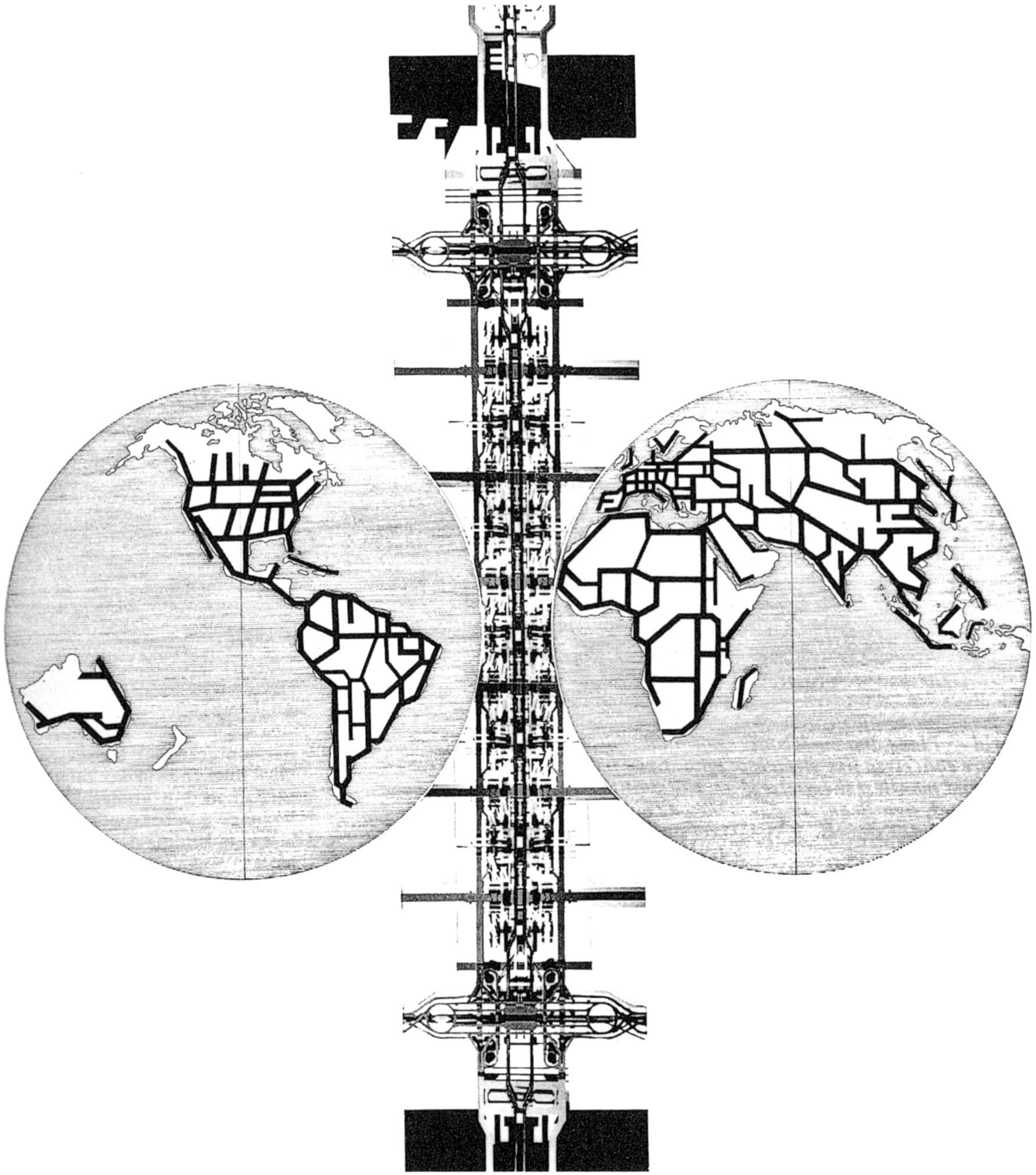

GLOBAL LINEAR CITY, 1963
This concept of a new global city model was based on the notion that a perfect infrastructure—including water supply, waste management, and mobility—forms the basis of a livable city. These infrastructures were designed to define the volume and density of the buildings and to serve them. Individual transport by cars was seen as a relic of the past and replaced, for medium distances, by elevators, funicular elevators, moving floors, and escalators, as well as subway and streetcar lines. Over long distances, people and goods would travel at high speeds in containers propelled through a tube mail-style system—see Elon Musk's Hyperloop project.

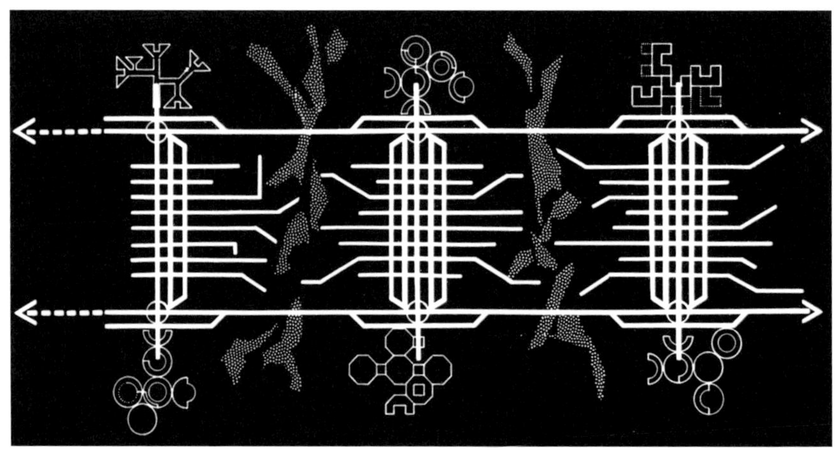

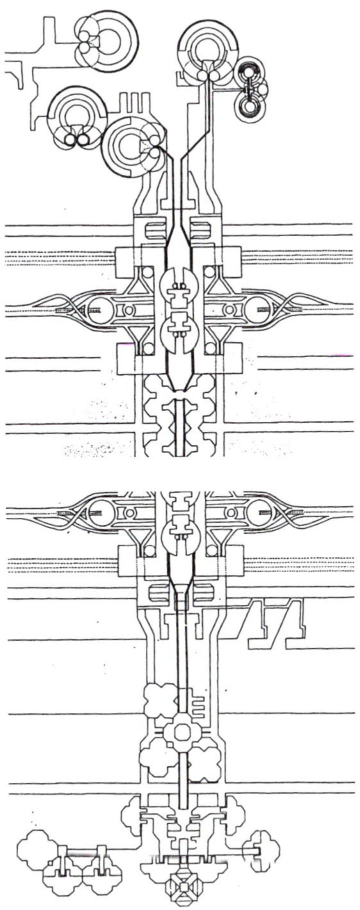

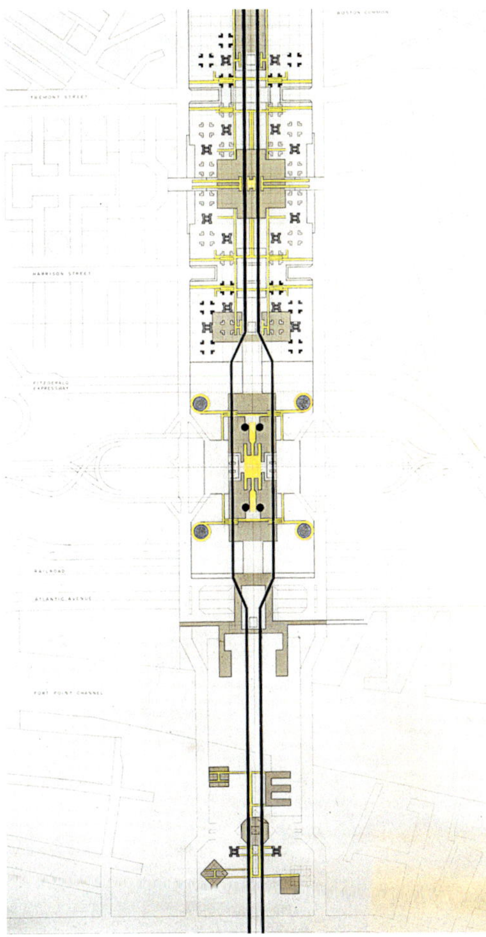

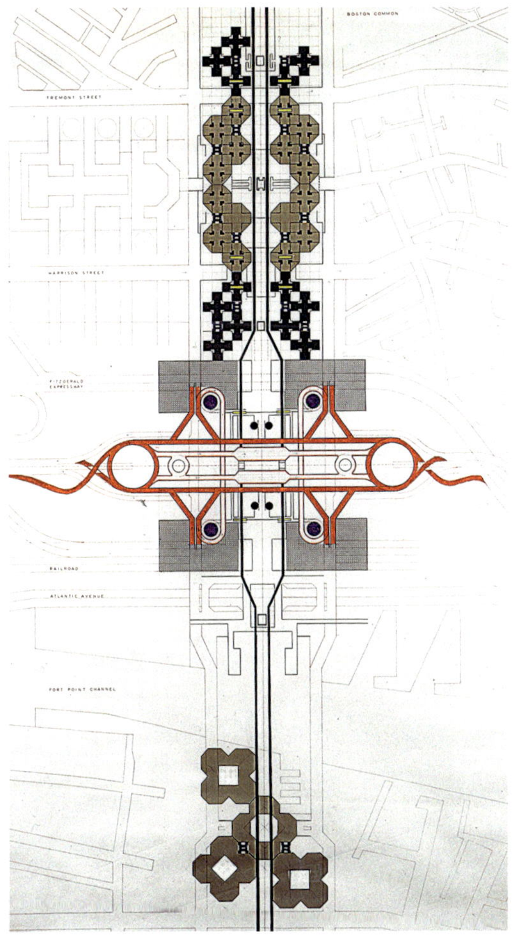
BOSTON COMMON
TREMONT STREET
HARRISON STREET
FITZGERALD EXPRESSWAY
RAILROAD
ATLANTIC AVENUE
FORT POINT CHANNEL

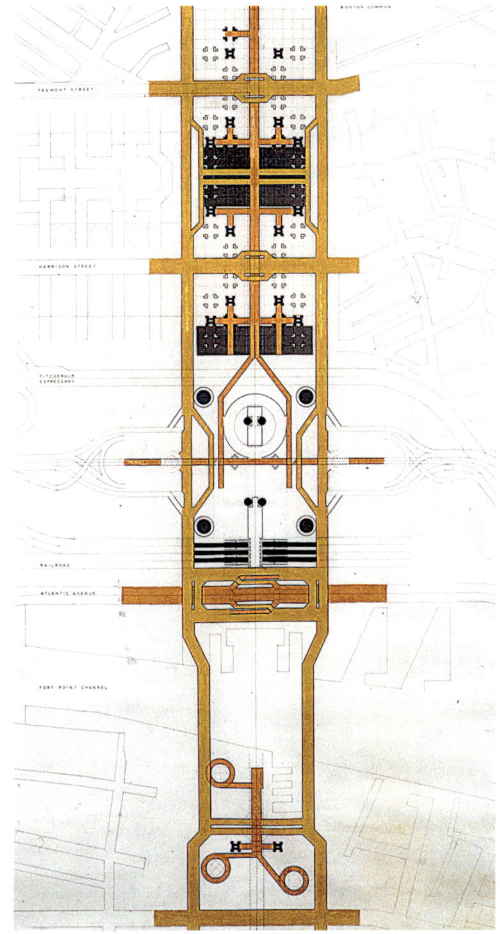

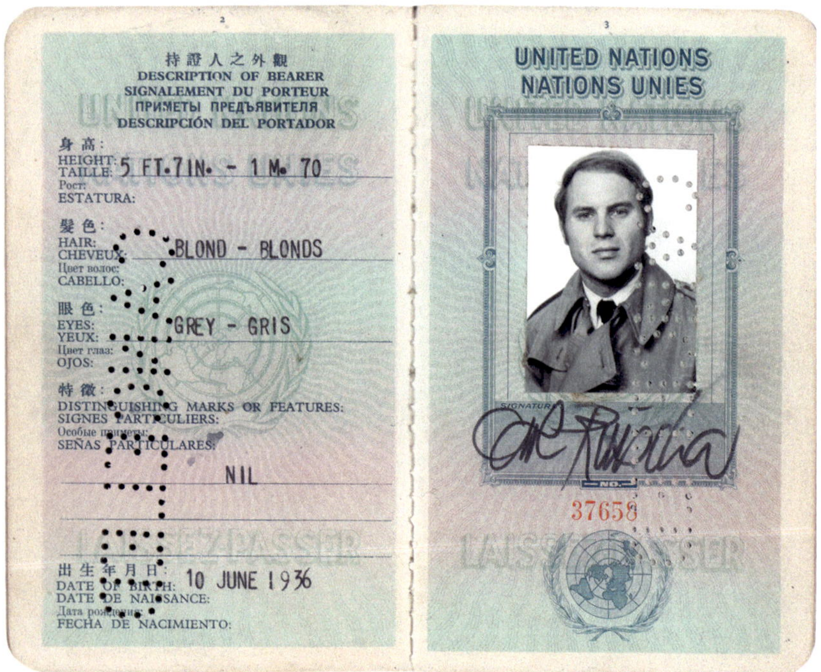

Carl Pruscha's passport when he was an expert for the UN, 1965

V. IN NEPAL ON ASSIGNMENT FOR THE UNITED NATIONS

1965–1973

I planted a tree, built a house for myself, started a family and even wrote a book—I was happy. This reality seemed so perfect that for a while, I forgot that I had set out to find the philosopher's stone.

CP

PRUSCHA'S SHANGRI-LA

Carl Pruscha found it, his small paradise: "In my quest for Shangri-La, my path had led me to the snow-covered Roof of the World, the Himalayas." The Kathmandu Valley is a basin that extends over an area measuring about 35 by 30 kilometers at an altitude of 1,400 meters above sea level, surrounded by the Nepalese mountains. For Pruscha it became a model valley, where he not only discovered a new universe but also embarked, in his words, "on a journey to the inner self and, at the same time, to the origins of mankind."

Even their arrival was magnificent. After a long journey with layovers in Canada, Hong Kong, and India, Edda and Carl Pruscha landed in a prop plane on what was then still the simple grass runway of the airport of Nepal's capital, Kathmandu. The snow-covered high-mountain scenery was intoxicating. An open-top Jeep picked the couple up. It was mid-March and in the streets of Kathmandu the Hindu Holi festival was in full swing. It celebrates the triumph of good over evil, the overcoming of winter, and the arrival of spring. People throw colored powders and water at each other or smear each other's faces and bodies with paint to drive away their sorrows and celebrate life in all its richness. When the Pruschas arrived at their hotel, not only their faces but also their white clothes were covered in dyes.

Pruscha was ecstatic and recognized in this ritual continuities between East and West. Only a few months prior to their departure, Edda and Carl had attended Carolee Schneemann's New York performance *Meat Joy* where the artist celebrated sexuality and sensuality. Among other things, naked couples smeared and daubed each other with raw meat, sausages, blood, and colors. Again and again, the parallels between traditional Asian rituals and the performances of contemporary Western art became apparent to Pruscha in Nepal. He would later take part in the sacrificial feasts for the goddess Durga where thousands of goats and buffalos are ritually slaughtered: "You really wade in the blood." He did find his sacrificial feast hard to stomach, but he was also fascinated with the ritual character of the culture. Vienna Actionism, which sparked scandals in Austria at the time, isn't something Pruscha gets worked up over; in his words it amounts to "harmless shenanigans compared to the great blood orgies of the Durga festival."

Initially, the two newcomers were accommodated in a small palace of the Rana dynasty, with servants and an official car. The same year, Pruscha's first daughter, Alexandra, was born in this house. Carl had known that Edda was expecting since the 1964/65 New Year's Eve party in New York. He had heard about it "by chance," as he puts it, just as everything private in his life more or less happened to him without his choosing. But this wouldn't interfere with the planned journey. And Pruscha, even though he never wanted to become a father or have a family, was soon delighted with the child. But he left the primary responsibility to his wife.

The more he discovered his new home country, the more he was spellbound. For instance by the unique centuries-old urban civilization with, above all, its formerly independent city-states of Patan and Bhaktapur, whose old architectural fabric was still well preserved. Additionally, there were a number of smaller towns, settlements, and villages. These were densely built-up areas with an urban character and, as Pruscha saw it, "exemplary structures." The settlements were mostly built on terraced hills near rivers and groves, "perfectly positioned in the landscape, always marked by economical use of land and urban density." They didn't spoil or destroy the natural environment and thus met precisely the demands that Pruscha thought urban and housing development had to live up to.

He also marveled at the narrow paths that cross the valley like a net. "The fantastic thing is that from the surrounding farm fields, you can get into town on simple gravel paths." The settlements were not designed to accommodate vehicles; all loads were carried. Using a traditional cultural technique, carriers shoulder a flexible bamboo pole holding a load at each end. As they walk, they adopt a swaying rhythm and this seesawing movement makes the load feel less heavy. The rhythm pushes them on, as it were, and motivates them to keep walking. When they have to stop or wait at narrow bridges to give way to oncoming traffic, they keep moving up and down so as not to fall out of rhythm, or walk in small circles—"like a jogger at a red light today," elucidates Pruscha.

INSCRUTABLE POLITICS, AN OVERHEAD PROJECTOR, AND A PLAN

The UN had sent Carl Pruscha to Nepal to serve as a consultant to the Nepalese government in the planned expansion of the city of Kathmandu. He soon realized that there was nothing awaiting him aside from the sign "Town Planning Office" and a couple of young people, who didn't know what they were supposed to do. "I was fairly naive and clueless, and they let me plunge in at the deep end." The government provided no support, everything seemed to be very complicated, he was put off over and over. Pruscha felt at a loss and condemned to inaction. At some point, though, he began to connect the dots. The planning office had been set up under the previous prime minister, Bishweshwar Prasad Koirala. He had been determined to lead the country out of its isolation, foster international contacts, and cooperate with the West, especially with social-democratic Scandinavian politicians. The aim was to advance social reforms and turn Nepal into a constitutional monarchy. City expansion plans were also part of his ambitious change program. He hired a Danish architect who was tasked with setting up the Planning Office. King Mahendra, however, had already removed the progressive prime minister from office and restored autocracy in 1960. Reforms were aborted, the Planning Office's ideas petered out, and the Danish architect had long left the country.

At first, Pruscha tried to collect material and find out what had previously been achieved, but the situation remained unsatisfactory. He started to look around for new fields of activity for himself independent of the Planning Office. Additionally, he wanted to learn more not only about Kathmandu, but about the entire country. He received unexpected help in this pursuit through a fortunate encounter with two interesting people: Nepalese geographer

Carl with Edda and their maid holding their newly born daughter Alexandra, 1965

The old Rana residence where the family spent its first year in Nepal, 1964

A proper means of transportation, 1965

Harka Gurung, who had studied in Edinburgh, and Arie Beenhakker, an economist from Amsterdam. Both were fired with enthusiasm and decided to explore the country with Pruscha—a prerequisite for the crafting of any development strategies. The three of them went on numerous trips, taking pictures, making sketches, exploring the terrain. It was a wonderful and productive cooperation. In the following years, Pruscha was to expand their results and development planning ideas and publish them as a book.[19]

Pruscha's ensuing development plan latched on to his utopian *Vision for Global Urbanization* from his New York days, which he now adapted for Nepal and took one step further. His plan included a number of linear cities, large developments along transport routes, and he placed them on the border with India. From there, roads connecting to the interior of the country would be lined with smaller towns or villages. He proposed that new housing should not be situated in the agriculturally valuable valley but at the foot of the hills; industrial and other economic enterprises were to be established outside of the Kathmandu Valley in neighboring regions. He recognized the danger posed by unbridled growth in the center of the valley. An "urban polyp" would destroy the integrity of settlement areas that had hitherto been respected—a dystopia that, sadly, has become a reality today, as Pruscha admits with a heavy heart.

When all data, sketches, and proposals were complete, he made plans, together with Gurung and Beenhakker, for a presentation to the National Planning Commission. Pruscha knew that modern presentation techniques could be used to great effect, and asked the Americans for logistical support. Three US institutions were present locally: the embassy, development-aid agency USAID, and the Peace Corps. The last-named would indirectly play a key role in Pruscha's future in Nepal. For now, the Americans provided him with the latest technology: an overhead projector, to be more precise, including transparencies, in those days, "an absolutely cool presentation medium and state-of-the-art!"

The reaction from the Nepalese government representatives was enthusiastic. Never before had anyone drawn up such a comprehensive professional plan for the area. However, it seems they were just as impressed with the overhead projector. The planning commission subsequently asked the United Nations to extend Pruscha's one-year contract. But first, Pruscha had to return to New York.

INTERLUDE IN NEW YORK, LONDON, AND VIENNA

People at the UN in New York were highly pleased to see that, obviously, cooperation with the Nepalese government was possible after all. Pruscha was congratulated on his success, but told the next minute that the tasks ahead were out of his league and more experienced UN staff needed to be sent to Nepal. He could, of course, join the team if he wanted to. Pruscha was shocked and adamant that he wasn't going to play a subordinate role in what he saw as his project.

But then things took a different turn. "In my life, there's always this kind of serendipity, it's unbelievable!" In New York, Pruscha

Carl on a short visit in Vienna with Hans and Max Hollein, 1967

Carl with his new red Jaguar, 1967

stayed with an American friend he knew from Nepal, the former head of the Peace Corps there, who was now working with the Ford Foundation. Pruscha told him about his troubles and complained about the way the UN was treating him. His friend suggested that wasn't a problem, he should just write his Ph.D. thesis on the Nepal project, the Ford Foundation would fund his work and send him back to Nepal. With this ace up his sleeve, Pruscha went into a further meeting with the department responsible for the matter. He would return to Nepal without backing from the UN and continue the project he had started on his own. Those in charge didn't like that idea either. By now they had realized how well connected Pruscha was in Kathmandu and how difficult it would be for someone else to operate there against his will. He was therefore presented with an alternative proposal where all those involved could save face. The UN was going to send him back to Nepal alone, but place him under the authority of the regional UN officials in Bangkok, Thailand, to whom he would report on the progress at his new Department for Housing and Physical Planning every few months. Pruscha could easily live with that.

In the meantime, Edda and Carl's marriage had suffered badly. This was a recurring situation in their relationship and like a common thread that ran through their life together. Edda had a hard time coping with phases where Carl's professional future became uncertain—first because she saw him as the breadwinner, and second because during these periods of his life Carl was difficult to be around. Edda filed for divorce. But a few months later when Pruscha already had his new UN contract in the bag, the two eventually got back together again and married a second time. Before they did so, Pruscha enjoyed a stopover in London, where he indulged in his love for expensive cars and cutting-edge fashion. He bought a "cool red Jaguar" and a long leather coat—"that was all the rage then."

A stint in Vienna followed, where Pruscha met Peter Noever who soon became one of his closest friends. A designer and exhibition curator at the time, he went on to serve as the director of the Museum of Applied Arts, Vienna. In the following eight years, he would become one of Pruscha's few sources of information from Vienna because, starting in 1970, Noever sent him his legendary Year Posters, a subjective commentary on the events of the year, which were mostly of a private nature but could also touch on political issues. Contact with his other friends, Walter Pichler and Raimund Abraham, largely broke off over the following years.

A HOME OF THEIR OWN AND PRUSCHA'S FIRST OFFICIAL BUILDING CONTRACT

The small Rana palace where Pruscha lived with his family during their first year in Kathmandu was no longer available. The equally small house adjacent to the wall of the king's palace, which they lived in temporarily, was not suitable for the family. For now, Edda and Alexandra stayed in Vienna and Pruscha enjoyed being single for a while. He began looking and asking around for a new home. Ultimately, a chief government engineer told him that he was building a house at the moment, the foundations had already been completed, and perhaps Pruscha would like to rent it when it was

Carl's newly built and designed house in Bansbari, Kathmandu, 1970

Carl Pruscha with his wife Edda Velim, 1970

finished. That made him sit up and take notice. If only the foundations were done, maybe he could take it from there and design the rest according to his own ideas? The two came to an agreement and Pruscha designed his very first house. See pp. 139–141 He built it around a small inner courtyard and from the traditional local materials of fired bricks and *sal* wood. The house was located in the hamlet of Bansbari, a little outside of the city center on the way to Budhanilkantha, "a fantastic temple complex" at the foot of the Shivapuri, which bounds the north side of the Kathmandu Valley. The cultic image at the center of the temple showed Hindu god Vishnu in a pond, resting on the world serpent. Pruscha was spellbound and knew that he wanted to explore many more of these magnificent places of worship. He would soon get a chance to do so.

Pruscha's job in Nepal was never just about architecture or development planning but also involved social and economic considerations. When the World Bank provided funds for the development of Nepal's most remote areas, a crucial problem soon became clear to him. Ethnic groups living far away from the capital and high up in the mountains lacked the know-how necessary to advance their interests with the central government. The funds therefore often didn't end up with those they were originally intended for. Pruscha consulted with the World Bank and USAID, the United States Agency for International Development. Together they arrived at the conclusion that the chiefs and representatives of these groups first needed to learn how they could articulate problems and wishes vis-à-vis Kathmandu or development-aid institutions. And so the idea emerged for a training and continuing-education center that would teach them the necessary knowledge and skills. At the same time, it was designed as a place where ethnic groups living in widely scattered areas could come together and maybe pool their interests. The Ford Foundation agreed to fund the project, and Pruscha was commissioned to design a suitable building complex. It was his very first construction contract.

Looking back, Carl thinks that his departure from America also had to do with his fear of building.[20] Now, in Nepal, he built more than anywhere else. However, scruples and concerns had to be overcome along the way. He felt not only the weight of his responsibility but also the interference with earth and nature. He almost sensed physical pain "when you bore into the ground and haul in unbelievable amounts of material." To him, every place has a certain balance, which is harmed by construction. Good architecture, however, heals this harm and leads to reconciliation.

But first, an appropriate location had to be found. Pruscha's credo was that "the choice of location is way more important than the architecture one builds." And he was determined to stick to a maxim he attempted to convey to the Nepalese at every possible opportunity, namely, that the fertile plateau should not be further compromised by development sprawl. He opted for a site at the edge of the valley, for a slope below Kirtipur in the midst of terraced rice fields. Pruscha modeled his building complex on these terraces of the natural environment by spreading it across nine levels that continue and reflect this landscape form. The terraced

Charles Correa's Visvesvarya Centre, Bangalore, 1974–1980

Charles Correa's Rahmkrishna house in Ahmedabad, 1962–1964

arrangement of the accommodation also repeats this theme. The roofs, in turn, can be walked on like the rice terraces. In order to integrate them even further into their surroundings as well as the seasons, Pruscha wanted to grow plants on part of the roofs. Architecture as built landscape, that was his goal. But it was not just the place and communicating with nature that was essential to him, so was the cultural context. What impressed him about Nepalese places of worship, aside from their architectural use of forms, were the ideas they represented, their spiritual dimension. In his own work, too, buildings and spaces cannot be conceived of as independent of a cultural, mythical, or historic meta level, and all his projects distinguish themselves through these added values. For this building project, the legend of the origin of the Kathmandu Valley provided him with an apt framework of ideas. Initially, the valley was filled with a lake from which protruded only one hill with a single lotus flower. The blossom symbolized Manjushri, the Bodhisattva of wisdom. One day, however, Manjushri decided to descend from the hill and cut through one of the valley's rock faces with his sword, so that the water of the lake could flow off. As the legend goes, this is how the fertile Kathmandu Valley was created. In the place where the lotus had stood rose Swayambhunath temple. Pruscha now made the axis of the central assembly hall point exactly at the stupa of this complex, so as to give the building a "spiritual footing" and let it become an integral part of the valley. Based on the forms of the circle, square, and triangle, the other buildings, in turn, are positioned diagonally to said axis. The construction of the complex was both traditional and innovative. The walls were built from bricks as they had been in Nepal for centuries. But when it came to the horizontal elements, Pruscha replaced the traditionally used, but by now very rare and expensive wood with a new building material, namely easy-to-produce concrete parts. To that end, he cooperated with Poland-born construction engineer Zenon A. Zielinski, who was working with the Ford Foundation in Calcutta and had already constructed affordable houses with prefab concrete elements there. Pruscha thought that his UCOPAN system could be perfectly adapted for Nepal. Zielinski and Pruscha had large, one-by-two-meter tub-shaped wooden casting molds made, which were patterned on the much smaller hollow molds used to dry bricks in Nepal. In these wooden containers concrete elements were cast on site, which could be used as staggered ceiling slabs instead of beams. The new construction method soon caught on in Kathmandu, such that Zielinski and Pruscha suggested setting up a small industry that could produce them in larger quantities. Zielinski regularly came to visit from Calcutta and became a close friend. Edda hit it off with Zielinski's wife Czeslawa, and she soon became the eponym of Edda and Carl's second daughter. Czeslavia was born in Nepal in 1969. Many years later when she had become a young grown-up, she was still in contact with her now Canada-based namesake.

Completed in 1969, the CEDA building (Centre for Economic Development and Administration) comprises conference halls, seminar rooms, and a library, as well as accommodation, and soon developed into a vibrant place of exchange. Just a few years later, however, the Nepali government recognized the explosive social

New friends to Carl and Edda: Zenon and Czeslawa Zielinski, 1970

and democratic potential of the ideas and demands developed there. Government funding was cut and the project became dormant. Today, Pruscha's building is part of the university that has risen around it.

Charles Correa soon joined the circle of his friends. He was an Indian architect and urban planner who had won international recognition with his Gandhi Memorial Museum in Ahmedabad and his commitment to the housing needs of the poor, among others. "We realized right away that we spoke the same language when it came to architecture, had the same ideas." Correa, too, sought to combine the architecture of Modernism with old local building methods or materials and develop a synthesis of the two. Pruscha was subsequently invited to teach at Ahmedabad University. Regarding his architecture in Nepal, Correa has noted that it invokes monumental images "as mythical and mysterious as the Himalayas themselves."[21] And he was certain that Carl had been guided to Kathmandu by some instinct—like birds of passage—and that he had only truly come alive there. Just as he had built his private home in Nepal onto a partly completed structure, he himself had become part of the Indian subcontinent.[22] Pruscha, in turn, could identify not only with Correa's architectural language but also with his fate. Both developed socially engaged visionary urban-expansion projects, but hardly any of these were ever executed. Both of them built very little, particularly in their respective hometowns. Pruscha remained in contact with Correa until his death in 2015, and he remembers how, "In the end, he complained bitterly that he had only been allowed to erect a single building in his home town. It was a small beautiful skyscraper!" Pruscha would fare similarly in Vienna. But for the time being, he was still in Nepal, where new building projects awaited.

PRUSCHA CONTINUES TO BUILD

In Kathmandu, people initially thought Pruscha's private home looked strange—after all, it was built from the traditional construction materials of bricks and *sal* wood, while the elite preferred Western-style bungalows. However, when the king's chief of protocol and later Nepalese foreign minister had Pruscha build a guesthouse for foreign diplomats and other guests of state in the style of Pruscha's private home, people began to reconsider. See pp. 156–157 They started to appreciate the qualities of archaic building methods—and, what's more, this almost created a boom.

A good example is his Taragaon Hostel in Kathmandu, built in 1970. A women's organization approached him after they had favorably taken note of Pruscha's previous buildings in the Kathmandu Valley. They thought that, as ever more foreign tourists were flocking to Nepal, they needed their own place to stay. "The women didn't want to accommodate those hashish smoking, sloppy hippies in their villages any longer where they would only spoil the children." They wanted Pruscha to build them their own "authentic" looking village, preferably consisting of straw huts, away from the center of town where they wouldn't bother anyone.

Pruscha saw this as an interesting task, even if he wanted to go about it in his own way and was in no way willing to set up

The Guesthouse for Jagadish Sumsher Rana, 1969

The Taragaon Hostel for the Nepal Women's Association, under construction, 1970

a pseudo-folkloristic tourist village. Still, he modeled it on a traditional type of building he had come across in his research on the country's places of worship. Many temple complexes are equipped with small brick houses that provide lodging to itinerant pilgrims, so-called *patis* or *dharmshalas.* In these vaulted single-story buildings, rooms are open on one side—a highly fascinating building type that Pruscha interpreted for his projects from a modern angle, "for the wayfarers of our time." Seeking a plot for his Taragaon Hostel, he again opted for a terraced terrain, this time near the holy Buddhist shrine Boudhanath in the northeast part of Kathmandu. With its 36-meter-high stupa, it ranked as one of the most important Nepalese pilgrimage destinations. The hostel consists of two larger community buildings and fourteen simple living units reminiscent of monks' cells. The walls, floors, vaulted ceilings, and even the built-in benches are made of bricks. On the outside, Pruscha had the barrel vault coated with bitumen and then added another layer of upright bricks. The rainwater seeped down to the bitumen and generated a cooling effect under direct sunlight by producing evaporation coolth. The rooms were open on both of their long sides and thus had good ventilation. Today, the building complex hosts a cultural-history museum.[23] See pp. 49–50, 150–155 In the following years, Pruscha built further structures, including accommodation for refugees fleeing Tibet, commissioned by the UNHCR. See pp. 142–143

In Pruscha's buildings, the bricks remain visible. He deliberately sought to counter the trend toward wall plaster painted gray or with synthetic colors, which was considered "almost a symbol of prestige" and was intended to show off the "progressive, Western mindset" of the builder-owners of such Nepalese buildings. He tried to show through model buildings that local construction methods and modern needs are a perfect fit. And, by and by, he was actually able to render the traditional red facing bricks, which are made from the earth of the Kathmandu Valley, socially acceptable again. In order to boost the population's appreciation of its own architecture and further the preservation of its cultural heritage, Pruscha proposed another exciting project. It would lead UNESCO to declare the Kathmandu Valley a World Heritage site in 1979.

AN EXPLOSIVE INVENTORY AND A PROJECT CLOSE TO THE HEART

Carl Pruscha's documentation of Nepal's cultural and scenic treasures was not conceived as an end in itself. Rather, his hope was that it would boost the country's awareness of its cultural identity and enable new developments on that basis. At first, he had no contract for this project, neither with the UN's development-aid program nor with the Nepalese government. He was even afraid the government might put a spoke in his wheel. After all, a couple of high-ranking officials were earning some extra income by secretly shipping statues and architectural elements of the old temple complexes out of the country and selling them off cheap on Western antiques markets. But when the director general of UNESCO visited Nepal, Pruscha presented him with his idea. The former liked it and sent an international team to the country to evaluate the project; fortunately this included Eduard Sekler, who

Carl Pruscha visiting the site of the Tribhuvan University, 1970

knew Nepal well and was Pruscha's "good old protecting power from Harvard." UNESCO decided to support the endeavor and the Nepalese government was on board, too.

Aside from daily development-planning tasks and interesting construction contracts, this project remained close to Pruscha's heart in the years between 1969 and 1973. He passionately immersed himself not only in the survey and documentation of architecture but also in the myths and cultural practices connected to it. To this end, he collaborated with regional religious-studies scholars. He marveled at how certain religious convictions were manifested in building designs. A case in point was the central place of worship in the valley, the Hindu temple of Shiva Pashupati, who is revered across the entire Indian subcontinent as the lord of the animals. For as far as this god could "see," it was not permitted to subject animals to "slave labor," meaning they could not be used as beasts of burden or draft animals. As Shiva's temple overlooks the entire Kathmandu Valley, no work animals were used there. That's why the only existing transport routes were said narrow footpaths, which were not suited for four-wheeled animal-drawn vehicles but only for the carriers whose seesawing gait had fascinated Pruscha. Year after year, the Night of Shiva in February was an "amazing experience" for him. Thousands of yogis gather at the foot of the temple, and the entire valley was "deeply immersed in clouds of hashish smoke."

Over the years, Pruscha and his team surveyed and documented more than thirty cities and settlement areas, about sixty cultic sites, some thirty landscape-conservation areas, and almost nine hundred individual buildings and ensembles. He did not limit his work to documenting the kingdom's rich cultural heritage, but also presented proposals on how it could be preserved and revitalized. He was aware from the outset that there was an explosive element to his work. As soon as UNESCO designates an area as protected, it's no longer easy to simply raze a building, designate a piece of land as a construction plot, or open a factory in a protected landscape. Pruscha knew he had to protect his material well, and took it home with him every night. He wasn't paranoid, as he soon realized; because one day a close acquaintance with ties to the state police warned him that the authorities were planning to seize his records. Pruscha didn't want to take any chances, and shipped his materials out of the country as fast as he could. That was no small feat in the days when there was no e-mail or other digital media in a "Third World" country. He contacted the US Embassy, which proceeded to send all his records to Delhi with a courier aircraft and, on Pruscha's urgent request, from there directly to the director general of UNESCO. He didn't trust officials on the lower rungs of the hierarchy; he knew of too many bribery cases. Coincidentally, a short while later the director general visited Vienna. He got into conversation with Austria's minister of science, Hertha Firnberg, brought up Pruscha, and suggested the publication of his fascinating records. The two-volume documentation appeared in 1975 and provided the basis for the inclusion of the Kathmandu Valley on the list of World Heritage Sites.

Book covers of *Kathmandu Valley I + II*, 1975

Pruscha was aware that he had a penchant for romanticizing archaic, collectivist societies whose mechanisms of social control were hard to reconcile with his individualistic inclinations. Social hierarchies and some legal concepts were not in keeping with his Western outlook. He was a member of the elite and, on top of that, came from another country, so many of these rules didn't apply to him. But on one occasion he nonetheless came into conflict with them. After a dinner one night, Edda had brought foreign guests back to their hotel in central Kathmandu and was driving home—"of course without street lighting"—when she accidentally hit a cow at full speed. The animal had settled down for a night's rest in the middle of the dark street. Edda emerged unscathed; in a state of shock she drove home and told Carl about the accident. The two felt anxious and concerned but went to bed as there was nothing they could do at the moment. When they woke up the next day, their house was surrounded by police. As they later found out, they were there to protect the Pruschas against the angry population. After all, a cow was a holy animal. It was still alive, and Pruscha had to have her transported to an animal hospital with a truck where he had to have a hut built for her care. Under Nepalese law, it would not be considered murder if the cow survived a certain number of days after the "attempted murder." "As ill luck would have it, the cow died the night before this period expired." Pruscha got off lightly by bribing the vet, who changed the date on the death certificate. The deceased cow was then thrown into the river, where Pruscha saw its cadaver decay over the following months. That irritated him not only for hygienic reasons but also because he was regularly reminded of the unfortunate incident when he drove by.

In 1973, Pruscha's stay in Nepal was drawing to a close. As UNESCO was highly satisfied with his work it offered to subsequently send him to Yemen. But Edda refused. From a Western acquaintance, she had recently heard the story of a gruesome and bloody vendetta in Bangladesh, likewise a Muslim-majority country. It was about another car accident, but one with more dramatic consequences. The little son of a couple they knew was killed in retaliation for the death of a boy in an accident. While these horrific events had taken place in Bangladesh and not in Yemen, it was nonetheless clear to Edda that with her two little daughters she definitely did not want to live in an atavistic society with this kind of vigilante justice. Carl reluctantly yielded to her demand, and the family moved back to Vienna.

PRUSCHA HOUSE, PRIVATE RESIDENCE, BANSBARI, 1967–1968
On the basis of the existing foundations of an already planned building, Pruscha developed his own house, which he built around a small inner courtyard with traditional local materials such as fired bricks and *sal* wood.
See pp. 132–133

UNHCR REFUGEE HOUSING, 1969–1971

After the Chinese occupation of the Tibetan territory in 1950, Tibetans crossed the Nepal border to seek refugee in areas where Buddhist practices and lifestyles were still in use. A part of Nepal's populace, the Sherpas of the Khumbu region, has traditionally been of Tibetan origin. And in the Kathmandu Valley there were a number of splendid monuments of Buddhist provenance, for example the stupas of Swayambhu and Boudhanath. Thus Tibetans settled preferably in the vicinity of these monuments but without the availability of housing. UNHCR took care of creating temporary housing for them. Pruscha was requested to design and build a number of units. He used available bricks and Zielinski's concrete elements, creating small but economical and useful housing units.

See p. 53

UNHCR Refugee Housing
under construction, 1970

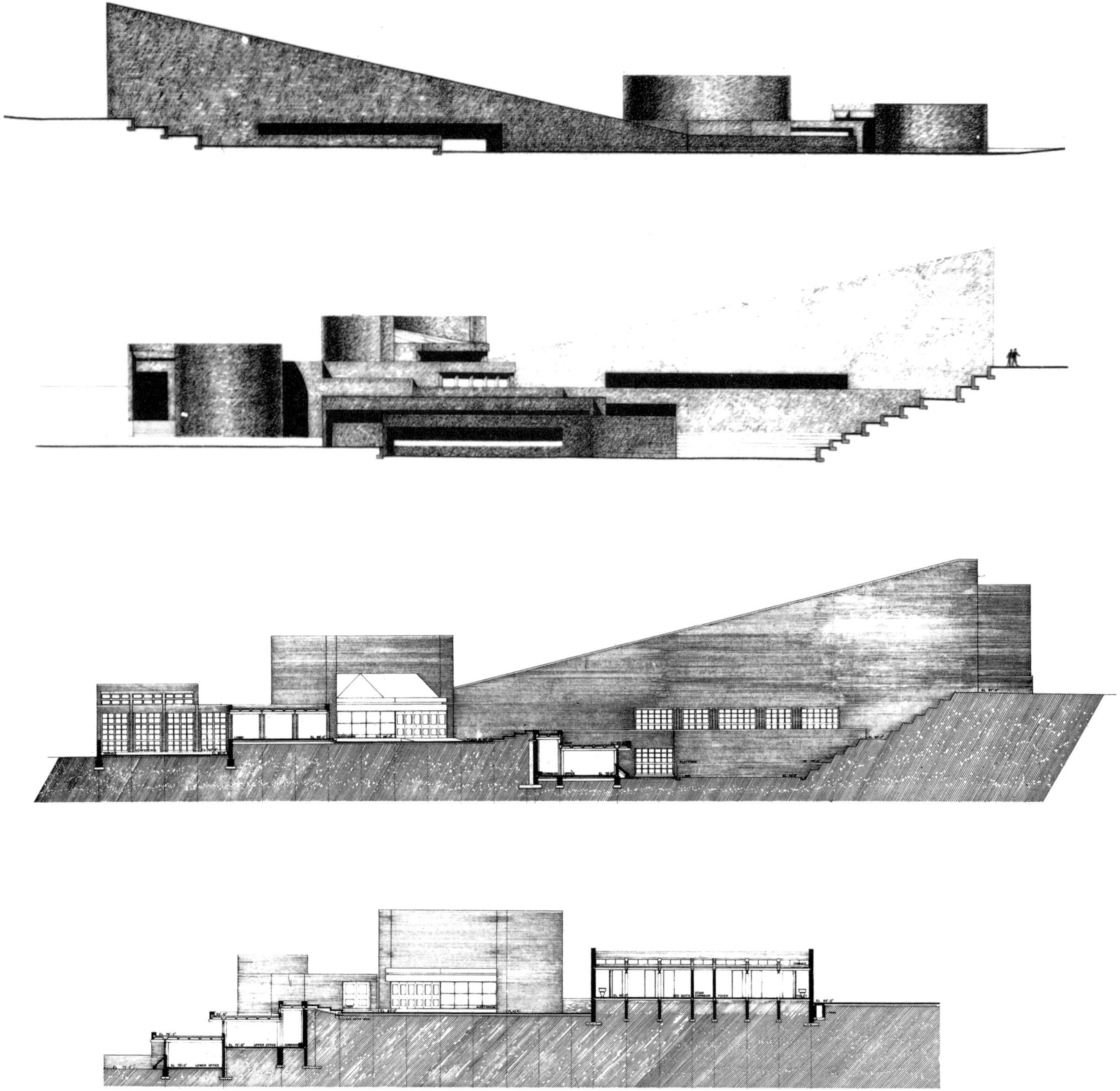

Design drawings of the CEDA building, 1967

CENTRE FOR ECONOMIC DEVELOPMENT AND ADMINISTRATION (CEDA), KATHMANDU, 1967–1969

The CEDA building was originally intended as a center for exchange, education, and training for the delegates and spokesmen of the different Nepalese tribes, and was primarily funded by the Ford Foundation. Pruscha designed a brick building that was integrated into the terraced landscape. For the construction of its ceilings, Pruscha invited to Kathmandu construction engineer Zenon Zielinski, who worked with the Ford Foundation in India. His system of prefab concrete elements made economical construction possible. The building design takes up elements of the mandala—the circle and the square—and is oriented toward the opposite side of the valley where the Swayambhunath stupa is located.

See pp. 18, 44–47, 55, 134

The CEDA building upon completion, 1971

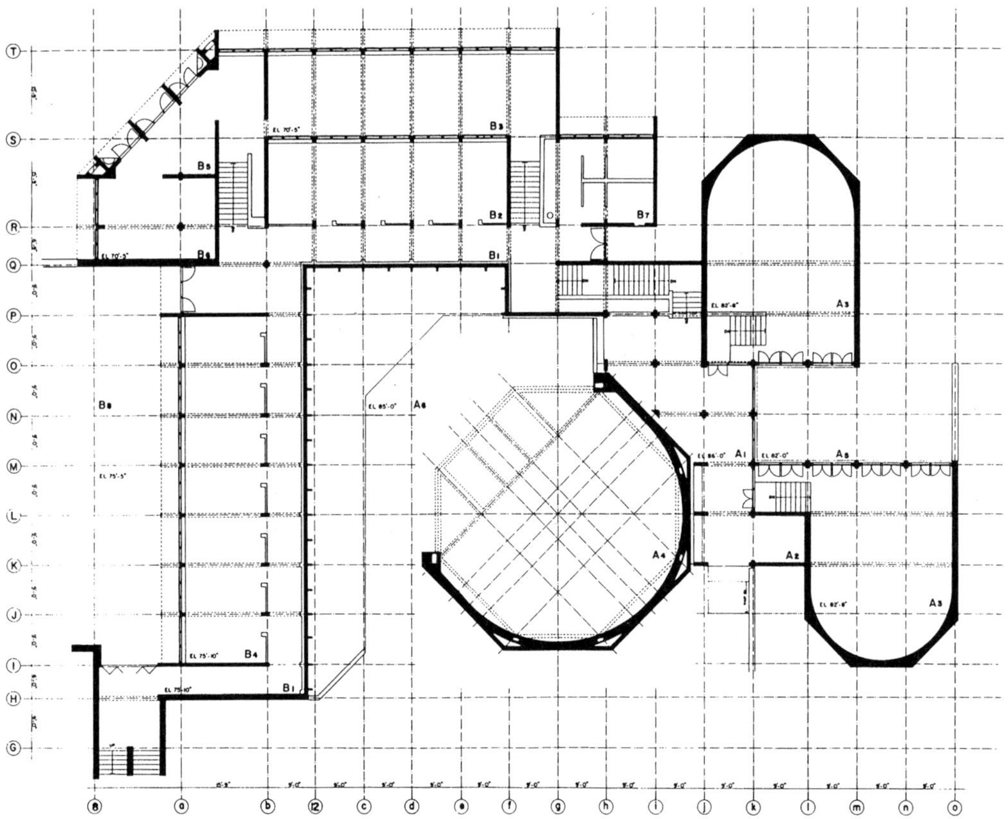

The stupa of Swayambhunath with its axial setting exactly opposite the CEDA building

The CEDA building

Groundplan of the CEDA building, 1967

The CEDA building upon completion, 1970

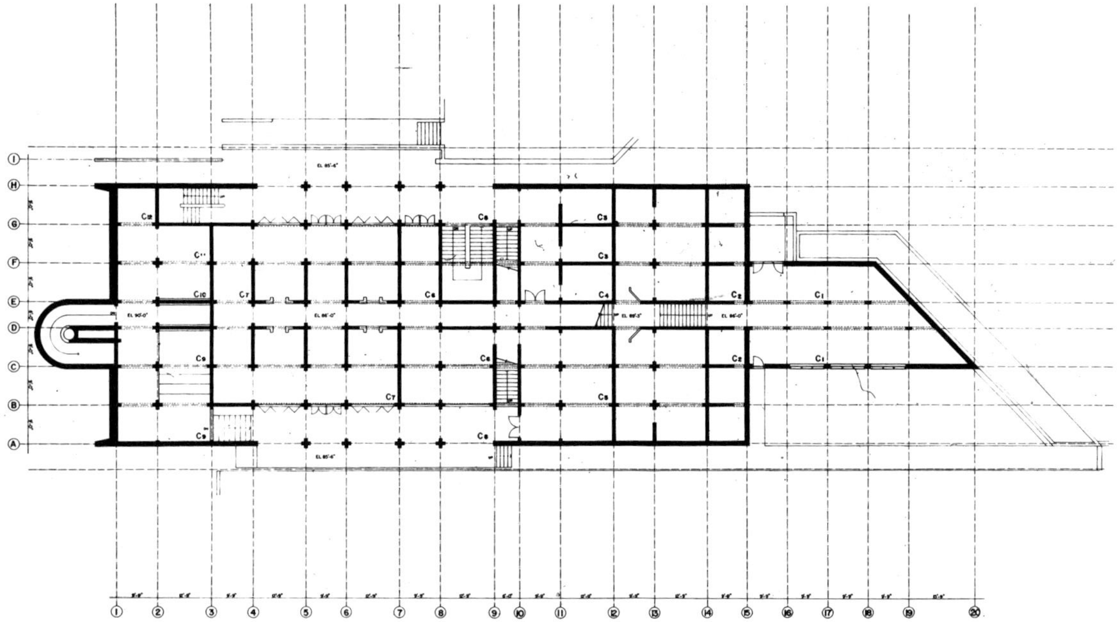

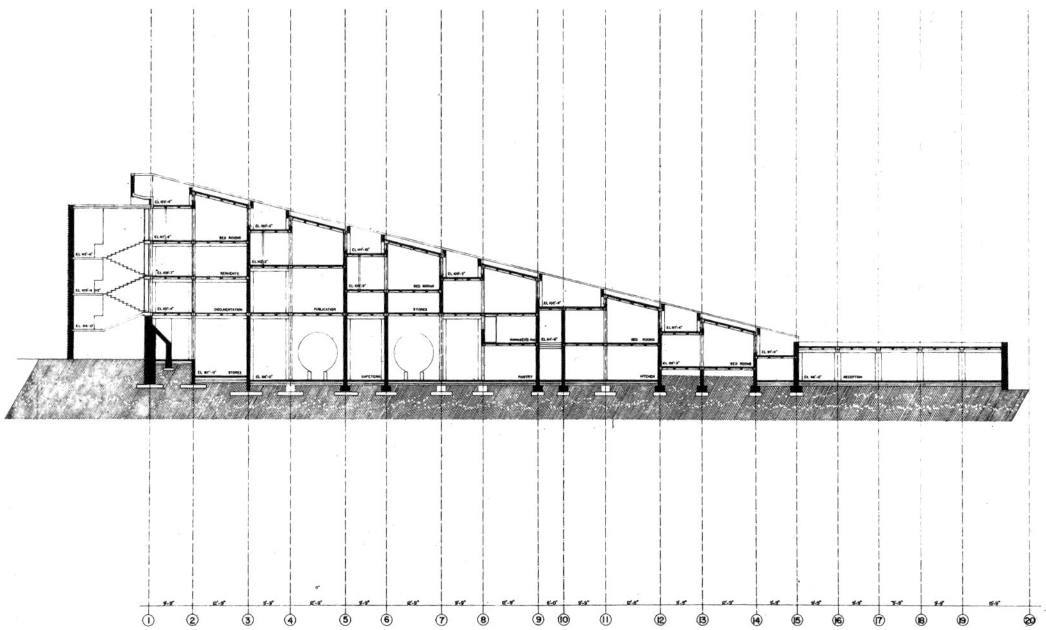

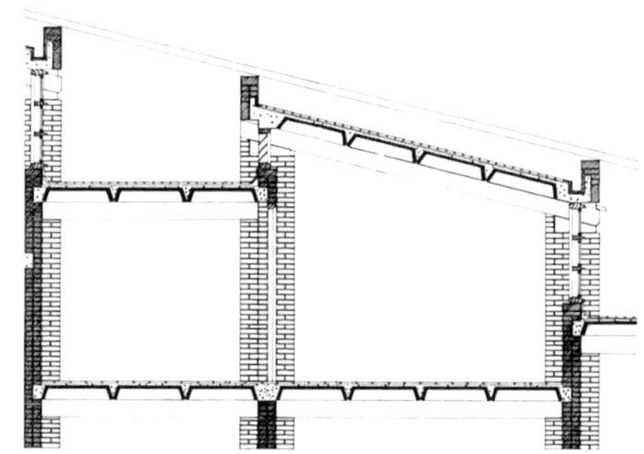

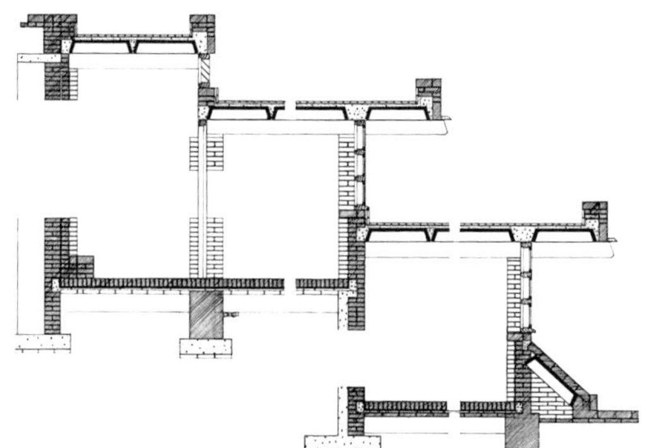

Construction drawings with Zielinski's concrete panels

CEDA building, exterior and interior view

TARAGAON HOSTEL, KATHMANDU, 1970–1972
A delegation of members of the Nepal Women's Association asked Pruscha to design a small "Nepali village" as a hostel for foreign visitors who wanted to spend time in the valley as scholars or artists. Pruscha researched examples of hostel buildings, of which there were a number in the extensive temple complexes in the valley. Called *patis,* these small houses welcomed pilgrims to spend the night there. The prototype of the Taragaon building was modeled on these lodgings. Following its renovation by the Saraf Foundation, it now hosts a museum of architecture.
See pp. 17–18, 49–51, 135–136

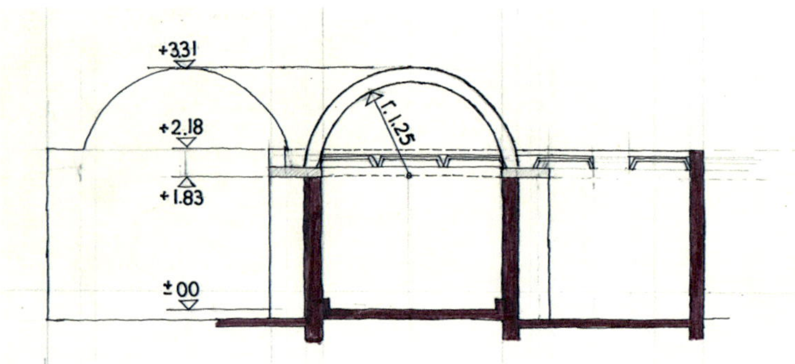

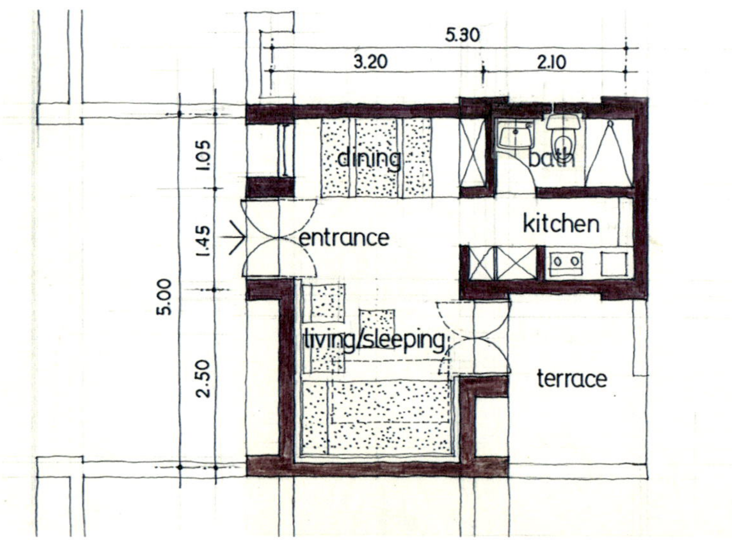

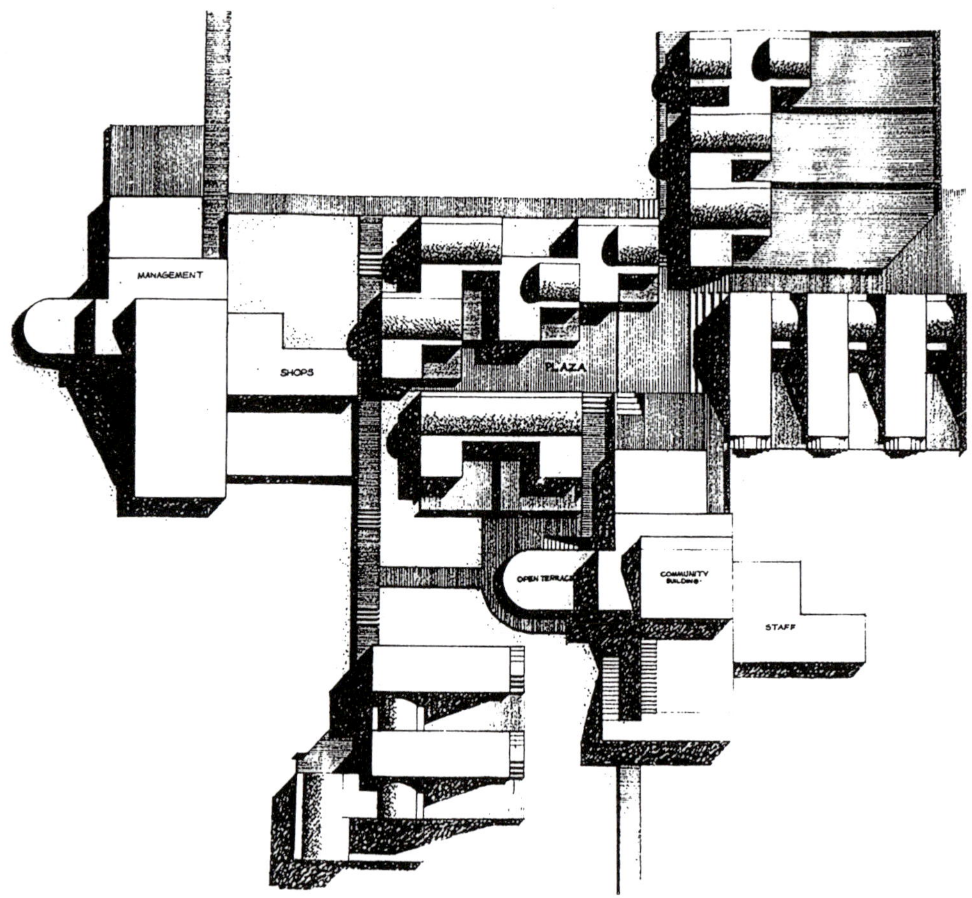

Taragaon Hostel, plan and unit

The Taragaon Hostel under construction, with the great stupa of Boudhanath in the background, 1970

GUESTHOUSE, KATHMANDU, 1969
At the time Pruscha was building his own house in Bansbari, it was common for wealthy Nepalese to have their houses built from concrete in a pseudo-Indian style. After the palace's chief of protocol, Jagadish Sumsher Rana, visited Pruscha at his house, he commissioned him to design a building where he, as the future foreign minister, could welcome foreign dignitaries. On a hill-shaped plot, Pruscha built a guesthouse, its three wings arranged around an inner courtyard with a big *sal* tree. He thus created a house prototype for a new Nepalese style. Even though traditional materials and construction techniques were used, it had the appearance of contemporary architecture.
See pp. 47, 135–136

The Rana residence, 1970

Carl Pruscha back in Vienna, working on his publication *Kathmandu Valley*, 1975

VI. BACK IN AUSTRIA

1974–1976

I think that in everything he did, Carl Pruscha was always an "enthusiast," obsessed by an idea, and to me that seems so much more important than if he had been "clever."
Roland Rainer

DISSERTATION IN GRAZ, A LOG CABIN IN INNSBRUCK

In the past, Carl Pruscha had repeatedly experienced radical breaks and departures in his life not as such but rather as turning points in an organic development that, in retrospect, proved consistent. This time around, however, it was truly a watershed moment for him, especially because, in his eyes, this was not a departure but a step backwards. He had never planned on ever living in Austria again for an extended period of time. And so his return was anything but easy. His financial resources were stretched thinly; he was aimless and disoriented.

During this period, his old friendship with Walter Pichler also fell apart. It went back to Pruscha's Innsbruck teenage years and had grown during their Academy years in Vienna and especially in New York. A small, ridiculous incident laid bare just how different they had become in terms of character, and they went their separate ways for good; his marriage was on the rocks, as well. Edda had a hard time coping with the uncertainties of Carl's future and was susceptible to depressive mood swings. At Edda's wish, they divorced for the second time.

Getting back into contact with Vienna's architectural scene after his long absence was difficult for Pruscha. But enterprising architect and architecture theoretician Günther Feuerstein invited him to one of his legendary "Open Office" evenings at his studio: a visionary forum on architecture, theory, and utopia. Already by the 1960s, Feuerstein had contributed greatly to advancing experimental, utopian, and most recent architecture in Austria. His students included Wolf D. Prix, Helmut Swiczinsky (soon to be known as Coop Himmelb[l]au) as well as Laurids and Manfred Ortner (Haus-Rucker-Co). Feuerstein had already invited Pruscha in 1967, when he was still based in Nepal, and presented his *Global Vision for Urbanization* at the *Urban Fiction* exhibition. Prix, then in his mid-twenties, remembers how fascinated he felt prior to the event. "The man was a legend. He was rumored to live and work far away from Vienna. He was designing fantastic buildings in Nepal—Corbusier and Kahn immediately came to mind—and was planning cities for the UN that ran around the entire globe."[24] That was the beginning of their friendship.

Now, almost ten years later, Pruscha again gave a talk at Feuerstein's studio about his ideas on anonymous architecture and their further development in Nepal. Timo Huber, founding member of the radically experimental architectural group Zünd-Up, reacted with a disparaging comment, saying, "So, that's what we've been waiting for, Pruscha has traveled the world and we thought he'd be laying out some great utopian ideas here, but he's showing us ramshackle huts and naked kids' heinies with flies on them." That was a blow to Pruscha. He had to recognize that this in-group had expected him to present something that was, in their eyes, more radical and technologically utopian, but that in the meantime he had moved in a different direction. "They thought I was this crazy guy with grandiose ideas, and then when I came back from Asia, I was too mild for them. Any further dialogue was pretty much impossible."[25] This put a damper on his once important friendship with Feuerstein. He wasn't going to make any friends

Edda and Pruscha, 1990

here either. He felt out of place in Austria, missed Asia, and found himself increasingly stuck in limbo.

As difficult as this period was, sitting idle was not an option for Pruscha. At first, he began preparing the publication of the material that had been shipped out of Nepal under bizarre circumstances; the two-volume *Protective Inventory* of cultural sites worthy of protection in the Kathmandu Valley appeared in 1975.[26] In the meantime, he was back in contact with his former professor, Roland Rainer. The latter was pleased to see his former student return, and once more assumed a paternal role. On the one hand, Pruscha was grateful for the support; on the other, he felt that the professor had put a tight reign on him. Rainer would not tolerate, for example, Pruscha's collaboration with Hans Hollein. That was too much for the former student who had become an architect in his own right and looked back on a career of his own. Still, he did follow Rainer's advice to turn the material collected in Asia into a dissertation. Rainer had an ulterior motive; he wanted Pruscha to get a professorship at the Academy. Hertha Firnberg, the Social-Democratic minister in charge, staunchly supported the idea as well. She went to great lengths to attract interesting people with an international experience to Austrian universities, which were outmoded and engaged in navel gazing much of the time. A professorship in Vienna was an entirely unexpected and new perspective for Pruscha. Rainer suggested he submit his dissertation at a remove from Viennese intrigues, preferably to Hubert Hoffmann, head of the Institute of Urban Design and Planning at the University of Technology in Graz. Hoffmann was "an old Bauhaus guy"[27] and appreciated Pruscha's approach to architecture. Pruscha was thirty-eight years old when he completed his doctorate in Graz in the spring of 1975. He was appointed professor at the Academy the following year.

It was roughly at this time that Roland Rainer, together with other internationally renowned architects, was commissioned by Farah Pahlavi, the wife of the shah of Iran, to develop urban-planning proposals for northern Tehran, a Western-influenced part of the Iranian capital. Rainer hardly spoke English and hired Pruscha as a junior partner. This was an exciting project, through which he got to know pre-revolutionary Iran. Their cooperation was not always free of conflict; it entailed a clash of two strong characters, and Pruscha was less and less willing to accept the role of the student. Ultimately, their plans hit a roadblock. In 1979 the Islamic Revolution broke out in Iran and the new regime shut down all Western projects.

Meanwhile, Pruscha was building his first house in Austria. Harmonizing with its landscape environment, it was a simple private home for his sister Hannelore and her husband Franz Strickner in Sistrans near Innsbruck. Years earlier, he and his sister had seen a Canadian log cabin at an architecture exhibition. He now went about building a modern Tyrolean log cabin. See pp. 166–167

As would so often be the case with his later Austrian projects, he was faced with obstacles. To begin with, the authorities refused to grant the building permit on the basis of an inflexible and hidebound building code. The planned flat roof, instead of a pitched one, was a particular annoyance to them. Another problem was posed by the round hewn logs needed for the building method Pruscha had opted for. Surprisingly, they could not be provided by any Tyrolean carpenters, and ultimately had to be ordered from a Finnish prefab-house company. In the end, a group of Finnish carpenters erected the house. Even though Pruscha's log cabin was economical, it stood out due to its exceptional spatial and atmospheric qualities. It can hardly be seen from the street as it is surrounded by tall trees and integrated into the environment. Yet upon entering the house, one is surprised by the spacious central living area with its both modern and archaic appearance. It was inspired by Pruscha's childhood experiences with the main front room in the Tyrolean farmhouse as well as his knowledge of anonymous Asian architecture. The logs are painted black and contrast with the white, midheight partitions and the handmade orange-brown terracotta tiles. Floor heating and a central tiled stove radiate enough warmth in the cold Tyrolean winter months. A terrace runs around the house, connecting indoor and outdoor spaces in an ideal fashion. Hannelore and her husband were thrilled. Carl Pruscha's father also loved the house and took pictures of it from all sides. "But it was all the same to Carl," his sister recounts. His father's appreciation still didn't mean anything to him, or, he was simply unable to see and accept it. When his sister talked about it decades later, many years after his dad's death, he appeared almost surprised: "I never noticed, I didn't know that."

Hannelore and Franz Strickner invited their numerous friends and acquaintances to promote the house. The basic idea behind it had always been an entire development of such homes. The Strickner house was conceived as a case study or prototype. But it was not at all in tune with the general Tyrolean aesthetic taste of the 1970s. People preferred to erect new *Lederhosen*-style homes or, from the 1980s, if not "traditional," then Postmodern ones. The neighbors referred to it as the "silly house" and pitied the Strickners for having to live in, what was to their mind, a cold and shabby barn. Thus, the intended knock-on effect did not materialize. Pruscha's first building in Austria proved to be exemplary for the difficulties and uninformed reactions that would repeatedly greet his highly functional, aesthetic, and innovative designs in his home country. They certainly didn't fit into the norm but, time and again, the force of the pushback was surprising.

To this day, Hannelore has a guilty conscience about letting her brother work for her for free without giving any thought to it. "When we built the house, he had nothing, because he was just back from Nepal. Still, he always drove up here to check on the construction site, and we never paid him a dime. That does cost money, the plans, the application! We could have at least paid for his train tickets. He was really generous. He was always like that with me."

PALACE AND CASTLE—"NEW" AND "OLD"

In the mid-1970s, Carl Pruscha's focus shifted to a palace and a castle. Over the years, whenever he came home to visit for a few

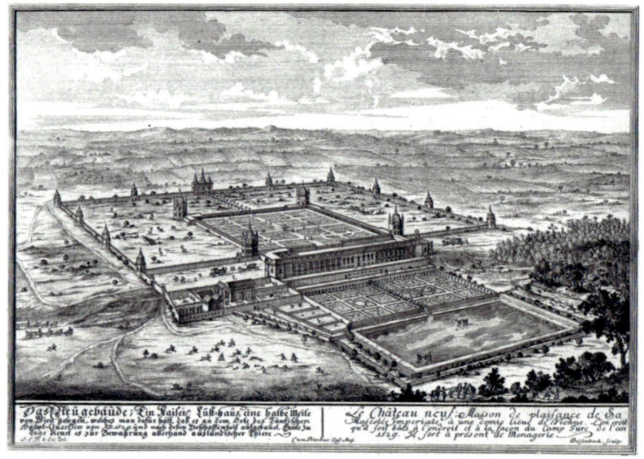

Kaiserlicher Waldspaziergang mit dem Schloss Neugebäude im Hintergrund (Imperial walk through the woods with Neugebäude Palace in the background), painting by Lucas van Valckenborch, 1590–1593

Das Neugebäude, engraving by Johann Adam Delsenbach, 1715

days, he had flown into Vienna and headed into town by car. On the way from the airport he had often noticed a fascinating, gigantic, gloomy edifice—a forbidding, 180-meter-long wall with three avant-corps rising high above Kaiser-Ebersdorfer-Strasse: "It became clear to me pretty soon what lay behind it. That this was not just a wall, but that really something highly intelligent formed the basis of it." The building was never completed and a ruin at the same time. Neugebäude Palace (Schloss Neugebäude) in today's district of Simmering is a "dream building" and "one of the most fascinating architectural creations of mannerism."[28] Emperor Maximilian II had it built, starting in the late 1560s. Pruscha sees him as "the only intelligent and visionary Habsburg ruler." The palace was conceived as a scholarly *Gesamtkunstwerk,* as a center of attraction for the scientific and artistic life of his time—with cabinets of antiquities, botanical gardens full of exotic plants from around the globe, animal enclosures, water installations, and a ball-game hall. Pruscha saw it as a "huge research center and not a building purely for purposes of representation. And that's something way more intelligent than the beautiful Baroque gardens of Versailles that had no other purpose than providing a venue where courtiers and their ladies could take a walk."

The palace, situated on a landscape terrace right above the then still unregulated Danube, offered a view across the floodplains. Unique for its time and place to the north of the Alps was the innovative dovetailing of inside and outside spaces, the interplay of building and nature—a theme that Pruscha, too, returned to again and again. But then the Ottoman–Habsburg wars emptied the state's coffers and construction began to stall. In the wake of Maximilian II's sudden death at the age of 49, his lifelong dream was left unfinished.

The name *Neugebäude,* which translates as "New Building," goes back to Maximilian's time and distinguished it from the nearby Ebersdorf Castle, where he had set up a menagerie with exotic animals that was sensational for its time. After Maximilian II's death, his son, Emperor Rudolf II, launched an unsuccessful attempt to complete construction on the palace. About 150 years later, Maria Theresa used it as a munitions depot and had individual parts of the building, especially the columned arcades, moved to Schönbrunn where they were used in the construction of the Gloriette. Pruscha thinks, "Stupid people like Maria Theresa didn't get it." During World War II, the Saurer-Werke company set up an armaments factory in the palace where forced laborers and prisoners from the Mauthausen Concentration Camp slaved away.

In the mid-1970s, the municipality of Vienna, which had owned the palace since 1922, decided to revitalize it and consulted Pruscha, among others. He came up with a revolutionary concept—in the truest sense of the word, because his idea was to "turn the building around," as it were. See pp. 210–211 With that, he reacted to the fundamentally changed topographic situation. The once sublime location and its sweeping view were forever lost. The floodplains no longer existed; urban sprawl, a few unattractive greenhouses, and the beginnings of commercial development had taken their place. Pruscha therefore decided to orient the palace toward its former rear side. He wanted to open the central avant-corps, formerly an immense triumphal arch, and create a stage in front of it. Thus, the entire rear side of the palace would be transformed into a tremendous theater backdrop. Inside, Pruscha planned to create a connecting corridor between the three avant-corps. The two outer Renaissance halls would be suitable as event venues. Originally designed as a hall of antiquities, the "fantastic halls" in the basement could serve as exhibition spaces.

To the left and right of the central room, which would be expanded to form a huge stage, Pruscha's plans included stepped auditorium seating areas in the style of an antique theater. This terraced concrete landscape would be situated exactly along the axis of the palace, just as the crematorium by Clemens Holzmeister from 1923. In order to build the auditorium, the cinerarium behind it would have to be relocated. Cemetery and castle, death and culture, dying and art would thus be intermeshed—an idea Pruscha thought was fitting for Vienna. The native Tyrolean is fascinated with Viennese necrophilia: the omnipresent cult of the dead, whose presence was felt much stronger before the fall of the Iron Curtain than today. This history and mentality of place was something he wanted not to negate but rather to address and integrate into his design.

It's not only this conceptual approach that makes Pruscha's design so intriguing but also its play with indoor and outdoor spaces, which, on the one hand, reflected Maximilian II's ideas and, on the other, is typical of Pruscha's approach to architecture: "In my mind, the essential thing about architecture is not built volume. To me, empty spaces are just as important. As shaped space or an accessible communication area it is often a lot more important than built-up space."

Of course, the officials in charge were overchallenged by this deeply engaged, lavish, utopian project. What they had in mind was a faithful restoration of the original Renaissance palace, something patently impossible as the landscape had fundamentally changed. As Pruscha puts it, "That would have been pure kitsch, a tourism gag. Disneyland!" But that, too, never materialized. Later, minor adaptations were made to prepare the premises for use as a summer movie theater. Pruscha cringed at the fact that "In these wonderful underground halls, in the hall of antiquities, they installed toilets. Unbelievable!"

He is perfectly aware that his ideas often demand too much of people. "My problem is always that I think about large-scale concepts and not about small, detailed solutions. And it just doesn't mean anything to them, they always dismiss it as utopian." He was to return to this project many years later when the Municipality of Vienna again asked him for an assessment in the late 1990s. He even suggested the Neugebäude could host an envisaged Manifesta, the roving European biennial of contemporary art. As might have been expected, these plans came to naught, as well.

There was, however, a castle project that Pruscha would be able to make a reality—without a public contract. Sure, he insists that it's a regular house. "That's no castle!" The notion of a feudal lord of the castle doesn't jibe with his self-image. And yet this "old castle," as it's officially known, has become his home. He changed its name to his "house in Lajtakatta":[29] Lajtakatta being the old Hungarian name of Gattendorf when the village marked the border between Hungary and Austria—the German *Gatter* translates as fence or gate.

In the meantime, Edda and Carl had grown closer again and married for the third time. Just as he had done in Nepal, Pruscha decided to build a house for his family. He sees place as the most important thing, and could never conceive of architecture independent of it. In the densely populated man-made landscapes of Vienna and its surroundings, the places that appeared interesting to him were already taken—"I didn't want to move into someone else's house." Seeking an alternative, he began to look for an existing building with historic structural fabric that would allow him to refashion and reconstruct it according to his own ideas. He found what he was looking for in Gattendorf in the Burgenland region, twelve kilometers from the Hungarian border. At first, his wife and daughters were appalled. All they saw was a forbidding ruinous façade, a dilapidated roof, and on an iron fence a hardly inviting sign reading, "Danger—Keep Out." Friends in Vienna advised against buying a property so close to the Iron Curtain, still a reality at the time, and asked him, "What are you going to do when the Russians come?" His response was that it still "attracted me like magic."[30] He also knew exactly why: "That was a ruin, but there was still a certain element of truthfulness to it." So, another ruin. And how could it be otherwise? The location of the building, with a park extending to the banks of the Leitha River, was fantastic.

Pruscha bought the property for a moderate price and, step by step, began remodeling it. At its core, the old castle is a Late Renaissance building like Neugebäude Palace, although its dimensions are much smaller. It was later converted in the Baroque style, and in the early twentieth century it was finally turned into a granary. Pruscha allowed himself plenty of time with his transformations, somewhere between twenty and thirty years. Every step had to be considered, and he didn't know in the beginning what the end result would be. The project remained full of suspense until the very end.

At first, Pruscha had to replace the crumbling roof truss with a plain timber truss-girder construction, whose elements were joined with American Gang-Nail connector plates. The wooden full boarding provides stability to the truss, while Torsteel rods bear the tractive forces and lend a sense of lightness to the entire roof structure. It was now ensured that the building would no longer suffer from a dilapidated roof, and Pruscha was able to proceed to the renovation of individual rooms, each "a lab" full of challenges. He began with the ground floor, where the historic structural fabric was best preserved. He removed redundant interior walls and created a large living and bedroom. The adjoining oblong room became the bathroom; then came an elongated dining room; and, finally, the kitchen took shape where Pruscha, following archaic principles, assigned to one of the long sides the element of water with the sink, to the other the element of fire with the stove. To him, this arrangement was a very natural choice: "All you have to do is listen to what these spaces tell you. Then you act on what

Old Schloss Gattendorf, around 1950

these spaces want to be, you make it come true."[31] It seems he not only listens but also speaks to the rooms, builds a relationship with them. Pruscha has an exceptional talent for communicating with spaces, which makes him a "room whisperer" of sorts and enables him like no other to elicit the most amazing things from old structural fabric. Pruscha thinks that it comes down to the architecture itself, because true high-quality architecture is not bound to a certain function but remains flexible. "Good spaces are always fascinating and you can use them in new ways over and over, and newly convert and re-interpret them."[32]

On this pleasantly cool first floor, the family has spent many a summer. With its historic vaults, Pruscha sees it as an archaic basis on which he built his "own new world." Unlike the ground floor, the vaults on the upper floor have only been preserved in the room that is now Pruscha's library. At the beginning of the twentieth century intermediate wooden floors were added to the upper floor for use as a three-story granary. The Renaissance windows were walled up save for narrow ventilation openings. On the one hand, Pruscha calls this misappropriation a "humiliation" of the castle; on the other hand, he thinks it has given the house a new energy. "Coming from Asia, for me the grain of rice or corn was the element of compact energy." Pruscha liked the idea of the house as an energy store, and it is a part of the history of the building that he by no means wanted to erase. He thus decided to leave the narrow window openings facing the village as they were, a cause of disappointment at the Federal Monuments Office. The façade with its fragments from various eras thus becomes a visual history book—from the remnants of the Renaissance gate to the pilasters added during the Baroque era, and the twentieth-century narrow ventilation openings reminiscent of an industrial building.

On the garden side, Pruscha opened the bricked-up large windows and in one place even inserted a narrow glass slit into the wall, which allows him to look into the green park from his workplace. In these "free spaces" on the upper floor he was able to unreservedly pursue his own ideas. The beams of the intermediate floors had long rotted away. Pruscha removed them and created two huge rooms. The transverse section, a six-meter-high room measuring twenty by eight meters, was turned into a new living unit, a kind of loft with a four-meter cube in the middle. It contains the wardrobe, kitchen, bath, toilet, and sauna—a kind of *cella,* reminiscent both of the inner sanctum of an antique temple and of a monk's cell. Of course, Pruscha doesn't sleep *inside*, but *on top* of this cell. The top of the cube forms a platform with a large bed. A parapet wall separates this sleeping spot from the surrounding room visually, but not acoustically or in terms of atmosphere. See pp. 174–176

The central hall directly above the entrance offers a full view of the impressive roof truss. The room is dominated by works of art created by friends and his daughter Alexandra, as well as wooden sculptures and brocade fabrics from Nepal.

Pruscha is an architect in the best sense: an artist of space. The different elements and various details, the individual rooms, and the extensive garden formed a well-matched unity. Just as important to Pruscha as the building itself, if not even more so, was the outdoor area, the garden. He gave it a new landscape design, dividing it into three distinctly separate sections that form interconnected spaces.

Following the refurbishment of the upper floor, the ground floor no longer had to serve as the living quarters. He therefore opened the large room to the terrace, transforming it into a *sala terrena*. Bounded by a box hedgerow, the terrace is tiled with old bricks. One of the castle's countless functionally unique details is a gutter crossing the terrace floor. It channels rainwater into a former cold room below, which has been repurposed as a cistern. From there, water can seep into the garden and irrigate the plants. This floor drain replaced the roof gutter, which Pruscha completely went without at his castle.

The second outdoor area is an extensive grassed area, which is bounded to the west by a vine bower, while the lower-lying third area comprises a swimming pool and a biotope. An opening in the hedges surrounding the property allows for a view of the old castle grounds behind it. Pruscha compares his newly planted trees, hedges, and bushes to "furnishings,"[33] intended as partitioning elements or to loosen things up. One of them is a willow planted close to the house which, by now, has grown into a tall tree. When a storm caused considerable damage to it in the summer of 2017, he was in despair—"That tree meant more to me than the entire house!" He was able to save the beloved plant even though one of its main branches had broken off.

HOUSE STRICKNER, SISTRANS, 1976–1977
House Strickner was conceived on the basis of Pruscha's memories of the traditional Tyrolean timber houses and barns of his youth. He designed a log cabin that was erected on a concrete basement by a Finnish company within a short period of time. The building seamlessly integrates into the landscape with its horizontal orientation; still, neither the local authorities nor the neighbors appreciated it as a contribution to a specific Tyrolean type of housing.
See pp. 160–161

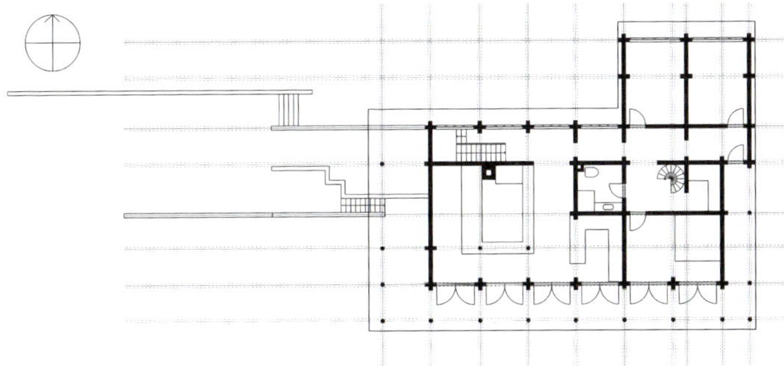

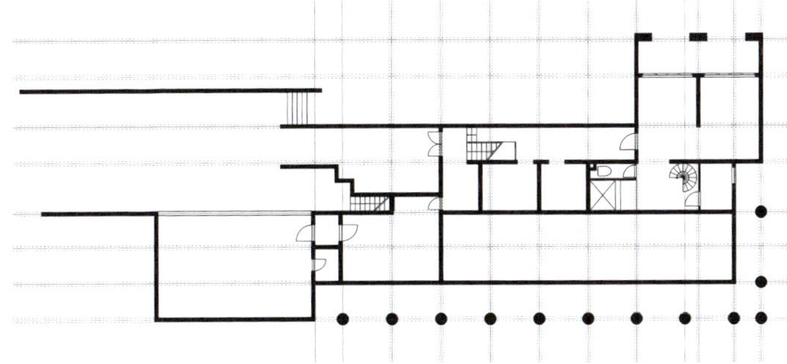

GATTENDORF CASTLE—HOUSE LAJTAKATTA, GATTENDORF, 1974

1500 Border station Austria/Hungary

1529 Village destroyed in the course of the Siege of Vienna

1594 Village destroyed again in the course of the Long Turkish War

1620 Village destroyed by Polish mercenaries

1683 Night quarters of the army of Grand Vizier Kara Mustafa during the second siege of Vienna

1711 Almost the entire village was pillaged during the Kuruc uprisings; properties were divided up among the Esterházy, Schlossberg, Babocsay, Renaud families, etc.

1733 Ladislaus Schlossberg rebuilt the Old Castle as a grand residence for himself; conversion of Renaissance elements to Baroque style; a high loan resulted in Ladislaus Schlossberg's bankruptcy.

1743 Johann Esterházy took over the debts and acquired the property

1809–1856 Castle owned by Barbara and Casimir Esterházy

1911 Romanian brewer Eugen Czell acquired the castle and the manor, which included extensive landholdings and an 18th-century garden palace

1936–1945 Eugen Czell and his wife fled from National Socialism to England

1945–1978 The manor was restituted to Gisela Czell, the widow of Eugen Czell.

1974 Carl Pruscha acquired the Old Castle from Gisela Czell and restored the building, which was slated for demolition, as a summer residence.

See pp. 163–166

Old photographs of Schloss Gattendorf, around 1950

Carl Pruscha's new summer residence, Gattendorf, 2010

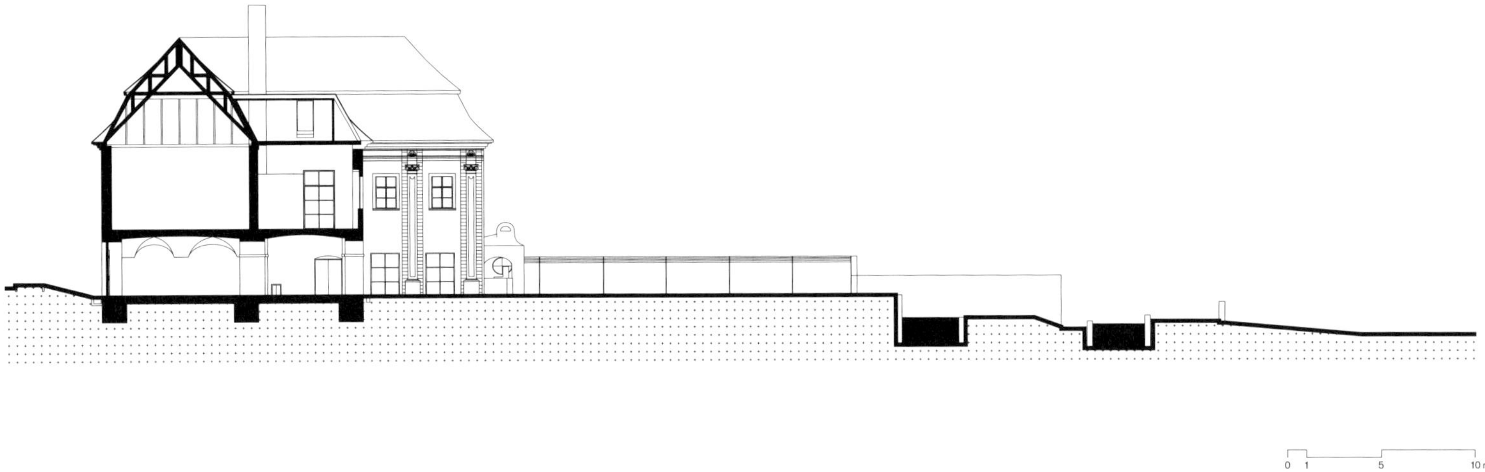

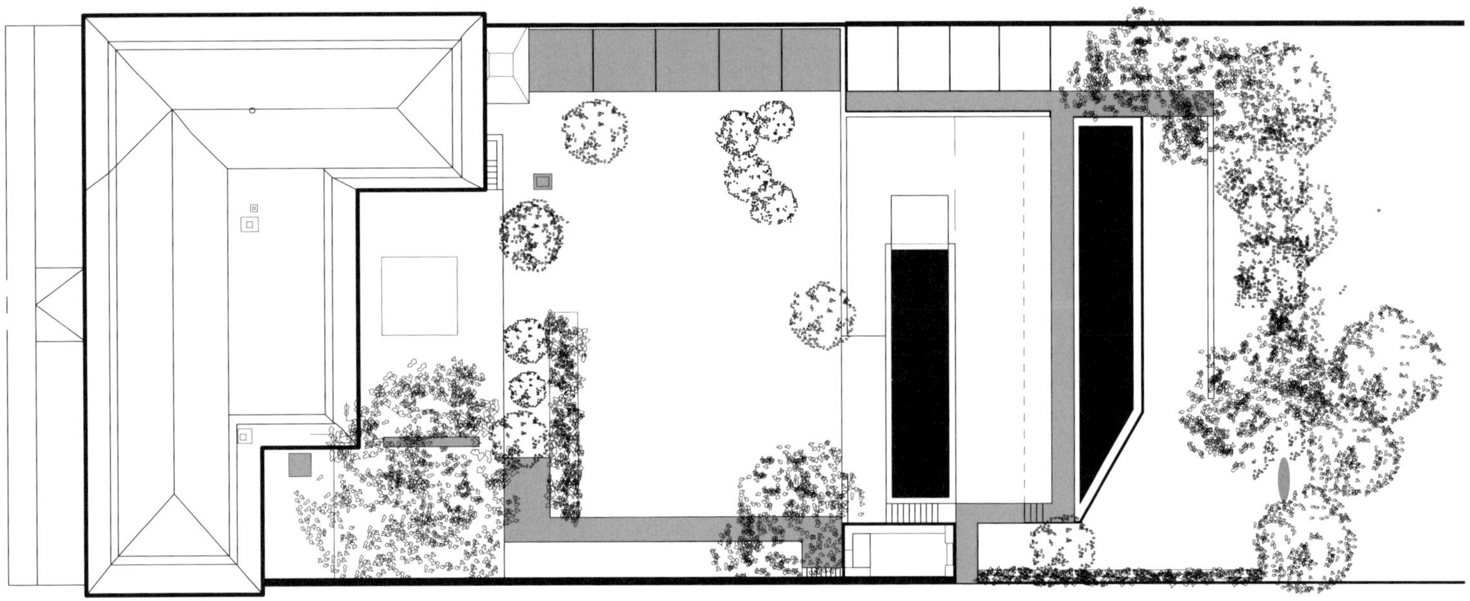

Section and site plan
of the summer residence
Gattendorf

Gattendorf's garden with
biotope, 2010

Interior views of the summer residence Gattendorf

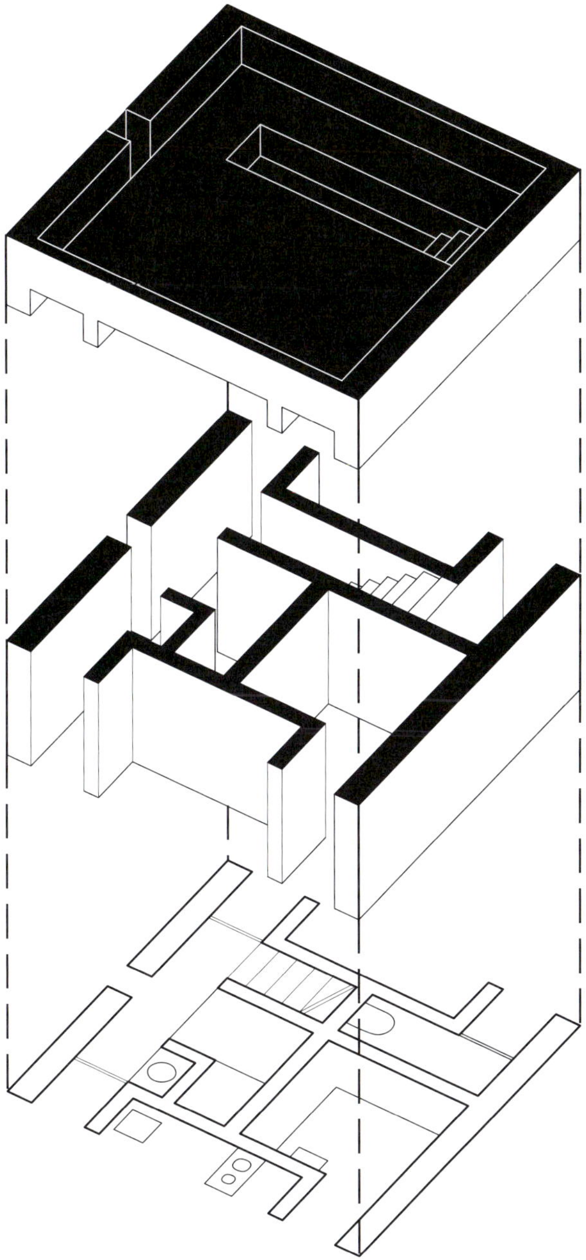

TWININGS

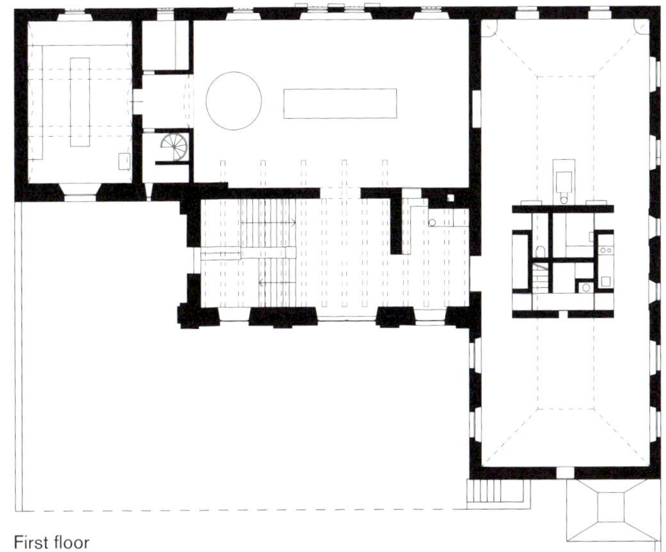

First floor

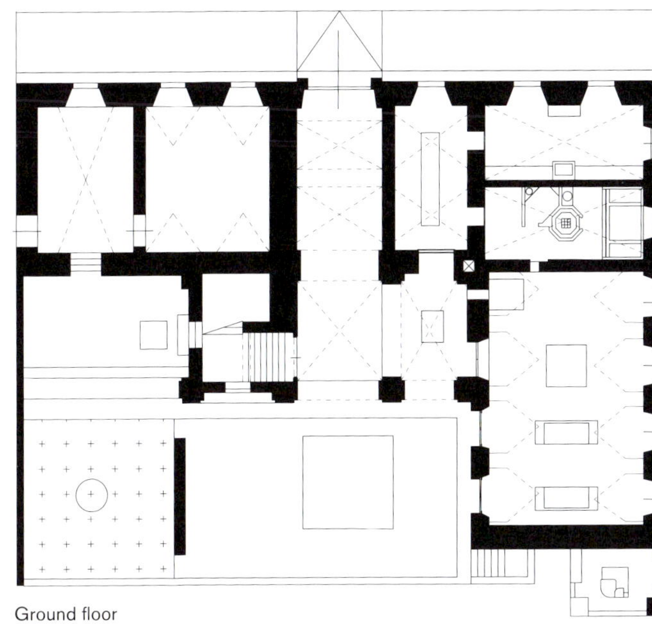

Ground floor

0 1 5 10 m

Garden of the summer residence, Gattendorf

Carl Pruscha, newly appointed professor at the Academy of Fine Arts Vienna, 1976

VII. BACK TO THE ACADEMY IN VIENNA

1976–1988

I always try to tell students that they must never create completed architecture! As an architect you can only provide a framework, then residents, if they get it right, need to develop within that framework.

CP

PROFESSOR PRUSCHA—"INOCULATING THE STUDENTS"

When Carl Pruscha left Nepal and returned to Austria in the mid-1970s, he was appalled at the way buildings were designed in Vienna. Both the monumental faceless multistory residential complexes on the outskirts and the private luxury villas were just horrible in his eyes. It was all, in his words, "both materially uninteresting and completely without merit in terms of attitude." In short, he considered it purely "commercial architecture."

When he became professor at the Academy of Fine Arts in Vienna in 1976, his primary objective in teaching his students was "to inoculate them against such tendencies." Accordingly, at his newly created "Essentials of Architecture" chair, students were taught what, from his perspective, must form the basis of serious architecture. Pruscha set high hopes in the architectural training at art schools, believing that their potential for resisting purely commercial design was greater than that at technological schools. He tried to raise awareness among his students to protect them against pitfalls lurking everywhere and the danger of corrupting influences—for instance against those whose argument is the power of the factual. "I have always fought back against the ideologies of the practical people who reduce everything to necessities."

Throughout his life, Pruscha remained true to classic Modernism. "To me, modern architecture is the invariable revocation of styles." What he defines as styles is any kind of decor, "forced on, uncalled-for elements that delude people with sham." In his view, the epitome of such phony architecture is the Historicism of Vienna's Ringstrasse era and, above all, Postmodernism. He is proud to note about his students that "postmodernism has not caught up with them." He hates it, "including the Haas Haus!" Pruscha is referring to the department-store building Austrian architect Hans Hollein built smack in the center of Vienna in 1990. What's wrong with it? "It gets you to believe something that corresponds neither to content nor to form. It deludes you into appreciating lots of insignificant details without returning to the essential."

The essential, that's what it's all about. It's what Pruscha calls the "archetypal systems" or the "return to the beginnings of architecture." This theme runs all through his life like a guiding thread, from his childhood experiences in the alpine Tyrolean cabin and the exploration of anonymous architecture in the Burgenland region with Roland Rainer all the way to his key moment in New York at Bernard Rudofsky's *Architecture Without Architects* exhibition and his experiences in Nepal.

In order to introduce students to this approach to architecture, he took them on extensive study trips "to the fringes of civilization," as Pruscha puts it: to the deserts or high mountains where these archetypal building methods can still be found today, for example in Yemen, Iran, Morocco, China, India, Bhutan, Nepal, and Tibet. There one could still witness what the true primal needs of humans are, how they reacted to climate and topography, and what spatial solutions they developed in dealing with them; which spaces correspond to the "basic concepts of life," to the rituals of sleeping, eating, cooking, and communicating. He wanted to teach that to his students, so as to keep them from "copying from some magazine models of home layouts from a highly civilized, expensive world of luxury." On these journeys, Pruscha was able to drum up some enthusiasm among his students.

The special thing about Pruscha is that there is nothing nostalgic about his insistence on the archaic and archetypal. "I'm in no way advocating blood and soil architecture or kitsch imitation."[34] The archaic leads him directly to the principles of Modernism: "It's important to uncover the archaic roots, then reinterpret them, and lead them to new solutions." What this boils down to is adapting them to contemporary needs. But, he maintains, it's impossible to create something original without digging up the roots. "Originality means nothing other than a quest for origins." In order to point students to the specific achievements of Modernism, he took them on further study trips, for instance to the Netherlands, "the most important country as far as housing is concerned." There, small new development quarters with low houses around Amsterdam and Delft form an alternative to colossal mass-housing complexes. In Denmark he showed them the buildings of Arne Jacobsen; in Darmstadt the artists' colony of Joseph Maria Olbrich, and the like.

A STUDIO IN THE TOWER

Initially, there was no room for Pruscha at the Academy, and "no one was willing to give up even the tiniest room." After all, the Essentials of Architecture chair had not existed previously. Pruscha had an idea and presented it for approval to Hertha Firnberg, the open-minded minister in charge. His plan was to convert one of the four big vacant corner towers of the Academy building into a studio. He wanted it to serve both as an office and a seminar room.

As always, it was all based on a conceptual idea that took the history of the building into consideration. The Academy of Fine Arts on Schillerplatz had been built by Theophil Hansen in the 1870s. In order to do justice to Hansen's strict Classical approach, Pruscha fitted the attic of his tower with a steel construction with riveted connections. A continuous ribbon window provided light from above from all four sides. The Historicist balustrade in front of it with its neo-Baroque sculptures obscures this ribbon of light from the outside. This was a respectful and at the same time nifty solution that complied with all preservation regulations. On the inside, Pruscha installed a "floating" gallery on a grillage suspended from the support structure, which created two levels. The open gallery became his office. See pp. 222–223

The degree of importance Pruscha attached to precision and functionality is illustrated by the following incident. When construction management chose a Burgenland-based low-cost supplier to produce structural steelwork, Pruscha already had his doubts about his ability to adequately carry out the project. And when the metal worker delivered the first steel beam, it was indeed welded and not riveted, as Pruscha had wanted it, in a nod to Otto Wagner. The rivet heads had been glued on "as quasi decoration." To Pruscha that was unacceptable. The metalworker now had to hire a master riveter from Germany's Ruhr district, who pounded the red-hot rivets into the steel beams. The company reneged on its cheap offer and ultimately even had to file for bankruptcy. In this

Academy of Fine Arts Vienna, front view

The Institute for Architectural Research in the tower of the Hansen building, designed by Carl Pruscha, 1979

case Pruscha stuck to his guns and got his way. Numerous other projects have taught him that his insistence on precision and quality is often perceived as utopian. Over and over, he felt disappointed that his work failed to produce a model effect, for example that the other three towers of the Academy were not modeled on his successful conversion. "It wasn't used as a prototype. Right after I left, the other three towers were also converted, but they added visible glass windows at the top. It looks abominable."

In any case, Pruscha was highly pleased with his tower, and he opened his studio with *Learning from the Kathmandu Valley,* a small exhibition on his buildings in Nepal. When only a few of his colleagues came to see his Nepal show in the tower studio, disappointment ensued. But some VIP visitors certainly did stop by, for instance Heinz Fischer, Hertha Firnberg's successor as minister of science. A friendly relationship has developed between them.

Many years later, in 2004, Fischer had just been elected federal president, and Carl Pruscha was appointed director general of The Arts and Culture Division of the Federal Chancellery of Austria. Federal President Heinz Fischer delivered the opening speech. "He made a point of once more mentioning his one-time visit to the exhibition," as Pruscha proudly remembers. During his tenure as director general of the The Arts and Culture Division, its newly elected members included Maria Lassnig, Valie Export, Eduard Sekler, Charles Correa, Zaha Hadid, Václav Havel, Peter Sloterdijk, Georg Baselitz, Marina Abramović, Bruno Ganz, Oscar Niemeyer, Nikolaus Harnoncourt, Elfie Semotan, Franz West, Rebecca Horn, Martha Jungwirth, Michael Haneke, Wolf Prix, and Gerhard Rühm—"Even though it wasn't easy at all to agree on someone!"

Incidentally, Pruscha's appointment as director general of The Arts and Culture Division resulted in the breach of his once deep friendship with, of all people, Peter Noever. The latter had also vied for the position and felt that Pruscha had stabbed him in the back. But Pruscha is adamant that he had not contributed to the outcome and that he hadn't even wanted to become director general. "It just happened!" There's that sentence again that runs like a thread through Pruscha's life, both in the private and the professional realm. There's a chance he's constructing a myth here. It appears that he often played a more active part in pursuing a certain career than he tends to realize. Over many decades, breaches with friends have also been a recurring theme; he recognizes "almost a pattern," adding, "I'm probably not someone who has many friends." It's often about the convictions, notions, and projects dearest to his heart. Friends ask him to design a house, remodel one, whatever. In the process, differences in opinion or conflicts of interest frequently emerge. Sometimes, it's simply about money, as many consider Pruscha's high-quality proposals too costly. He doesn't know how to deal with that situation. To him it's insulting, a lack of appreciation of his work.

PRUSCHA'S SENSITIVE SLEDGEHAMMER—KUNSTHAUS HORN

In the 1980s and 1990s, the Academy of Fine Arts was lacking spaces suited for new developments in the arts, such as larger installations. The search was therefore on for new locations.

Friedensreich Hundertwasser, head of a painting master class since 1981, suggested they try to acquire the former Piarist school in Horn, Lower Austria. He deplored the fact that this historically intriguing building, an anti-reformationist Piarist convent from 1657, was increasingly falling into ruin and was now even threatened with demolition. But it would make for a magnificent summer studio for the Academy. The faculty was delighted with the proposal. All the concerned authorities gave their consent and provided the funds for the revitalization effort. The contract was awarded to Carl Pruscha.

When he inspected the Renaissance edifice, his infallible spatial instinct and knowledge of architectural history told him that the Baroque wall running toward the courtyard didn't chime with the building as a whole. He was convinced that there was something older and more interesting hidden behind it, but no one shared his judgment and everyone thought it was an irksome distraction. Furthermore, the Baroque wall was deemed to be valuable old structural fabric. But Pruscha remained stubborn, secretly had a hole drilled through the wall, and was proven right. Behind it lay Renaissance arcades, a rare architectural jewel in Austria, which were uncovered after 200 years. See pp. 214–215

Construction work involved in the refurbishment took two years to complete and Pruscha encountered numerous problems. On the one hand, because political authorities were involved definitions of responsibilities were unclear; on the other hand, his approach to the project was, as always, highly sensitive and thus uncompromising. Every time he inspected the progress of the works, he discovered modifications of his plans caused by ignorance, laziness, a know-it-all attitude, or misguided pragmatism. Pruscha protested verbally and in writing, but to no avail. So he resorted to more radical methods. He went and bought a sledgehammer. "So I walked through the building dangling this hammer, and if something was not to my liking I smashed it." At a first glance, sensitivity and brute force, the respectful treatment of historic structural fabric and such a destructive tool appear to be mutually exclusive. In Pruscha's case, however, they are mutually dependent. Precisely because of his keen sense for precision and details he cannot suffer any deviations from his well-thought-out plans.

It was no surprise to him that his sledgehammer did not gain him many friends. Some politicians from the State of Lower Austria, who provided a crucial part of the funding of the projects, thought Pruscha's solutions were too unorthodox. For example, that one had to step outside of the students' rooms to get to the toilets and bathrooms. When the conversion was completed, Pruscha was not even invited to the opening. Nevertheless, the result was convincing and Pruscha himself was pleased with it. The building now comprised a large painting hall, smaller studios, a lecture theater, a library, workshops, exhibition galleries, and student accommodation, which proved popular in the following years, especially in the summer. The setting allowed for intense workshops that could not have been conducted at the Vienna Academy, and it was suited as an accommodation and seminar location for visiting professors and exchange students from around the world.

ARKANEUM–UTOPIAN TREASURE HOUSE FOR CONTEMPORARY ART

All through his life, Carl Pruscha has admired singular and extraordinary architecture—from Oscar Niemeyer's designs and Mies van der Rohe's Seagram Building all the way to Coop Himmelb(l)au's Musée des Confluences in Lyon. Even so, he didn't want to build anything of that kind himself. He was not interested in running a large architect's office with its many employees—there's no other way to tackle such complex competitions and contracts. Another reason was his fear of having to bring to the table a willingness to compromise and engage in discussions that he could not muster.

But there was one important exception. In 1986, a competition was held for the transformation of Vienna's former royal stables, which had been used as exhibition halls since the 1920s, into a cultural forum. Called the MuseumsQuartier today, this project was hotly contested over many years. The task piqued Pruscha's interest for two reasons. Firstly, it allowed him to go through ideas on a large urban scale since this was "the largest and most important project Vienna ever had"—since Gottfried Semper's never realized Imperial Forum, which was originally conceived as the crowning ensemble of the Ringstrasse boulevard. Additionally, there was the appealing historic structure. The royal stables had been designed by Johann Bernhard Fischer von Erlach, the star architect of the Austrian Baroque. Secondly, Pruscha interpreted a building for the arts as a kind of cultic site, because he saw art as Modernism's substitute for religion—"The belief in the continued existence of art is of religious provenance." Conceptualizing such a spiritually charged place in a central location in Vienna was a fascinating challenge to him.

And thus he decided, against his own principles, to take part in this competition. Even though he wasn't expecting his proposal to win, he still hoped to touch off a process of discussion and reflection. From the outset, he approached the project not in a realistic and pragmatic manner but with a utopian design. Pruscha was convinced that a new museum of contemporary art was less an architectural and more a conceptual task, which required a new philosophical approach to the exhibiting and collecting of such art.

He was not planning on any changes to the historic Baroque architecture, but wanted only to eliminate "the artistically worthless historistic riding hall." In its place on the large center courtyard he placed a new exhibition hall, the "Konche," a kind of gateway building to a complex subterranean system of underground galleries, which he called an Arkaneum or treasury of art. He aligned the building to one of the key city-planning axes of Vienna, which leads from Michaelerplatz across Heldenplatz, through the castle gate, and on between the two imperial museums to the flak tower on Stiftgasse, an indestructible giant concrete cylinder from World War II. Here, Carl envisaged an exit from his subterranean Arkaneum. His terrace overlooking the rooftops would have offered a view across almost all of Vienna—"the actual museum." The Arkaneum, on the other hand, was conceived as an infinite archive that would take in the entirety of the contemporary art of every day—a utopian and megalomaniac idea. Pruscha owed the

Carl Pruscha with Roland Rainer, 1987

Carl Pruscha with Hans Hollein, 2005

inspiration to his students. Day after day he watched their inexhaustible artistic accomplishments, their unbelievable creativity, which usually goes unnoticed by the outside world and just evaporates. "In contrast to what Museums do these days, where only the art of the victors is shown, so to speak, I wanted people to preserve at least prototypes of that, in order to document the zeitgeist of a certain era. An infinite number of tunnels could have been built, you know, on top of and below each other." See pp. 216–217

Pruscha was clear about the utopian character of his plan from the outset, because the actual job was to design two museums for two specific collections. His project, one out of a total of 88, was knocked out of the competition at an early stage. The winning design was that by Ortner & Ortner, which was, however, completely transformed and adapted in scale in the following years due to public protests.

Today's MuseumsQuartier with its Leopold Museum and MUMOK (Museum of Modern Art) only elicits biting commentary from Pruscha. It almost takes on the qualities of a Thomas Bernhard rant: "The eye doctor's ridiculous museum and MUMOK over there, which is even more ludicrous, in a certain sense; just looking at that, the funny way these two massive lumps just sit around [...] And in the middle, the only building that was truly ugly and could have been razed, this Emperor-Franz-Joseph riding hall! That's now the folly in the middle, converted in a terrible way, with only the façade left, which has nothing whatsoever to do with its content and what it was turned into. It's so absurd that it hurts when I think about it."[35]

RADICAL HOUSING DEVELOPMENT—COURTYARD HOUSES INSTEAD OF "SLAVE SHIPS"

Carl Pruscha has no kind words for Vienna's large-scale housing projects of the 1970s—all he can see is dismal "container and slave ships." To him, this is especially disappointing because, when it comes to innovative and progressive housing, Vienna can look back on a riveting history that has attracted a great deal of attention internationally. After all, in the 1920s and early 1930s the students of pioneer and big-city enthusiast Otto Wagner built the most important large public-housing complexes (*Gemeindebauten*) of "Red Vienna", the so-called superblocks. Karl Ehn designed the Karl-Marx-Hof, Hubert Gessner the Reumann-Hof, Engelbert Mang the Victor-Adler-Hof, and Rudolf Perco the complex on Friedrich Engels Platz. Pruscha concedes that these buildings certainly betray "a masterful sense for monumentality and a keen sense of space." Aside from the large-scale, multistory residential blocks preferred by the City of Vienna, there were also developments in the opposite direction through the so-called settler and garden-city movement, their objective being clusters of affordable small and single-family homes with kitchen gardens. Adolf Loos, Josef Frank, and Margarete Schütte-Lihotzky counted among their protagonists. Their achievements included Vienna's Werkbundsiedlung in Hietzing, one of the most important manifestations of Modernism in Austria, as well as Adolf Loos' and Hugo Mayer's model housing development on Heuberg in a row-house arrangement. Loos, in the early 1920s chief architect of the Settlement Office of the City of Vienna, was an especially important

C.P.P.N. (Carl Pruscha with Peter Noever), project for a house for artists in old Havana, exhibition, 1991

Covers of the magazine *Umriss*, edited by Peter Noever, 1985, 1992

source of inspiration for Pruscha. With National Socialism, all the traditions of Austrian Modernism were lost, and it was only in the 1950s and 1960s that Roland Rainer took up the idea of the low-rise housing development again.[36] In the decades after the war, however, the Municipality of Vienna focused, just as it had in the 1920s, on large-scale, multistory projects, such as the Trabrenngründe on Rennbahnweg in Vienna's 22nd district, built between 1973 and 1977, or Wohnpark Alterlaa in the 23rd district, built between 1973 and 1985, one of the largest housing complexes in Austria. In Pruscha's estimation, there was no life in these high-rise blocks. Only in the 1980s did the conceptual tide turn. The City of Vienna tried to embark on a new start in public housing, and the tradition of the small-house development was at least partially revived.

Residential building is one of the most important tasks of urban development and was one of Pruscha's passions, at the latest since his New York years. He therefore accepted an invitation, together with architects Otto Häuselmayer and Heinz Tesar, to develop new ideas for the faceless outskirts of Vienna's 22nd district and design a model housing development on Biberhaufenweg in Aspern. What the officials in charge of the commission had in mind was the revival of the concept of the village center, and each of the three architects therefore focused on a basic typological pattern. Heinz Tesar took on the "square," Otto Häuselmayer the "street," and Carl Pruscha the "village green." Pruscha interpreted the village green as the "prototypal poetic whole" between city and country. He designed two row-house developments whose towers were to form the last clear signs of urban life while their gently curving corrugated roofs symbolize the transition to the wide-open landscape. The model housing development was built in 1985. See pp. 196–197

One year later, Pruscha was invited again. Unlike in the case of Biberhaufenweg, this was an invited competition for a housing development at Traviatagasse in the middle of the commercial belt in Inzersdorf, a part of Vienna's southern 23rd district. Pruscha's ambition was stirred, not least because Raimund Abraham also took part, a friend he respected highly as an architect. Since their first encounter at the Academy, their relationship had been marked by friendly competition—so the challenge was on. "It was clear to me that if he was in the game, I'd have to come up with something interesting to stay in the game."[37] It was a boon to their friendship that both won the competition ex aequo, and thus could both realize their projects.

What was initially shocking to some was that on the outside, Pruscha's three-story houses have no windows, doors, balconies, or ornaments: "My planning was inspired by my oriental experiences." Entering his closed square complex of thirty-six homes can actually feel like walking into an Arab city district. The buildings are accessed on foot via narrow paths, their entrances are located in their respective courtyards. And it is the courtyards that distinguish these houses and mark their character. Toward the outside they guarantee ultimate privacy, they are oriented entirely inward. All three floors open exclusively to five-by-five meter courtyards, which are partially spanned by grillage-floor terraces. Pruscha drew inspiration not only from archetypal anonymous architecture around the world but also from Adolf Loos, who expressed exactly what Pruscha felt when he wrote, "The house should be discreet on the outside; its entire richness should be disclosed on the inside."[38] Loos loathed any transparency of private life and called buildings with large glass windows "bird cages."[39] Another inspiration was Loos' legendary system "house with one wall," which he had even filed a patent for. The outer walls were self-supporting and contained all installations; the rest was built from wood. Thus the "house with one wall" allows a highly flexible structure, and Pruscha took the idea one step further. For his courtyard houses he planned an L-shaped concrete wall that formed a courtyard. Part of his original concept was that prefab lightweight construction rooms would dock on to these walls. But here, the responsible Vienna officials put a spoke in his wheel. They dismissed wood as substandard—that was still the consensus in the 1980s. As was often the case, Pruscha had been ahead of his time, had to build his courtyard houses entirely in massive construction, and he was "pretty upset about that."

He designated the bottom floor a basement. It was thus not counted as usable floor space, which was important to be eligible for residential-building subsidies. With this "trick," Pruscha provided residents with more living space, about 130 square meters in all. He was thinking of workshops or hobby rooms. The bath, bed, and children's rooms are located on the floor above, which is connected with the yard via an outside staircase. The communal rooms, which is to say, the living and dining room as well as the kitchen, are found on the top third floor. Pruscha thus turned the traditional arrangement of rooms on its head. This interesting approach ensures ideal lighting conditions in the fully glazed living area, which faces exactly south. From here, a staircase leads to the roof terrace, which offers a view into the distance as well as visual cover from neighbors.

The compound is based on a strict geometrical system, its primary element being the square. From the outside, it's a closed, compact block measuring one hundred by one hundred meters. Pruscha accentuated the four corners of the square with cube-shaped community buildings. They comprise the Kaminhaus for festivities and events, a children's playhouse with a two-story slide, a youth house, and a bathhouse (*hammam*) with a sauna. Within the square there is another square, which is again divided into four quadrants by the housing complex's system of main access routes. See pp. 193–195

A development of small houses can also achieve high housing density, which is what Pruscha sought to prove with his courtyard dwellings. His message was that his clusters of atrium houses are suited as a form of urban housing and can compete with multi-story apartment buildings. His one-time professor and fatherly friend Roland Rainer was delighted. He had always found Pruscha's "striving for vitality, clarity" to be convincing. Rainer, however, doesn't forget to mention that these qualities "were never appreciated in Vienna, today less than ever."[40] It was little surprise then that Pruscha's radical concept was not met entirely

Carl Pruscha with Eva Schlegel, Ursula Krinzinger, Richard Schmitz, and Klaus Albrecht Schröder, 1999

Carl Pruscha with Eva Schlegel, Josef Ortner and Kathrin Messner, Colombo, 2002

with applause. Architect and architecture critic Judith Eiblmayr posed the question, whether the development on Traviatagasse was architecture "on the wrong track," this being a pun on the Italian *traviata,* which translates as "a woman who has strayed from the straight and narrow" or even "The Fallen Woman."[41] The reasons she cited for her critique were, not least, feminist ones. As she rightly observed, housework was still mostly carried out by women and condemned many of them to isolation from public life. The focus on courtyards fails to do justice to humans as social beings, Eiblmayr maintained. She considered it problematic "[i]f in your own house you are denied the right to cast a glance into the street, out of mere curiosity, which is to say, when even superficial social interest is deliberately curtailed." In a highly polemic manner, she referred to "neurotically excessive introversion" and a staged "'petrified' turning away from the rest of the world,"[42] which was more in tune with oriental than with Western social notions and climates. In the *Wiener Zeitung,* Hans Haider countered such criticism from a conservative perspective, writing that "social engineers drunk on theory view this retreat behind ten-meter high walls with suspicion. They want citizens to be constantly available to them for communication and interaction."[43] Pruscha himself also reacted to these accusations, pointing out that "[p]eople go to a Vietnamese restaurant, but they cannot acquire a taste for a form of housing that has indeed proved successful somewhere else. These are things where one should be free to think in new ways, to collect examples from the traditions of many cultures and work with them."[44]

But, contrary to expectations, Pruscha's courtyard houses were highly popular. This was illustrated, for example, by Julia Zillinger's studies on housing satisfaction. A women living there went into raptures about the light conditions, "the different lighting angles due to projections and recesses, terraces, windows, and skylights." A houseowner, in turn, explains how much space the house created for people. What's more, for children the building was "an adventure, because it takes them time to figure it out" or, as others said, it's "a fairy-tale castle." And the kitchen on the top floor does not necessarily entail that—mostly—women were lugging stuff up the stairs all the time. Aside from the fact that to this end Pruscha had planned to install pulleys with baskets, it seems none of the women were complaining. On the contrary, "I see that as my gym." Some, of course, fear that they will be unable to make it up the stairs when they grow old. But, there was always the possibility of installing a small elevator, some residents added. They also did not experience the social isolation Eiblmayr thought the sealed-off courtyards could cause. Rather, neighborly relations were very good because they were able to decide how much social contact they wanted to engage in. And residents particularly appreciated the seclusion that had been called into question.[45]

Fifteen years after Traviatagasse, Pruscha again aired the idea of his model housing development, but in a modified form. Together with his young Team Habitat—Franz Loranzi, Julia Nuler, and Andreas Pfusterer—he developed a successor project and called it Quadrangle Housing. This time it would be constructed from wood, as originally intended. The team now almost doubled the

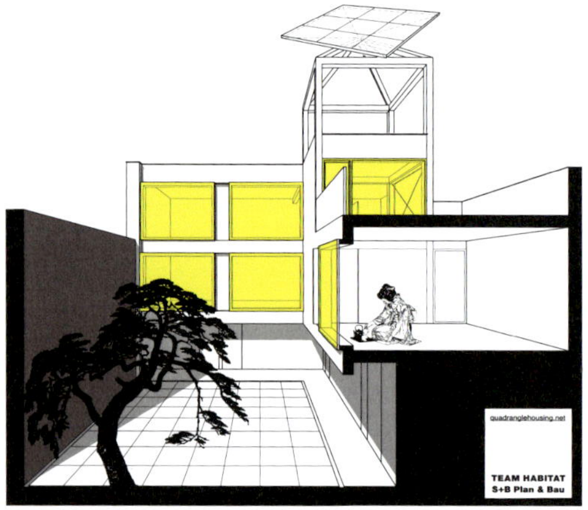

Cover of the Quadrangle-Housing folder, 2009

size of the courtyard to seven by seven meters; the maximum living area was now 150 square meters. A photovoltaic sail above the roof terrace provided for a partially off-grid power arrangement.

See pp. 198–199

Pruscha and his Team Habitat submitted the project in a competition held by the City of Vienna's creative center *departure,* which functions as a hub between the creative and the classic industries. Pruscha's hopes were high, after all he was deeply convinced of the qualities of his Quadrangle Housing. There was much enthusiasm in professional circles. The Museum of Applied Arts acquired the model and showed it at an exhibition, as did Architekturzentrum Vienna. To Pruscha's disappointment, the much-praised project never materialized. "The city of Vienna is interested in high buildings, they are not interested in low houses," he noted in resignation, adding, "If people don't want it, there's nothing you can do about it." And there was an additional factor: Carl's quality standards are, to say the least, utopian. When a potential developer calculated the project, he concluded that it wasn't appealing to him because it didn't turn enough profit.

Pruscha's friend Wolf D. Prix also set store by the Quadrangle Housing project, and proposed it in Saudi Arabia when he himself got a housing contract there. The local decision makers declined. Their middle-class society wanted to live in high towers with gleaming glass façades and not "in a souk of yesteryear." Over and over, Pruscha was driven to desperation by the fact that these societies have no appreciation of their own heritage and make no attempts to renew them—"Those are my romantic ideas …" Both Romantic and utopian, as he was far ahead of his time. The elites of the non-Western world currently fall, above all, for something Pruscha calls "neocolonialist architectural adventures." It is likely going to take more time before they proudly remember their own magnificent building traditions.

TRAVIATAGASSE, VIENNA, 1992

The competition for this housing development was won by Raimund Abraham and Carl Pruscha ex aequo. It was decided that the complex would be further developed on the basis of Abraham's urban-planning concept, and Pruscha was commissioned for the design of the central residential area. His radical idea included L-shaped concrete walls into which three-story apartments would be built. They would be constructed from prefab wooden elements around an open courtyard, their structural introversion creating a special form of privacy. Since, at the time, it was legally impossible to build wooden structures, the entire development and its concept had to be adapted to allow for massive construction throughout.

See pp. 189–190, 260

A contemporary *hammam* for the Traviatagasse housing project, model and realization, 1992

Plans and construction drawings, 1990

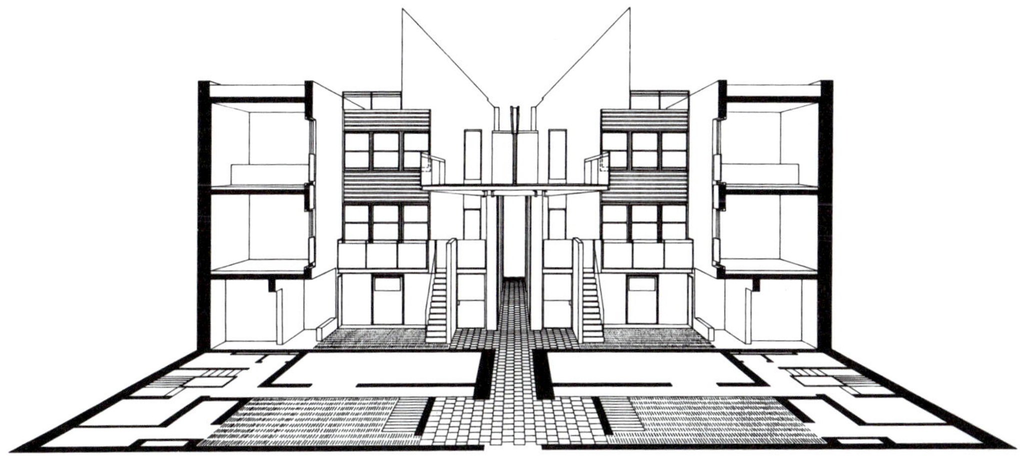

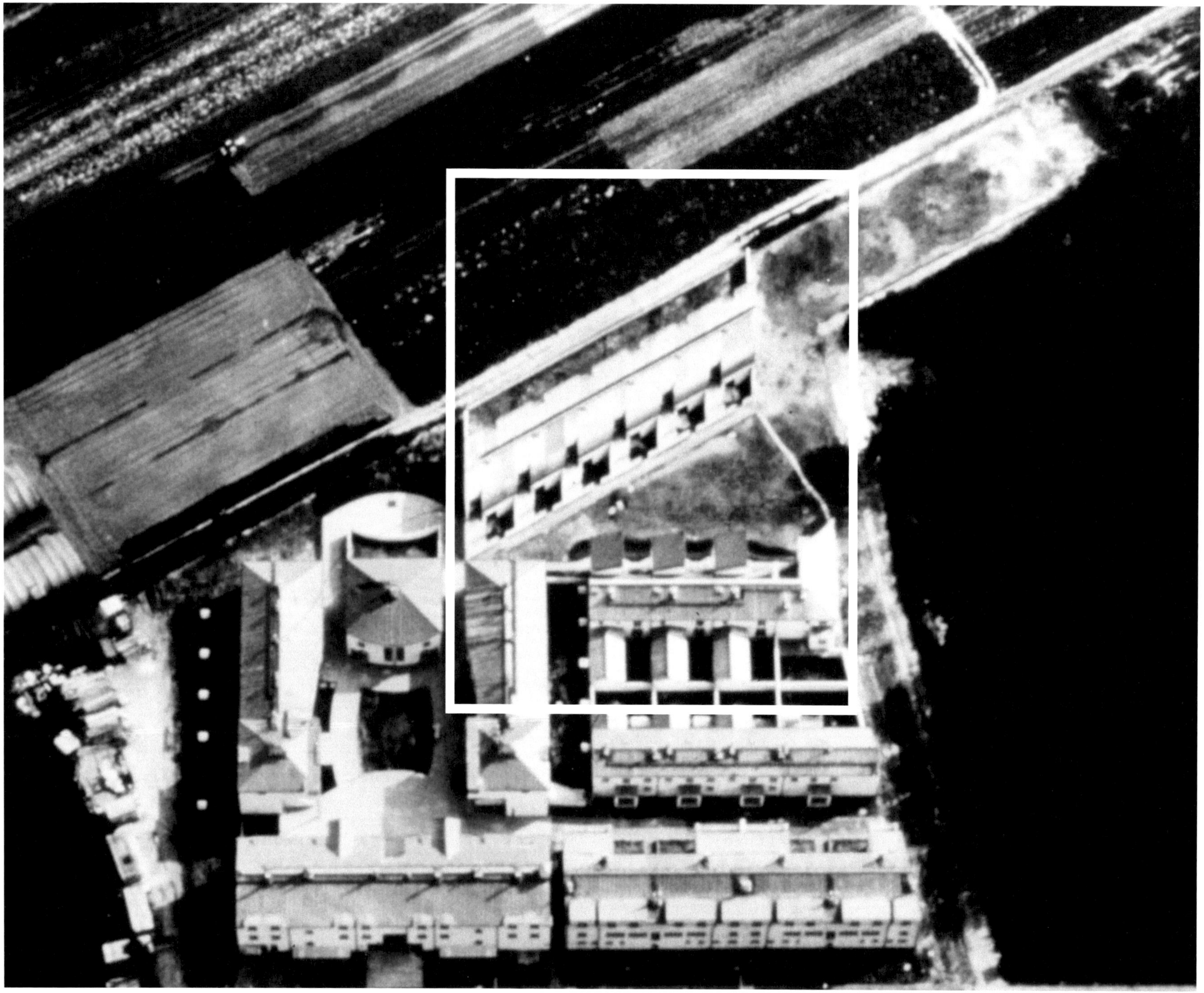

Aerial view of row houses in Aspern, Vienna, 1985

Front view of the housing project in Aspern, 1985

HOUSING DEVELOPMENT IN ASPERN, VIENNA, 1985
Since the initiation of democracy in Austria the socialist city government of Vienna was concerned about the housing problem of the growing population. Two alternate approaches were adopted: multi-story mass housing with courtyards and subsidiary services for its habitants and "settlement" schemes as practiced in England's suburban developments. After World War II, the preference in Vienna was predominantly the mass-housing concept.

It was a surprise when the city started a small initiative to return—in some instances—to the settlement scheme at the beginning of the eighties. Three architects were invited to develop a small scheme together but with individual preferences. So one of the three chose the plaza as its topic; the other the *Gasse* (alley); and the third, Carl Pruscha, the *Anger* (village green) to create a link between the built-up area and the open fields beyond.

See p. 189

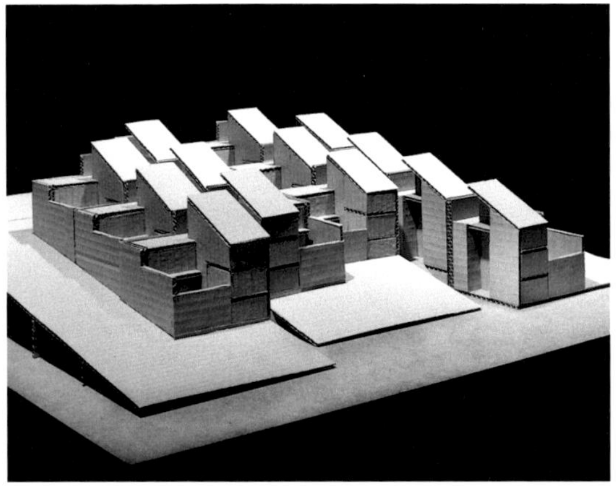

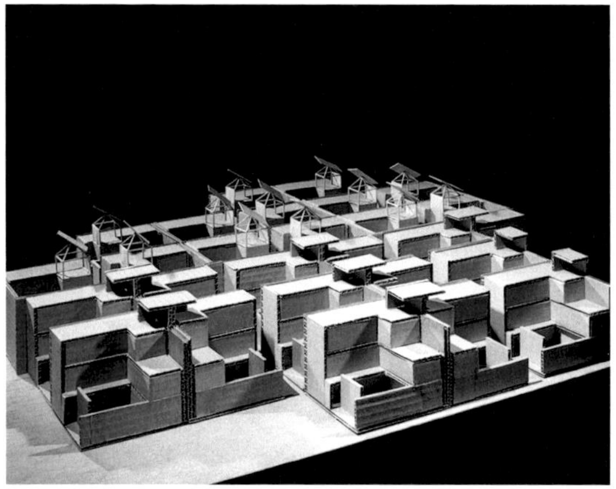

TYP A			**145,43 m²**
Grundfläche	144,00 m²	Wohnfläche gesamt	145,43 m²
Hoffläche	34,30 m²	EG	31,55 m²
Kellerräume	19,07 m²	1.OG	65,18 m²
Terrasse, 2.OG	18,20 m²	2.OG	48,70 m²

1:200 | 2m | 5m | 10m | 50m | 25m | 10m | 1:1000

14 Wohneinheiten

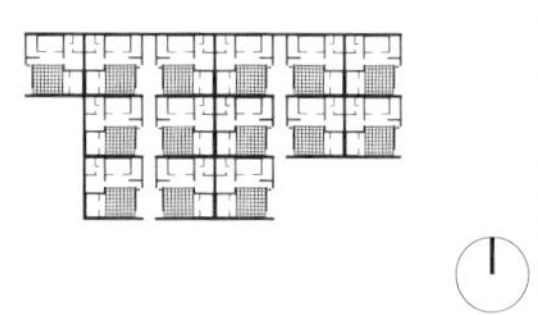

TYP B			**147,56 m²**
Grundfläche	144,00 m²	Wohnfläche gesamt	147,56 m²
Hoffläche	46,80 m²	EG	25,78 m²
Kellerräume	19,92 m²	1.OG	68,28 m²
Terrasse, 2.OG	18,20 m²	2.OG	53,50 m²

1:200 | 2m | 5m | 10m | 50m | 25m | 10m | 1:1000

13 Wohneinheiten

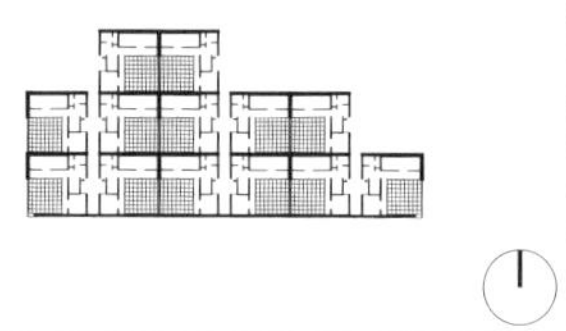

TYP C			**129,92 m²**
Grundfläche	121,00 m²	Wohnfläche gesamt	129,92 m²
Hoffläche	31,71 m²	EG	38,10 m²
Kellerräume	4,46 m²	1.OG	41,47 m²
Terrasse, 2.OG	10,08 m²	2.OG	50,35 m²

1:200 | 2m | 5m | 10m | 50m | 25m | 10m | 1:1000

13 Wohneinheiten
am Hang

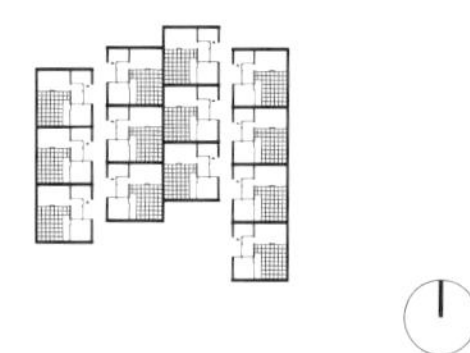

QUADRANGLE HOUSING, VIENNA, 2009

The basic elements of this urban-development concept are individual residential "fields"—so-called clusters. Each of these consists of 27 courtyard houses and forms compartmentalized neighborhoods. The "houses," while individual units, are conceived as a horizontally structured residential complex. Compared with the usual row house or single-family home developments, the arrangement of courtyard houses in "clusters" is distinguished by an intriguing spatial concept, which includes both extensive public open spaces as well as private and secluded inner courtyards and roof terraces. Project development was carried out by Pruscha and his Team Habitat.

See pp. 191–192, 260

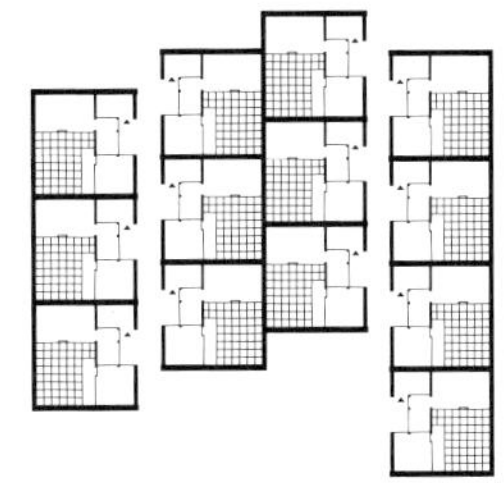

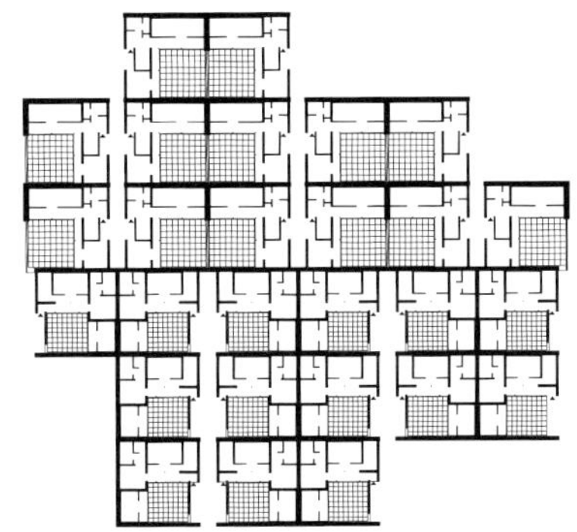

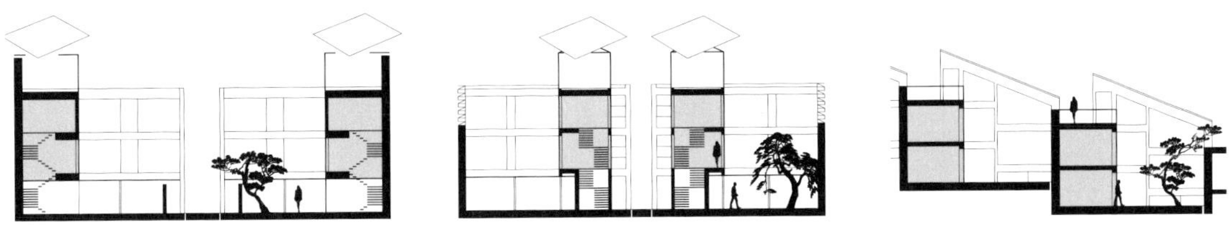

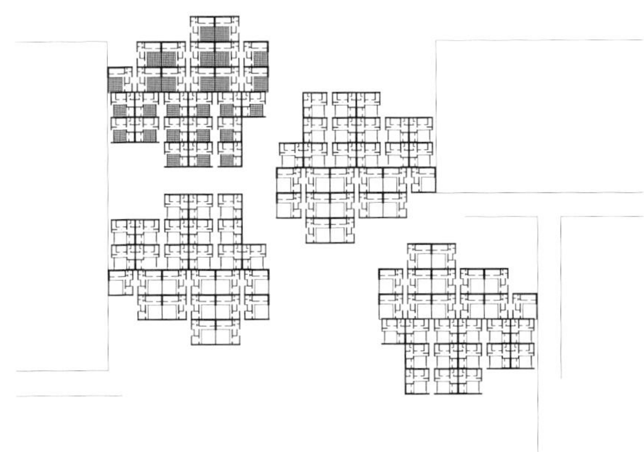

Carl Pruscha, rector of the Academy, at the Semper Depot, 1993

VIII. RECTOR AT THE ACADEMY OF FINE ARTS VIENNA

1988–2001

Pruscha's talent for power derived from being a natural in dealing with paranoiacs. He allowed everyone to not take him seriously; he got almost everything he wanted; he relished in the vibration of his fortune, pushed through what he thought served the cause. He didn't need the position to be what he was; he filled it, until he overflowed.

Peter Sloterdijk

"THE MAN OF THE HOUR"

When Carl Pruscha took the helm of the Academy on Schillerplatz in 1988, he was, according to philosopher Peter Sloterdijk, "the right man at the right time at the right place." As a visiting professor, Sloterdijk witnessed the radical changes at the art academy almost from the very beginning. In his eyes it was no doubt thanks to Pruscha that "the last bastion of Kakania" has been transformed into "a house of the present."[46] In the 1980s, the Academy of Fine Arts was indeed regarded as a venerable, but also antiquated institution. It was still dominated by the two art currents of the postwar era, Austrian Informalism, which flourished especially in the circles around Galerie St. Stephan starting in the mid-1950s, and the so-called Vienna School of Fantastic Realism, the Austrian variant of Neo-Surrealism founded by Albert Paris Gütersloh. The protagonists of these two antagonistic currents were still teaching at the Academy. Innovative or even revolutionary over thirty years ago, they were now stagnant, busy navel gazing, and hardly interested in present-day international currents. Innovative trends had taken hold at the Academy of Applied Arts, Vienna's second art school, not at the Academy on Schillerplatz.

In the stale air of an outmoded institution Carl Pruscha became its rector—once again, as he maintains, without much effort on his part. He was actually planning to leave town, Austria had become too narrow for him. And he sided with Otto Wagner on the point that one should not teach architecture for more than ten years. The fact that his innovative housing projects were met with limited interest only reinforced his decision. But then things took an altogether different turn. Being elected rector was a surprise not just to him but to many of his colleagues as well. It was a thrilling new task and there was a lot to do. He aimed to turn the Academy into one of Europe's leading art schools. Of late, the winds of change had also been blowing from the relevant government ministry. As a result of the revolutionary events of 1968, belated by twenty years, the so-called Art Academy Organization Act brought new participation regulations. No longer could a coterie of professors settle all issues between them in a restaurant back room; decisions were now made with the equal involvement of professors, assistants, and students in democratic committees. This new balance of power made possible not only Pruscha's election as rector but also his reforms. With his characteristic stubbornness and creativity he was able, above all, to implement three agendas, namely to open up the master schools, give art theory its rightful place, and anchor contemporary art currents at the Academy.

The master schools had long developed into isolated little princedoms. Studying under a professor meant that it was virtually impossible to also attend the class of another professor for a change. That was deemed tantamount to high treason or apostasy in a fundamentalist sect. Pruscha was convinced that this unproductive system, which was ultimately inimical to art, had to be broken up. An exchange had to be launched internally and with the world outside. And the Academy had to start seeing itself as a unity, as a whole. Through publications and exhibitions, Pruscha endeavored to present the work of professors and students to a public audience.

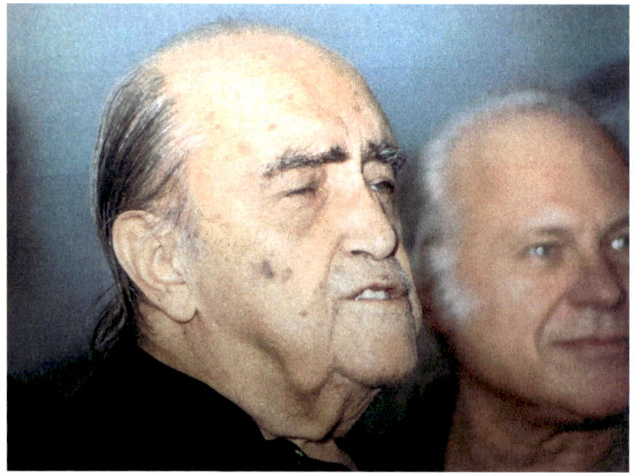

Carl Pruscha and Prorector Köb in Japan, 1995

Carl Pruscha with Oscar Niemeyer, Rio de Janeiro, 2007

Carl Pruscha with the rector of the University of Applied Arts, Oswald Oberhuber, 2002

Up until the 1980s, art at the Academy came only "from the guts of the initiates" ("aus den Eingeweiden der Eingeweihten") as Peter Sloterdijk pithily summed things up, but now Pruscha greatly stepped up the role of art theory. In 1960s' America, he had become familiar with the important role of theory. Now he was determined to establish it as a course at the Vienna Academy. To this end, he definitely needed a new chair. In order to get it approved, he resorted to a "trick," as he himself calls it. This was about persuading not only the Academy professors but also, above all, the Ministry, which needed to fund the academic chair.

What was this "trick" about? Pruscha staged a two-day symposium in 1990, the so-called *Philosophengespräche*. On two rows of chairs in the Academy's auditorium the "masters" and the "philosophers" sat facing each other. It was a theatric staging with almost Monty Python-esque qualities. Among others, Pruscha invited Gottfried Boehm, Boris Groys, Herta Nagl-Docekal, Hanspeter Padrutt, Giovanni Vicario, Manfred Frank, Peter Sloterdijk, and Francisco Varela. While they had the ability to eloquently present their theses, the artists had a hard time doing the same. After all, language was not their home medium. Still, after a while, several artists came out of their shells and found the culture of discussion that had hitherto not existed in this form intriguing—including, for instance, Wolfgang Hollegha.[47] Newly appointed Minister of Science Erhard Busek also participated in the symposium and was excited. And it wasn't long before Pruscha got his chair for Cultural Philosophy and Theory of Perception, which was first held by Peter Sloterdijk.

It really was high time to establish at the Academy new positions in art, such as video and media art, performance, and installations. Since 1983 there had at least been an Institute of Contemporary Art, initially headed by Johannes Gachnang and subsequently by Burghart Schmidt. In 1988, Erika Billeter was the first woman to be appointed professor at the Academy. Billeter remembers that "at first, there was a lot of skepticism among the professors."[48] But Pruscha had also set out to end the dominance of male fraternization at the Academy. Moreover, in Billeter he found an important ally in pushing his reforms through. The same was true for Elisabeth Schweeger, who focused on innovative exhibition concepts. Together they were able to enlist renowned international curators such as Harald Szeemann or Kasper König for the annual closing exhibitions.

Appointing international and younger artists to new and vacant positions slowly but surely drove away the stuffy provincial atmosphere. Participation by the students made it possible to bring new faces and new positions in art to the Academy. For example, Michelangelo Pistoletto from Turin took the helm of the sculpture class and Michael Sorkin from New York now headed the Institute of Urbanism. Sorkin arrived from the US in Vienna with typical American, naive, and positive expectations. He had not anticipated the "Baroque cultivation of the high art of intrigue and moral execution—the favorite local form of sport hunting," he recounts. It was only after a few months that he realized what role Pruscha expected him to play, namely "that I was to be nothing short of the torpedo that Charlie was thinking of firing at the

Carl Pruscha with Raimund Abraham and Wolf Prix, 2008

Carl Pruscha, Raimund Abraham, and Michael Rotondi, 2006

Carl Pruscha with Rafael Moneo, 2000

heavy battleship of the master school system and the somber masters ruling it then."[49]

One of their most inveterate foes, it turned out, was Gustav Peichl, the former rector, who had headed a master class in architecture at the Academy for over twenty years. He was well connected in Austria and had already tried to prevent Pruscha's appointment as rector. Pruscha had known Peichl since the 1950s when he had done an internship with him. The relationship between the two was ruined for decades when, after a night of drinking in Peichl's live-in studio, he got into the bathtub instead of sitting down at the architect's table and answered the door in his boss's bathrobe when he returned earlier than expected. What's more, at the Academy Pruscha was regarded as Roland Rainer's protégé and, as people liked to think in terms of feudal power relations, that alone made him appear highly suspect. When Pruscha was appointed rector, Peichl had had a different successor in mind. And on top of that, now there was this young architect from the US who thought he could lecture these long-established gentlemen about architecture. Peichl left no stone unturned to make life at the Academy hard for Michael Sorkin. The latter was frustrated by the absurd intrigues, which mainly affected the students, but being twenty years younger than the old guard, he also knew he had the advantage of age. "Ultimately, I simply outlived these academic dinosaurs who were pensioned off, each to their own Jurassic Park."[50]

That did not come to pass without conflict, either. When the venerable generation of those born in 1928/29 reached retirement age and Pruscha actually wanted to pension them off, all hell broke loose. The artists were outraged and tried to intervene with the Ministry, or to at least have a say in the choice of their own successors. But it was precisely these continuities that Pruscha wanted to thwart. What ultimately tipped the scale were the students, who were less interested in big names and more in good and regular support—which busy "stars" could not offer them. When it came to choosing a successor for Gustav Peichl, they gave preference to young Iranian architect Nasrine Seraji over the internationally famous Zaha Hadid or the renowned Raimund Abraham.

For Pruscha, the retirements resulted in a tough battle with sensitive, egomaniacal artists' souls that could not be won without deeply insulting them. But by and by, the rector got his way. A new, younger generation took over, among them Heimo Zobernig, Franz Graf, Renée Green, Peter Kogler, Hubert Schmalix, Elisabeth von Samsonow, Sue Williams, and Eva Schlegel. Despite the conflicts that came with them, Pruscha experienced the days of these new appointments as the happiest of his rectorship.

Peter Sloterdijk lived through countless college meetings: "In order to appreciate Carl Pruscha's achievement, you have to know that structurally, a conference hall full of grand Austrian artists is the most democratically inept group in the world. A bunch of wrangling suicide bombers would look like a harmonious chamber orchestra by comparison."[51] For Michael Sorkin, these meetings were a mixture of a "UN General Assembly meeting and an opera evening," where Pruscha acted as the "captain of a Ship of

Carl Pruscha with Raimund Abraham, 2004

Carl Pruscha, Raimund Abraham, and Peter Noever, 1995

Carl Pruscha, Ute Woltron, Peter Noever, and Zaha Hadid, 1990

Fools." "As a mercilessly brilliant self-promoter and manipulator he was never more in his element than when he orchestrated the tumultuous democracy of these monthly meetings he presided over."[52]

When Pruscha thought that gentle efforts at persuasion weren't getting him anywhere, he put his foot down in an authoritarian manner and launched into bouts of hotheaded shouting at colleagues. He played bad cop, while his prorector, Edelbert Köb, took on the role of good cop. Pruscha saw Köb, the later director of Kunsthaus Bregenz and the Museum of Modern Art in Vienna, as the best possible person for his job: "He's honest, concise, precise, super loyal, but still critical." Often Köb acted as a buffer and mediator between the rector and the others. For his part, Köb speaks of Pruscha in high terms, saying that he was the only rector since 1945 who took on the crucial issues pertaining to art and art education and led the Academy "out of its glass tower."[53]

Edelbert Köb was also the one Pruscha called in one of the worst crises of his life. In recent years, his relationship with his wife Edda had taken another dive. Edda wanted to file for divorce a third time. Carl did not. Nevertheless, they lived separate lives, albeit under the same roof. One morning in June 1992, when Pruscha wanted to bring her coffee, he found her dead in her bed. The autopsy showed that she had suffered a heart attack. She only lived to be fifty-two. Pruscha was in a state of shock and, without so much as a thought, called Edelbert Köb, the most reliable person around him. Köb immediately took charge, called the police and a doctor. Pruscha was in a state of complete numbness, and Köb suggested he travel to the Confederation of European Union Rectors' Conference in Naples as originally planned to get some distance. He left without informing his daughters. Czeslavia was in Greece, but Alexandra was just returning from India and had to be informed of her mother's death by the rectorate secretary. This added further strain to the already difficult relationship between the father and his daughters.

ANOTHER "TRICK"—PETER GREENAWAY AT THE SEMPER DEPOT

Barely a few decades after Theophil Hansen had built the Academy of Fine Arts on Schillerplatz in the 1870s, it turned out that the building with its small and medium-sized rooms did not meet the current requirements of an art school. By 1898, Otto Wagner was thus already working on plans for an expansive new building in Vienna's Schmelz area. In 1910 he presented a further plan, but none of this was ever put into effect. At the beginning of the twentieth century, some sculptors' studios at least were added in the Prater, but over the following one hundred years, nothing changed about the basic lack of adequate spaces.

When Carl Pruscha was appointed rector, he was determined to tackle this perennial issue and find a new studio house for the Academy. He soon had a suitable object in his sights: one of the most unusual and impressive buildings in Vienna, not far from the Ringstrasse and within sight of the Academy. It was the so-called Semper Depot, the former Imperial-Royal Court Theater's scenery depot, built between 1874 and 1877 by Gottfried Semper and Carl

Carl Pruscha with Elisabeth Schweeger and Peter Greenaway, 1992

Previous rectors of the Academy visiting Pruscha at his rector's office: Maximilian Melcher, Ferdinand Welz, Roland Rainer, Carl Pruscha, and Franz Mairinger, 2003

Hasenauer. This extraordinary four-story building is marked by its unusual ground plan, an irregular triangle with a truncated tip. A transversal wall divides the interior into two sections. The markedly smaller one forms the so-called Prospekthof (indoor courtyard used to store stage backdrop panels), which is open all the way to the roof with galleries on its sides; the other has two hall-style rooms on each floor that fan out and are structured by elegant six-meter-high cast-iron columns. See pp. 218–221 Until the early 1950s, it was used as a scenery depot by the Bundestheater (Austrian Federal Theatres); it then fell into oblivion and stood vacant for decades. Unbelievable as it may seem today, in the 1970s it was nearly razed.[54] In the early 1990s, it presented itself to Pruscha as a "mysterious, dark, erratic block," and what could be more fascinating to him? He thought the spacious rooms would be ideally suited for studios, the Prospekthof could serve as venue for art events. And so he lodged his interest with the responsible authorities. However, as he soon learned, numerous willing occupants and conversion-happy architects had already found this building to be a tough nut to crack. Monument protection and fire-safety regulations were simply irreconcilable, he was told, and he would not fare any better. But he accepted the challenge. In order to reach his goal, however, he had to resort yet again to one of his "tricks"—as he recounts with a mischievous smile.

Up until that point, Pruscha says, "atrocious proposals" had been made, for example to coat the wonderful cast-iron columns with concrete to guarantee fire safety. To him, that was out of the question. The existing construction would not be altered, that was clear from the start. Next, a smart proposal had to be drawn up to convince the authorities that fire-prevention regulations could nevertheless be met. At the same time, he needed to communicate to the public that a unique building lay dormant right in the middle of Vienna. On this front, a big event came to the rescue, namely the tricentennial celebrations of the Academy in 1992. Pruscha and his colleagues began to plan exhibitions, workshops, symposiums, performances, and more. The opening was staged on the Ringstrasse and reached a broad audience. Elisabeth Schweeger, who was on the staff of Erich Wonder, head of the Master Class for Stage Design, directed a theatrical performance titled *The Eye of the Taifun*. A thirty-meter-long transparent mobile stage, a hybrid of icebreaker and spaceship, rolled through nocturnal Vienna. Huskies on conveyor belts, a ginormous astronaut, a unicorn, and snow flurries of bath foam mesmerized onlookers. And in the middle of it all, rock band Einstürzende Neubauten performed to words written by Blixa Bargeld after Pliny the Younger, Adalbert Stifter, and Heiner Müller. Paulus Manker produced a documentary about the event. It was a magnificent prelude, which made the Academy the focus of public attention.

But what Pruscha was really aiming at was to convey to the public the unique character and attractiveness of the Semper Depot. He quickly realized that to achieve this goal he had to make it accessible, and arrived at the idea of an exhibition curated by a famous artist. In order to also illustrate the blurring lines between art genres, he opted not for a fine artist or curator from the art world but for British film director Peter Greenaway. He had

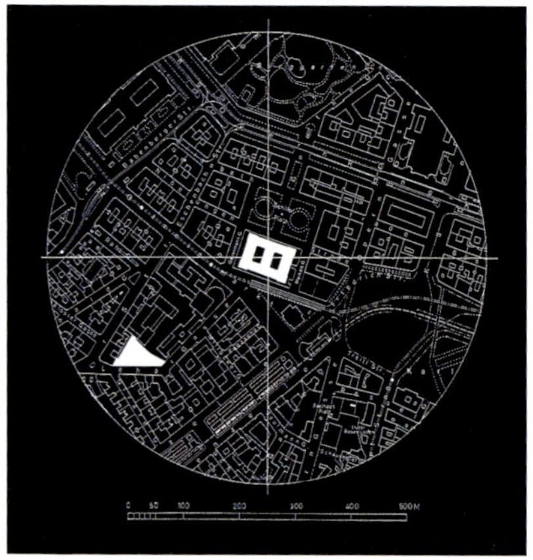

Poster for Carl Pruscha by his assistants, for continued rectorship, 2002

Plan of Vienna with Academy and the Semper Depot, 1993

Widerstand (resistance) banner on the Academy against Austria's right-wing government, 2000

become famous internationally in the 1980s with movies such as *The Draughtsman's Contract* (1982), *The Belly of an Architect* (1986), and *The Cook, the Thief, His Wife & Her Lover* (1989), and had just landed another success with *Prospero's Books* (1991). Greenaway curated two exhibitions for the tricentennial, one of them was *100 Objects to Represent the World*, with thirteen objects at the Semper Depot and eighty-seven at the Hofburg. At the Semper Depot he presented, among others, one hundred umbrellas, which were rained down on from an enormous cotton-wool cloud. It was a virtually ideal spectacle for Pruscha, one of his "tricks" that attracted the public attention he needed. At the same time, he had demonstrated that you could make it rain in the Semper Depot. That was exactly what his fire-control plan provided for: a sprinkler system and a big pool in the basement with fire-fighting water. Furthermore, he had experts calculate how many people could leave the building in the required period of time in case of a fire. He added two new large outside staircases as emergency exits. Double-glazed fireproof windows, a firewall between the studios, and a fire door to the Prospekthof provided further protection. All the original iron and wooden constructions remained untouched by all this. Pruscha's plan worked. He successfully convinced the authorities and got the building permit. See pp. 218–221

With his very own sense for old structural fabric he applied highly sensitive modifications that neither ingratiate themselves with the old nor pretentiously push to the fore. New elements are clearly identifiable as such, don't intend to hide or try to compete with the old but enter into communication with it. On the three upper floors, Pruscha installed lightweight containers with toilets, showers, kitchens, storerooms, and lockers. In the Prospekthof, the ceiling was removed, opening the view to the fabulous steel roof truss above. On the ground floor he built, in miniature, an antique theater, a semicircle-shaped auditorium with six ascending steps. During the renovation of the façade, a conflict arose that was quite typical of Pruscha. The specialist firm contracted by the Federal Monuments Office began treating the brick façade with high-pressure cleaners to make it shine "like new." It was the opposite of what Pruscha wanted, which was to preserve the patina and history of a building. He immediately had the work stopped. The funds originally earmarked for the company were given to willing students who now went about cleaning the outer wall by hand using small brushes, segment by segment. It was thus possible to preserve the historic character of the façade, including traces of time such as bullet scars from World War II. The same is true for the interior. Pruscha had the cast-iron columns simply cleaned rather than painted. He didn't want to restore the building like the Marchfeld castles "that look as if they had just been built yesterday." But no one understood that at the time, says Pruscha.

That's not true. His work was cheered as an exemplary refurbishment of an "architectural jewel."[55] His former teacher, Eduard F. Sekler, saw Pruscha as "a sensitive and creative successor" of Hasenauer and Semper, and compared the building "with the best international examples of successful revitalization."[56] The press celebrated the Semper Depot as "one of Vienna's most beautiful 19th century buildings" and as a "model dialog of old and new."[57]

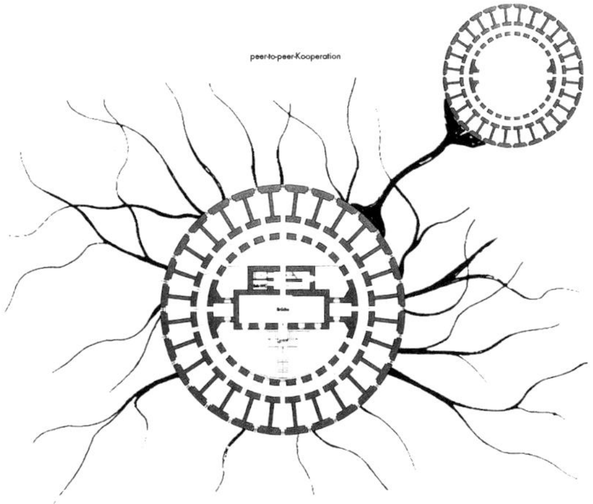

Fool's Tower Vienna, drawing

Carl Pruscha at the inauguration of the revitalized Semper Depot for the students of the Academy, 1995

A TOWER FOR FOOLS AND SCHOLARS (AND CHILDREN)

Carl Pruscha has an instinct for spotting and sensing the potential of extraordinary historic buildings, as his interest in the Neugebäude Palace or the Semper Depot has shown. He now began to shift his focus to another curious building, the so-called Narrenturm (Fools' Tower) on the premises of the Old Vienna General Hospital (Altes Allgemeinen Krankenhaus, or AKH) in the Alsergrund district—"My God, that's a building that fascinates me." Built on a round floor plan, the five-story tower has something clumsy about it and the Viennese have quite disrespectfully dubbed it the *Gugelhupf* (Bundt cake). It not only looks grim, it also looks back on a dark history. This tower was the world's first building for psychiatric patients and was specifically built for this purpose. At the time, in 1784, this was considered a progressive idea, in line with the policies of enlightened monarch Joseph II. In keeping with the times, the "fools" were separated from the other marginal groups, the poor and criminals, taken out of poorhouses and prisons, and provided with the treatment then considered appropriate. The twenty-eight cells on each floor measure about twelve square meters and form circular sectors with narrow, slit-shaped window openings. In the Narrenturm, up to 300 patients were crammed into small prison-like rooms. Ten years after it was opened, this institution was already considered outdated, but it was only closed for good in 1869. In 1998, the entire building complex of the old AKH was handed over to the University of Vienna as a campus and became home to sixteen social-sciences and liberal-arts institutes. The Narrenturm, too, is on the university premises and its rector wanted to find a new use for this historic building. Pruscha was commissioned to conduct a study.

As always, he didn't look at the new use of the building independent of its former function. He toyed with the notion of the fool. The building had been put there to isolate people from their surroundings in extreme mental situations. He now upended this concept. The tower was to become the epitome of exchange and networking. "What are fools? They're people whose minds are completely free. Who therefore have no limitations, no conditions." The fool's license became Pruscha's leitmotif. The tower was to turn into a place to think for the mentally freest, the fools of today: the scholars. But he didn't intend to produce any ivory-tower occupants; the building thus had to become open. The old lock-up cells would therefore be turned into networked knowledge cells, aluminum-lined gleaming spaces of insight. The highly functional furniture included a cabinet, sofa, and desk with a retractable computer built into it. Glass doors replaced the stern, isolating cell doors and opened the workspaces to the ring corridors on the inside of the tower. There were community, communication, and event rooms. The tower was thus conducive, on the one hand, to focused, solitary work and, on the other, to intense exchange between people. Pruscha wanted to see the building filled with students and researchers from around the world, as a beacon of networked international research. He developed a visual metaphor, displayed for all to see on the outside. As soon as a researcher entered their respective cell and turned on the computer, a one-meter-long gleaming stainless-steel antenna would jut out

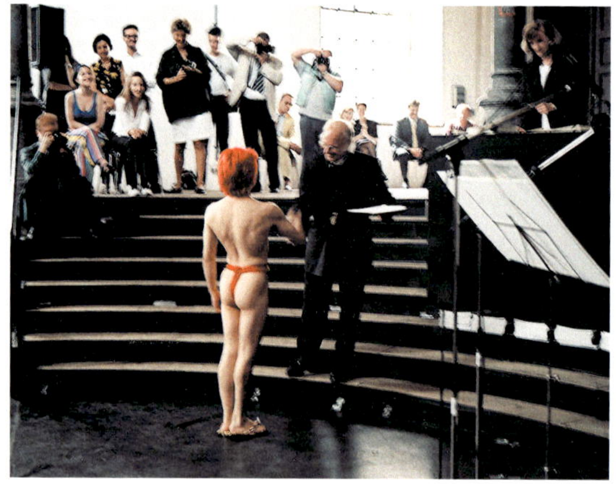

from the round façade as a signal to the outside environment, an image conveying connectedness with the world. The tower would thus change its outward appearance depending on the goings-on inside it. It would turn into a "hedgehog" with delicate defensive spines, which would simultaneously serve as antennas that maintain contact with the world. This was a wonderfully ambivalent image illustrating the way successful scholarly inquiry works, requiring both solitary concentration and intense exchange. Pruscha wanted not only "crazy scientists" to enjoy the privilege of fools on the premises of the Narrenturm but also the children, their kindred spirits. To the south of the tower, his plans included a daycare center for the offspring of teachers and students. Pruscha loves to reflect on such correlations, to charge a building with philosophical and metaphoric content. His idea was met with approval, but then the year 2000 brought not only the appointment of a new rector but also a change of government. Elisabeth Gehrer, the responsible science minister of the new right-wing conservative government, had no interest in the planned revitalization of the Narrenturm.

Pruscha was disappointed, even hurt. His feeling was that precisely the things that piqued his interest—such as linking a construction project with an idea—were not understood or simply not wanted by decision makers: "A concept is always a dream, a vision. The banality of reality is the opposite." And all too often, the mundane, real implementation triumphs over fantasy, creativity, and utopia.

Wolf Prix and Carl Pruscha at the Venice Biennale, 2010

Carl Pruscha and Okwui Enwezor, Academy of Fine Arts Vienna, 2001

Carl Pruscha during the annual graduation ceremony, Semper Depot, 2002

Rector Carl Pruscha at his introductory speech for the exhibition on his role model Lois Welzenbacher, 1989

NEUGEBÄUDE PALACE, VIENNA, 1976–2015

The late-Renaissance building was commissioned by Maximilian II and originally designed as a venue for dialog between scholars and artists on the issues of the day, but it was never completed and left to stand vacant. The building comprised a linear pillared grand corridor that connected three halls of different sizes. The complex also included buildings with animal enclosures and gardens for the cultivation of special plants as well as aviaries. Pruscha's concept proposed changing the orientation of the complex—due to the extensive development of the Danube floodplains—toward the former pleasances, which today serve as an urn cemetery. He envisioned a venue for theatrical performances and open-air events with a touch of "necrophilia" that would provide a space for contemporary culture, something unique for Vienna.

See pp. 162–163

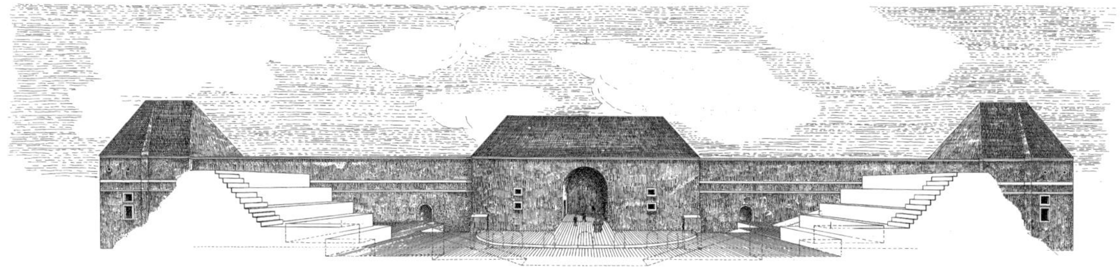

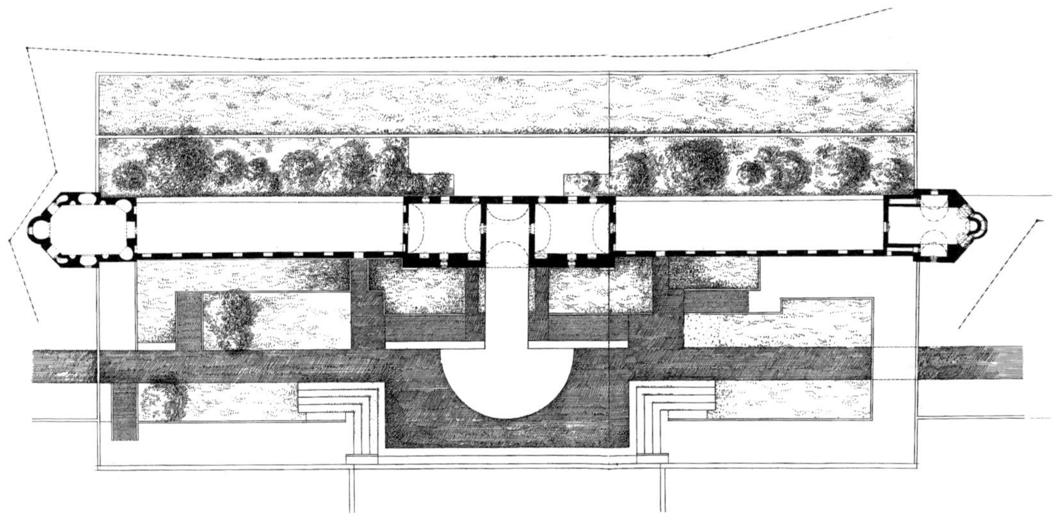

Proposal for a revitalization of Neugebäude Palace. First phase: Turning toward the rear side, 1976

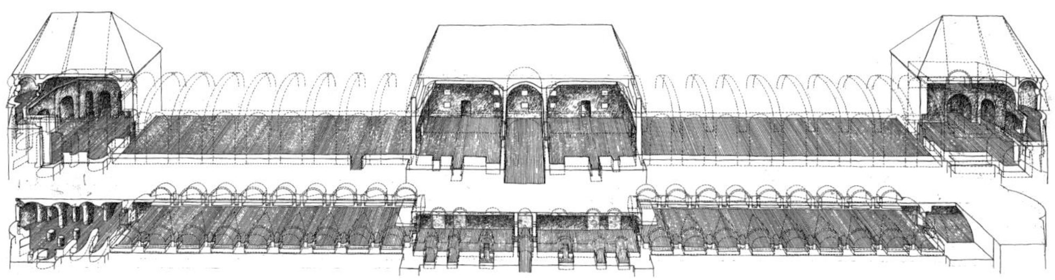

Second phase: Expanding toward the cinerarium, 2002

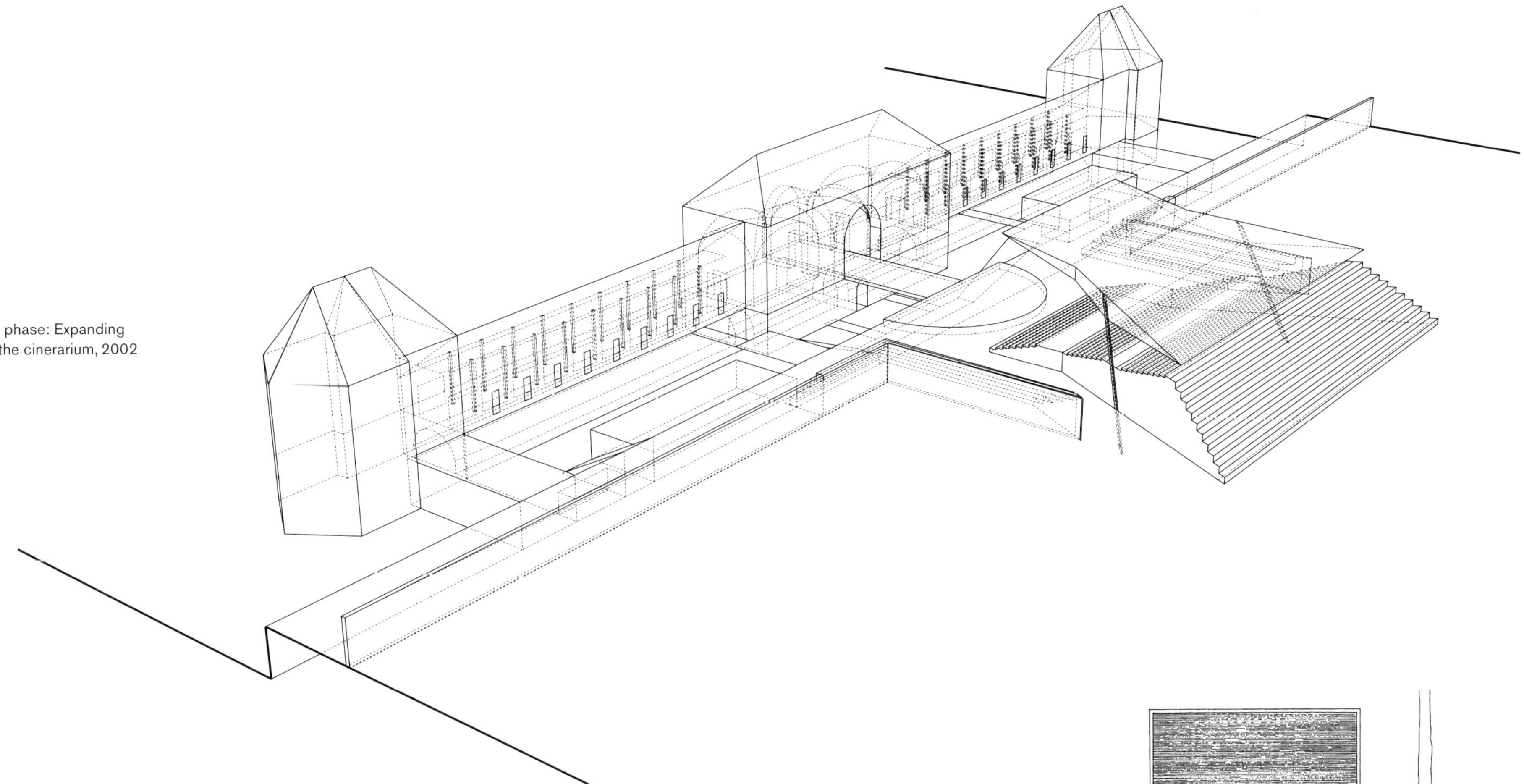

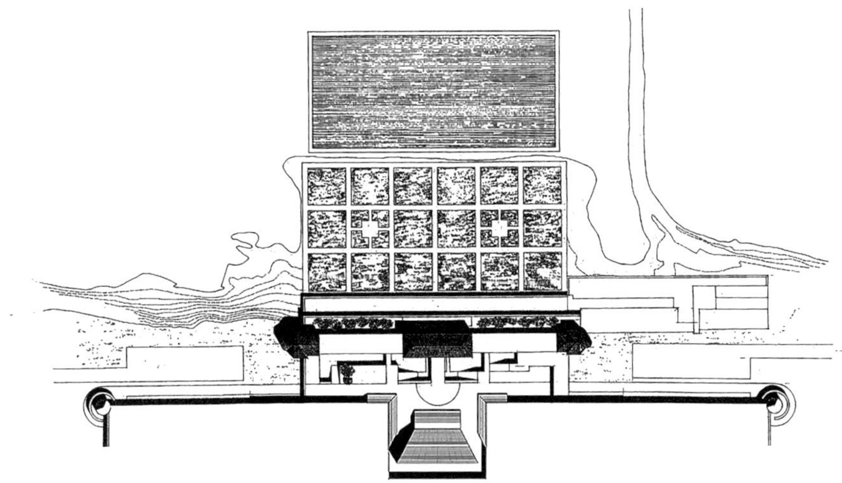

FOOLS' TOWER, VIENNA, 1997–1999

The so-called Fools' Tower (*Narrenturm*) was the first "psychiatric Hospital" in Europe and was handed over by the City of Vienna to the university, together with the historic hospital complex. In a study, Pruscha proposed repurposing the building as a home for complex scholarly projects and converting its cells into rooms for interdisciplinary thinkers. Establishing connections between knowledge potentials by means of modern network technology was designed to facilitate exchange across disciplines, spaces, time, and continents. The solitary cell thus becomes a window to the world.

See pp. 207–208

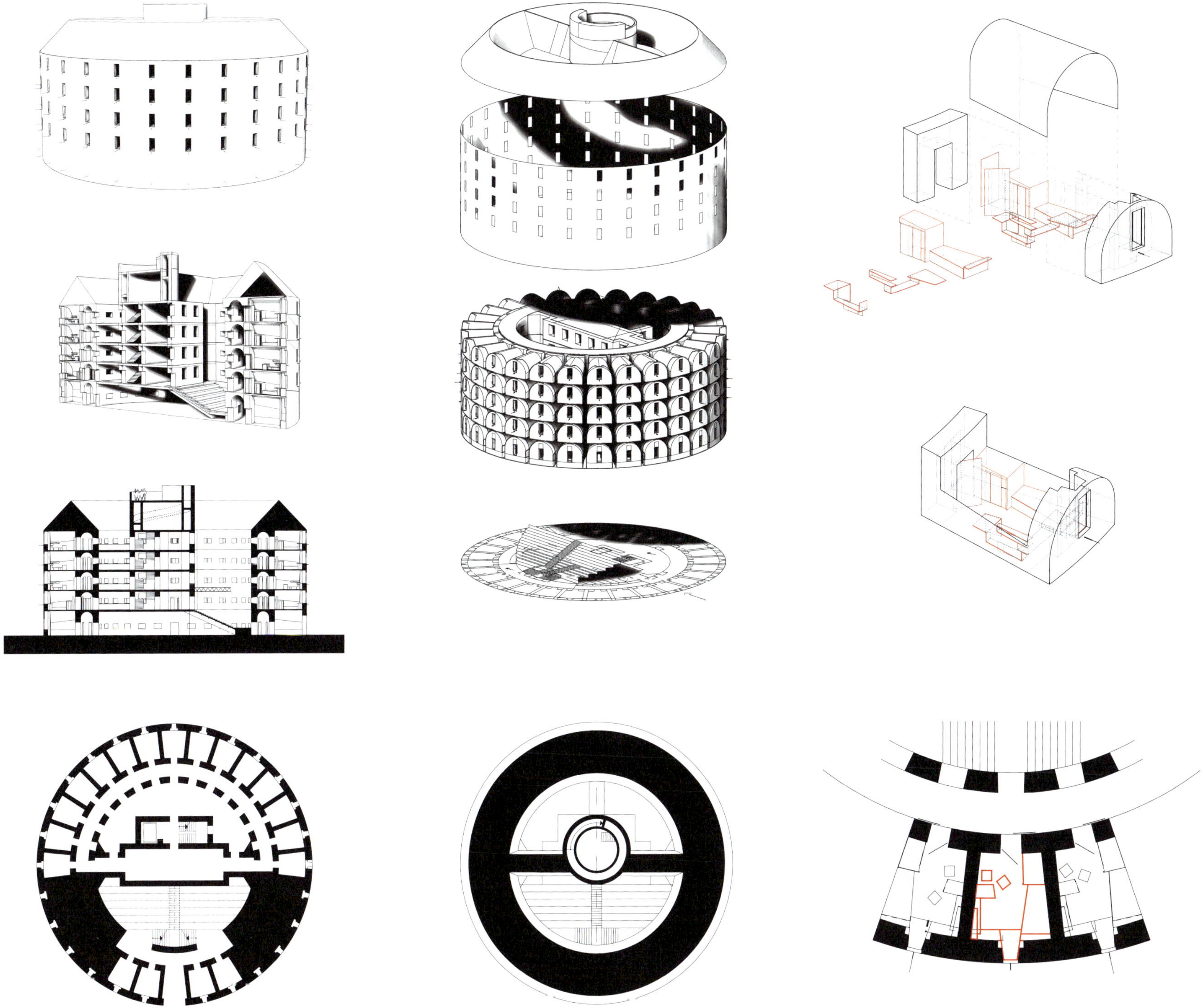

Vienna's General Hospital with *Narrenturm* (Fool's Tower), engraving by Peter Schaffer, 1781

Proposal for a revitalization of the Fool's Tower to become working cells for scientists of the University of Vienna, model, 1997/1998

Revitalization of a former Catholic monastery into a studio home for art students in Horn, Lower Austria, 1986–1988

KUNSTHAUS HORN, 1986–1988

A vacant former anti-reformationist convent building in the center of the town of Horn was converted by Pruscha into a branch building of the Vienna Academy of Fine Arts. It was intended to provide students with additional studio spaces that could be used for special projects and workshops. This was also aimed at stepping up the Academy's international relations by facilitating exchange programs with art schools and their students. During restoration works Pruscha discovered Renaissance arcades, hidden for centuries behind the Baroque walls, and had this architectural jewel uncovered again.

See pp. 185–186

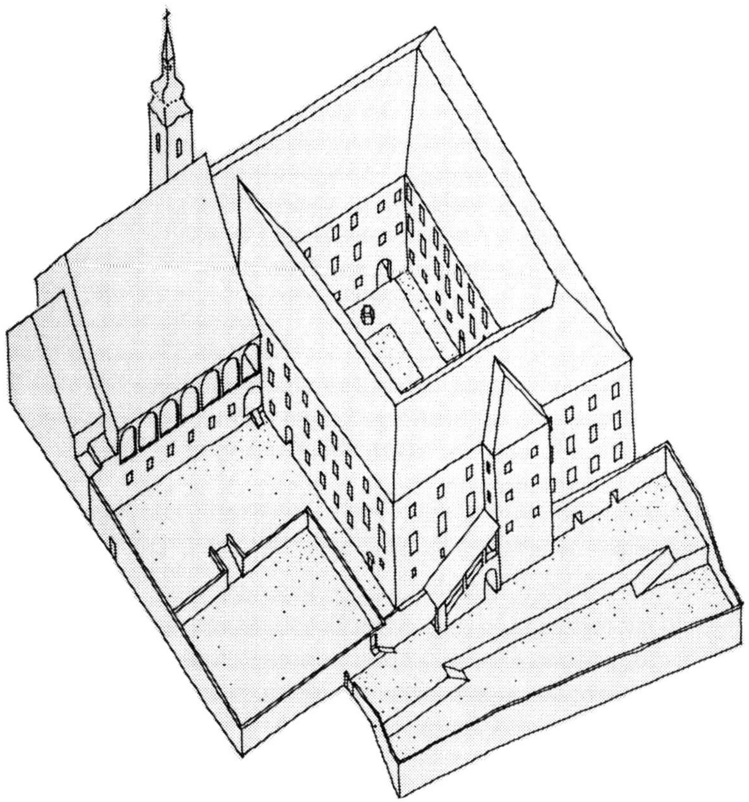

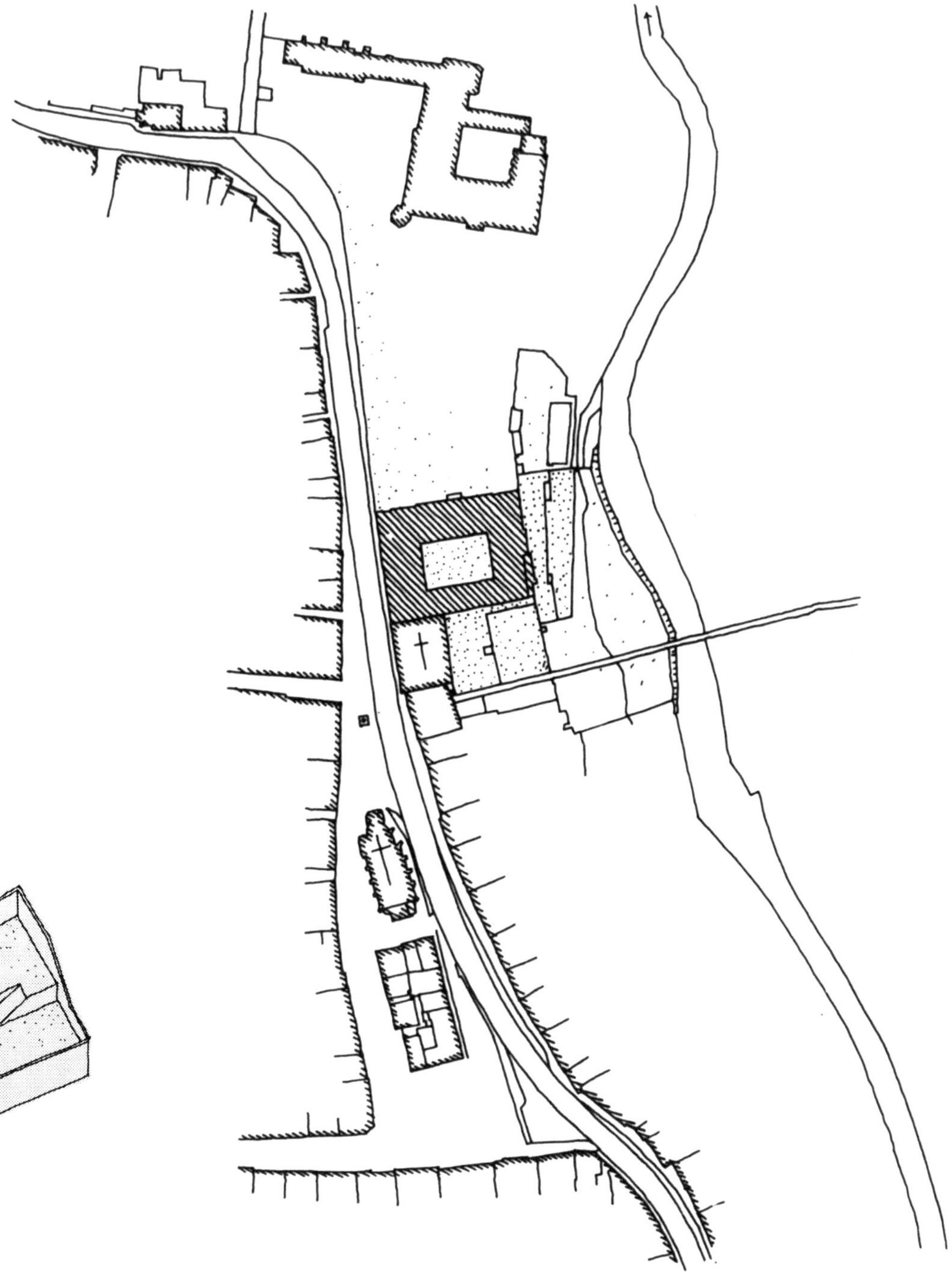

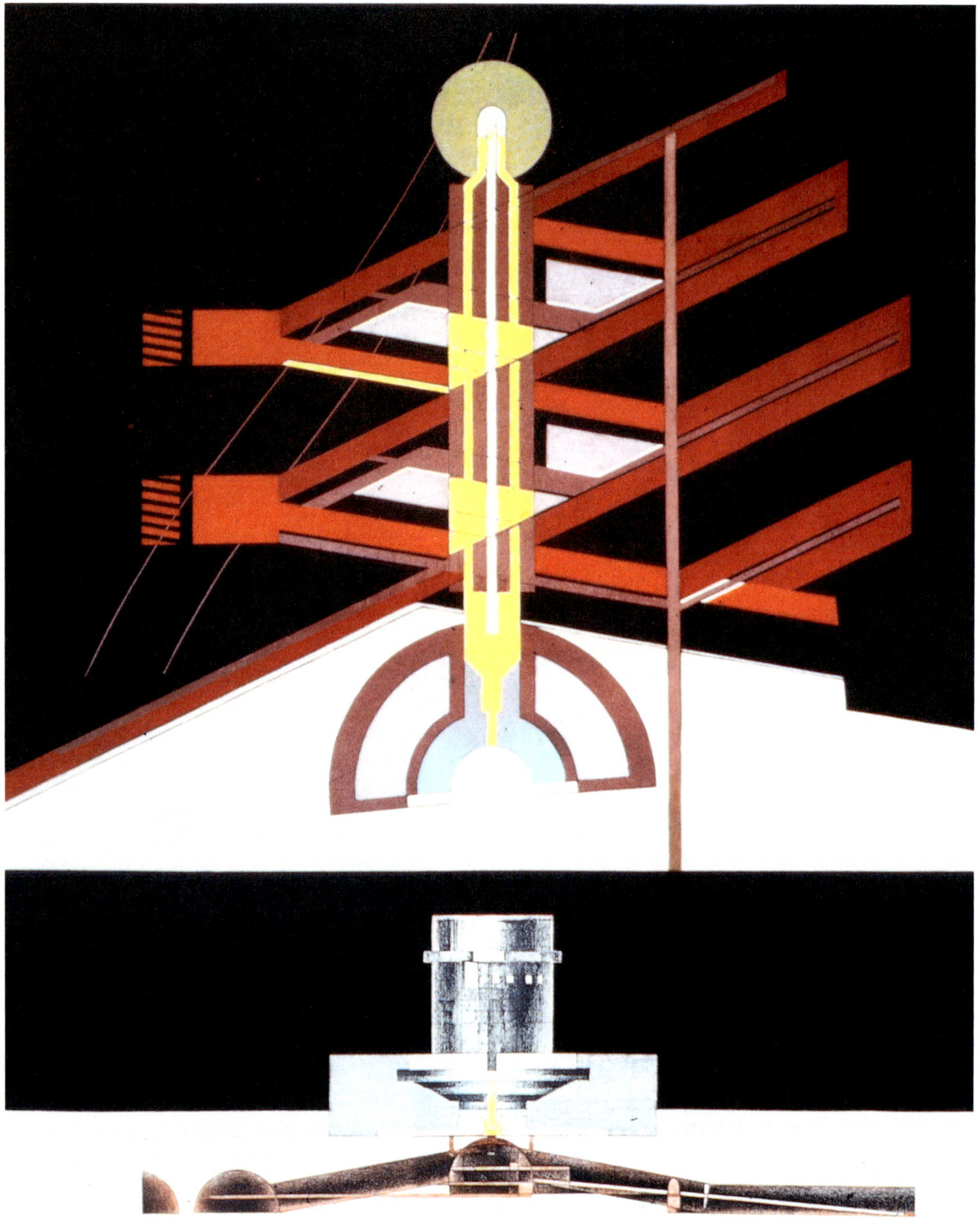

ARKANEUM, VIENNA, 1986

At the time, the competition held for the new MuseumsQuartier was Vienna's biggest and most important cultural project. Pruscha's concept was based on the idea of creating for the city an infinitely expandable system of tunnels as an art repository. It could have potentially been expanded into the Spittelberg neighborhood all the way to a former flak tower from World War II. Along the urban-planning axis starting at the Hofburg and crossing between the museum buildings by Gottfried Semper, an exhibition space for contemporary art would serve as an entrance to the MuseumsQuartier, while the tunnel-like repository would be used as a kind of "treasure house of art" for the preservation of artistic creations.

See pp. 187–188

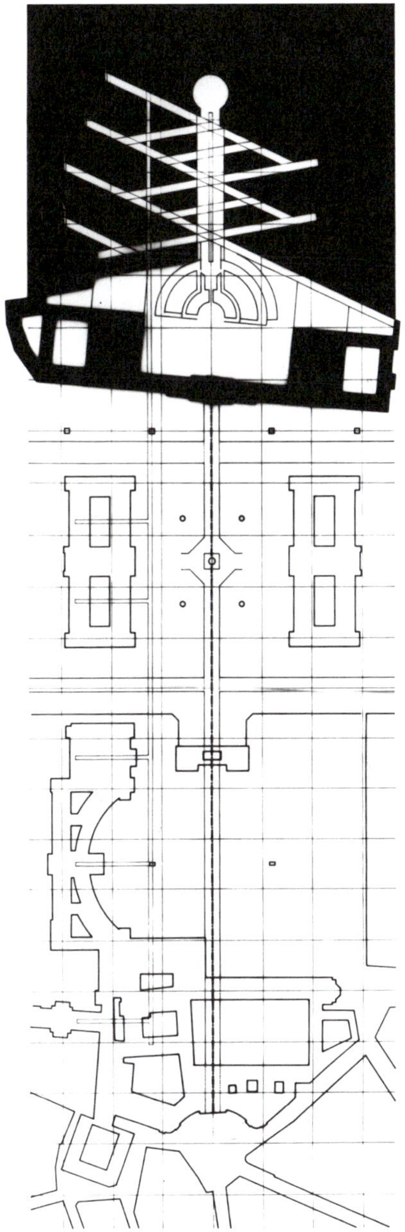

SEMPER DEPOT, VIENNA, 1993–1995

The conversion of the former scenery depot, designed by Gottfried Semper, into a studio house for the Academy of Fine Arts provided the basis for the expansion of its course offerings. One event played a crucial role in drumming up interest in the revitalization of the building, which had stood dormant for decades. It was the exhibition by Peter Greenaway on the occasion of the Academy's tricentennial celebrations, for which the so-called Prospekthof (indoor courtyard used to store stage backdrop panels) was chosen as an exhibition venue. For the conversion, Pruscha deviated from recommendations set forth at the time by the Federal Monuments Office and developed his approach of a sensitive restoration, which enabled him to largely preserve the building's historically grown appearance and patina.

See pp. 204–206, 256

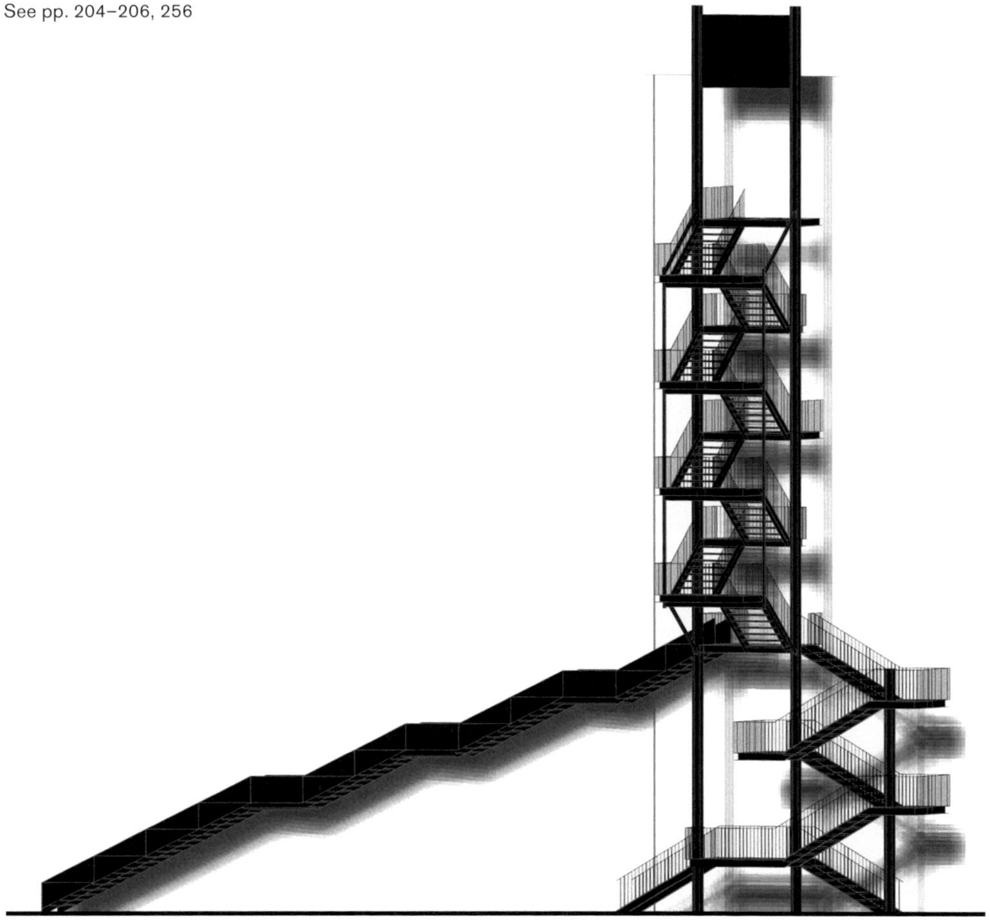

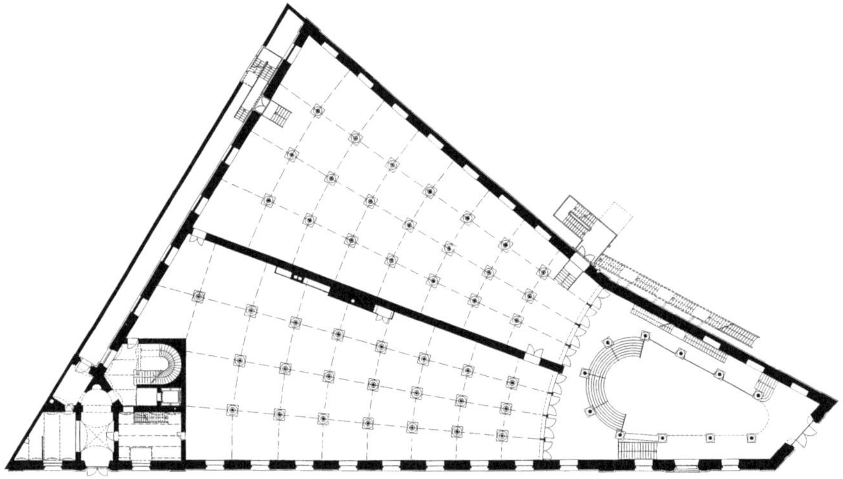

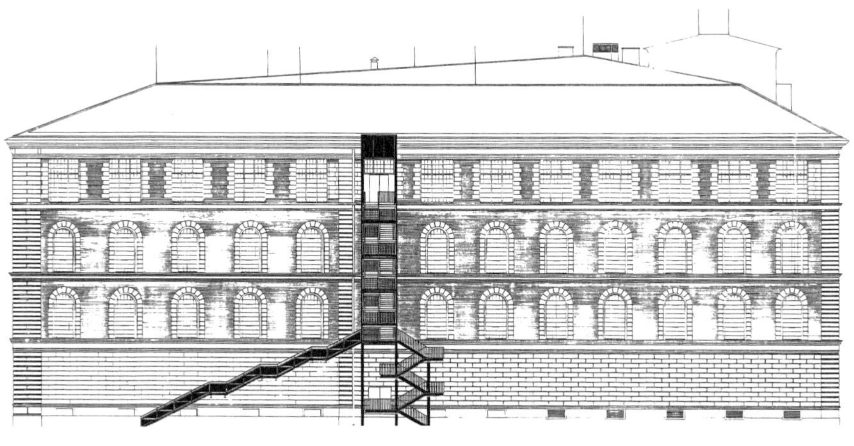

Groundplan and elevation of the Semper Depot

Revitalization of the depot building by Gottfried Semper as a studio house for the Academy of Fine Arts Vienna, 1996

STUDIO CONVERSION IN THE CORNER TOWER OF THE ACADEMY OF FINE ARTS VIENNA, 1978

The founding of the Institute for Architectural Research by Carl Pruscha required additional space in the Academy building. A then vacant corner tower proved to be an ideal location for the new institute, which was intended to host teaching events, seminars, lectures, and exhibitions. The steel construction made possible a continuous ribbon window that did not interfere with the shape of the tower's roof.

See pp. 184–185

Carl Pruscha's office in the Academy's tower

Carl Pruscha and his Aston Martin DB7, 2002

IX. NO RETIREMENT

2002 TO THE PRESENT

Carl Pruscha is known the world over as a great architect. Not only because the world knows him. Whenever I meet famous architects abroad, they ask me to send their regards. No, it's also because he knows the world and it can be read in his buildings and designs.

Wolf D. Prix

Elevator Villaseca, Valparaíso, 2013

DISASTER PROJECTS, CITY ACUPUNCTURE, AND TRUE UNIVERSALISM

Disaster projects, that's how Carl Pruscha characterizes his new field of activity, which he turned to in 2001 when he ended his successful tenure as rector of the Academy of Fine Arts at the age of sixty-five. He founded the design studio Habitat, Environment, and Conservation at the Academy, which he headed until he retired from his professorship in 2004. His stated goal was to keep his students from making the same terrible mistakes that, in his view, destroy the urban environment, namely building residential high-rises and spoiling the urban vicinity with a sprawl of detached single-family homes. "Both are extremely anti-urban, without being rural. Both are completely uneconomical with regard to infrastructure, maintenance, and land use. Nonetheless, both are inexplicably copied the world over."

He wanted to pass on to the young generation that there are alternatives. To make his argument, he chose highly specialized example cases. He calls them *Disaster projects* because, as a rule, they had been preceded by actual catastrophes of various kinds. What can you do when wars, conflagrations, earthquakes, droughts, or even economic problems destroy a town and its environment? A case in point is the old caravan and commercial town of Bhuj in northwestern India, which was largely reduced to rubble by an earthquake in 2001. Or the oasis town of Ksar Tamnougalt in Morocco, which, nowadays, is regularly stricken by droughts. Or the small town of Počitelj in Bosnia and Herzegovina, which was completely destroyed during the war. Or the old Chilean port town of Valparaíso, which has deteriorated due to economic problems. Are there alternatives to demolishing everything and rebuilding it, Western-style? Could development draw on grown traditions and existing stock? Can something sustainable be created? These are the questions Pruscha is interested in, which he goes through with his students based on specific cases, and to which he finds unusual and creative answers.

For Valparaíso he thus recommended interventions at individual focal points. The port town extends across numerous hills, accessible via stairways and inclined elevators, in Pruscha's eyes a fascinating and promising transport system that should be developed further by all means. He recommended preventing further sprawl from encroaching on the plain and striving for intelligent densification on the hills. This once largest port in the Pacific region has rapidly declined in importance since the opening of the Panama Canal in 1914. In order to bring new life to the area and raise its value, Pruscha proposed a building complex in the harbor basin that would host United Nations offices and a newly founded UN department dedicated to the preservation and protection of the oceans. A notorious prison of the Pinochet dictatorship, on the other hand, could be turned into a vibrant cultural center.

This urban-renewal project was not only fascinating to Pruscha and his students, it also elicited praise from the Chilean colleagues who evaluated it. In their assessment, it was a successful attempt at reviving an ailing city with the methods of "acupuncture." This analysis captured the essence of what Pruscha is heading for—namely, "to find exactly these points where new energy, new activity could again be implanted into an ailing system."[58]

Visiting Iran, 1998

Experts were impressed but politicians took little appropriate action, a recurring experience for Pruscha. But all his frustration never dented his zest for action and his creativity. After retiring from his professorship in 2004, he continued the Habitat Studio as a self-employed architect.

Another project close to his heart was to preserve autochthonous architecture in Asia, in the Himalayas, to be more precise, which is to say in Nepal, Tibet, and Bhutan. Since his time with the UN he couldn't stop thinking about the subject. He watched from afar as the region was rapidly and irreversibly changed by globalization, industrialization, urban sprawl, and tourism, often gradually destroying old grown structures. In the once so peaceful, secluded Kathmandu Valley, the cities that used to be clearly demarcated from cultivated land had sprawled from their outskirts into the entire valley, so that the lines between urban and rural areas have increasingly disappeared.

A research semester at the renowned Getty Conservation Institute in Los Angeles 2003 allowed Pruscha to once again pore over the problem.[59] His published findings were a passionate plea to preserve unique extant architecture and, at the same time, think about it in new ways on the basis of answers provided by Modernism.[60] He was in no way intending to blindly preserve everything old, seal off the non-Western world, or vilify new technologies. Pruscha was convinced that new construction doesn't need to be synonymous with destruction, even though past and present practice often suggests otherwise.

His counter model to globalization is critical regionalism. This does not imply any nationalist blood-and-soil notions, much less corny pseudo-regional architecture for tourists. Pruscha calls both "architectural pornography." Tradition should never be allowed to ossify but must always keep developing; it otherwise turns into folklore bereft of meaning. Critical regionalism means creating a balance between globalization and local tradition. Pruscha's utopian vision is a truly universalist architecture—"a lot more universalist than the International Style of the 1930s"—which links Modernism and tradition, West and East, allowing for regional adaptations. In his words, this would amount to an "avant-garde in the truest and broadest sense of the word."[61]

To prove his case, he cited highly diverse example cases in Nepal, Bhutan, and Tibet. He particularly followed the development of projects in Tibet with great passion. After all, Tibet had already been a place of yearning for him in his youth and was later his first choice for a United Nations assignment.

Gyantse, then the fourth-largest town in Tibet, is famous for its monastery, which boasts a huge stupa. The city is situated between the monastery and a fortress at its opposite end. It was the only town in southern Tibet that had largely retained its original character, not least because it was spared by China's Cultural Revolution between 1966 and 1976. But now this vibrant old part of town faced the risk of being replaced by a new district and thus being marginalized. With an international team of scholars and students —including from China—he wanted to develop a plan for the city and its immediate surroundings. In this way, Gyantse could become

Visiting Morocco, 1985

a prototype for a sustainable, ecologically reasonable revitalization of historic city centers and urban expansion. Museification of the old town would have to be avoided at all costs, and it should not be left to decay—two equally bad options. Pruscha's goal was, rather, to bring it up to speed with the requirements of the twenty-first century. That would in no way preclude sustainable tourism facilities, but it would also not be reduced to it. The Chinese authorities, however, showed no interest in these ideas. It was an altogether different story with the government in Bhutan. At the beginning of the twenty-first century, the country remained one of the most remote, inaccessible regions in the world, without agglomeration but with a widely dispersed population of about 600,000. Pruscha is no naive romantic. He knows that in the coming years and decades, Bhutan will be completely restructured and urbanized. That's inevitable. What he envisioned was innovation that integrated autochthonous culture. "But not the way it's done now where gas stations are colorfully decorated like Buddhist temples." Rather, this is a question of preserving the spirit of a community while also creating it anew. This time around, the project was thwarted not by local authorities but by a lack of financing. The Austrian support Pruscha had hoped for failed to materialize; among others, the Austrian Science Fund (Fonds zur Förderung der wissenschaftlichen Forschung, FWF) and the Austrian Development Cooperation declined. This upset him because their money was invested in other projects. "They have used Austrian funds, for example, to build the ugliest and most expensive hotel you can imagine in Bhutan—something unbelievably stupid, but with fat cash from Austria."

SRI LANKA, TSUNAMI, AND FINALLY A HAPPY MARRIAGE

Eva Schlegel was the new and certainly the right woman in Pruscha's life. An artist born in Tyrol like Carl, she had headed a master class for art and photography at the Academy of Fine Arts since 1997. Pruscha and Schlegel got to know each other on the job and soon became a couple. As so often when it comes to private matters, Pruscha calls it "pure chance." They came together because his apartment had burned down and he was looking for a place to stay. Things just fell into place. In the wake of his experiences with his first wife he had no intention of marrying again. Once more, "it happened" to him: "Eva married me."

As much as this has a passive ring coming from the otherwise so dynamic Carl Pruscha, he sounds nothing like that when he goes into raptures about his relationship with his wife: "That's probably one of the big secrets about my wonderful relationship with Eva that we both have our very own life, are successful and fulfilled by it." And that both respect and admire each other's work, talk about it, and provide support. The two married in May 2002. All those who have known Carl for decades say that the marriage has done him a world of good, and that it has made him more mild and tolerant.

At first, Pruscha's daughters had a tough time accepting a new woman in their father's life, but things soon took a turn for the better; the lifelong complicated relationship between the father and his daughters improved and became a more loving one.

Visiting Yemen, 1996

Carl Pruscha had long been dreaming of a home in Asia, preferably in India, where he would spend his retirement years. "I tried to talk Eva into taking a trip to Goa with me to look for a plot of land there. But properties there have become very expensive by now." Then he came across an alternative in Sri Lanka. Artist Josef Ortner was a former fellow student of Eva Schlegel's and the founder of the "museum in progress" project. Together with his partner Kathrin Messner, he started the One World Foundation on the southwest coast of Sri Lanka in 1995. Their goal was to foster educational projects and finance them through sustainable tourism. They built a guesthouse for tourists and a school, initially for one hundred children. Over time, more than 1,100 children, adolescents, and grown-ups have attended it. When Eva Schlegel and Carl Pruscha visited the project, a new idea was born. Ortner and Pruscha decided they wanted to build three additional bungalows on the premises, which would also be rented to guests. At the same time, those who finance these accommodations receive a lifelong right of residence and a holiday home.

For himself and Eva, Carl built a lagoon bungalow—again an outstanding example of his ability to connect local construction methods with new modern needs. He was disappointed to see that these Sri Lankan traditions had largely fallen into oblivion during the Portuguese, Dutch, and British colonial periods. Already during his first visit, it struck him as awkward how European-style buildings—thick brick walls with small windows, foundations sunk into the ground, and heavy roofs with ceramic tiles—were at odds with climatic conditions. The monsoon rains regularly swamp the buildings, the walls become damp, the small windows allow only insufficient ventilation. "Up to one meter from the floor, everything turns green from algae and mold!"

Pruscha remembered how in Thailand and Indonesia wooden bungalows were built on stilts and walls were made from air-permeable and shade-giving materials. "It was clear to me that that was the only way to build there." As logging was now prohibited in Sri Lanka and wood had to be imported at great expense, Pruscha opted for a different solution and used metal beams. "The profession of the carpenter has long died out there, you know, the young people are all mechanics or welders. They built cars for themselves from truck parts—they're very skilled. These welders also put my house together." See pp. 234–239

Like so many coastal areas in Southeast Asia, the hamlet of Wathuregama, where the Foundation is located, was hit by a catastrophe at the end of December, 2004. The tsunami destroyed the school and large parts of the premises. It so happened that Schlegel and Pruscha were on-site in their bungalow near the ocean. When the first, only knee-high wave came, they didn't yet worry. They even thoughtfully tossed the fish that had been washed ashore back into the ocean. Then they went a bit earlier than usual to have breakfast at the guesthouse, which was located a little further inland. Suddenly the fishermen came running and yelled "Run, run, run!" They knew what it means when the water level drops so low. Everyone started to run. They ran uphill for two hours, farther and farther inland. That saved them. Between 30,000 and 40,000 people lost their lives in Sri Lanka that day. The school

Visiting Bhutan, 1997

of the One World Foundation was completely destroyed. Pruscha's bungalow, however, withstood the deluge surprisingly well. The moveable furniture and partition walls had been washed away, but the fundamental iron framework and the roof had remained intact. Eva Schlegel soon came to the rescue of the school project, launching an initiative whereby Austrian artists donated works for an auction at Vienna's Dorotheum. The proceeds amounted to €230,000 and Pruscha was able to rebuild the school, larger than before and this time at a safe distance from the coast, a little outside of Ahungalla. He constructed it from light concrete parts, again relying on the local welders who had helped build his bungalow. They produced the molds in which the concrete modules were cast directly on site. Long open hall construction ensured good ventilation, even without air-conditioning, and protected from the monsoon rains. Even when flooded, their cross-shaped concrete supports can withstand the deluge. The opening celebrations for the new school took place two years after the devastating tsunami. The minister in charge was delighted and concluded that all schools in Sri Lanka had to be built that way. The 2010 Venice Biennale of Architecture presented the architect's plan. Pruscha's guest bungalow is the one most often booked at the One World Foundation. See pp. 230–239

Nevertheless, Carl Pruscha was unhappy, as "Nobody liked it!" He arrived at this conclusion because the project didn't form a precedent—as the minister had suggested—and no further schools were built using the flexible modular system he had developed. "That's what really hurts me about Sri Lanka, that it didn't trigger a bandwagon effect there. The idea that you can have an authentic building that is still modern." He had held out hope that his critical regionalism, his new universalist architecture, which takes local conditions into consideration, would be recognized as a prototype.

SCHOOL PROJECT FOR THE ONE WORLD FOUNDATION, AHUNGALLA, SRI LANKA, 2005–2006

Artist Josef Ortner and his partner, Kathrin Messner, founded the so-called One World Foundation in Sri Lanka with the aim of providing children of low-income parents with a free school education. The project became a great success until the 2004 tsunami ultimately destroyed the old wooden schoolhouse. With the help of Austrian and international artists as well as tsunami aid provided by the City of Vienna it became possible to realize a new school together with architect Carl Pruscha on the basis of a concept by Josef Ortner.

See p. 228–229

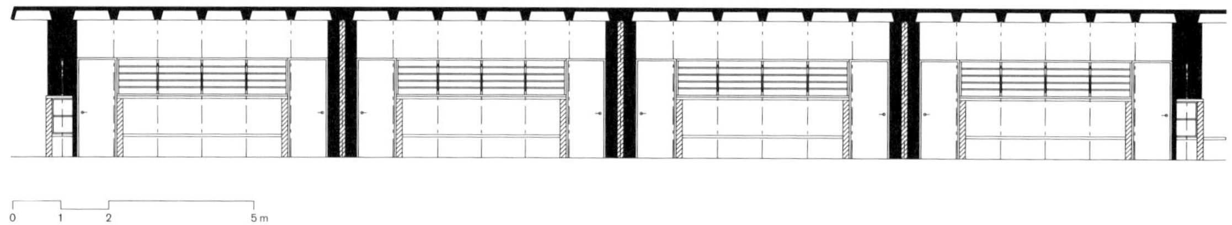

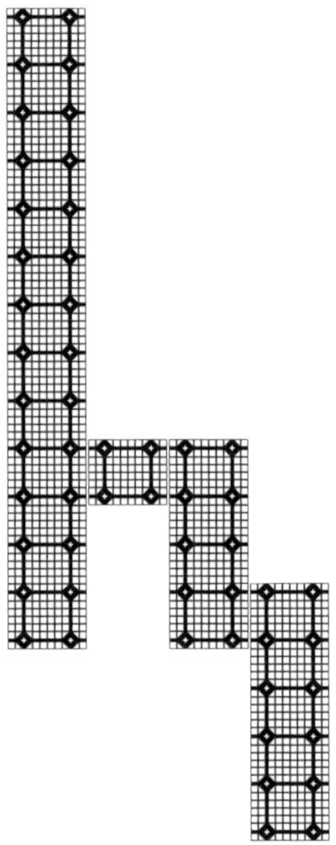

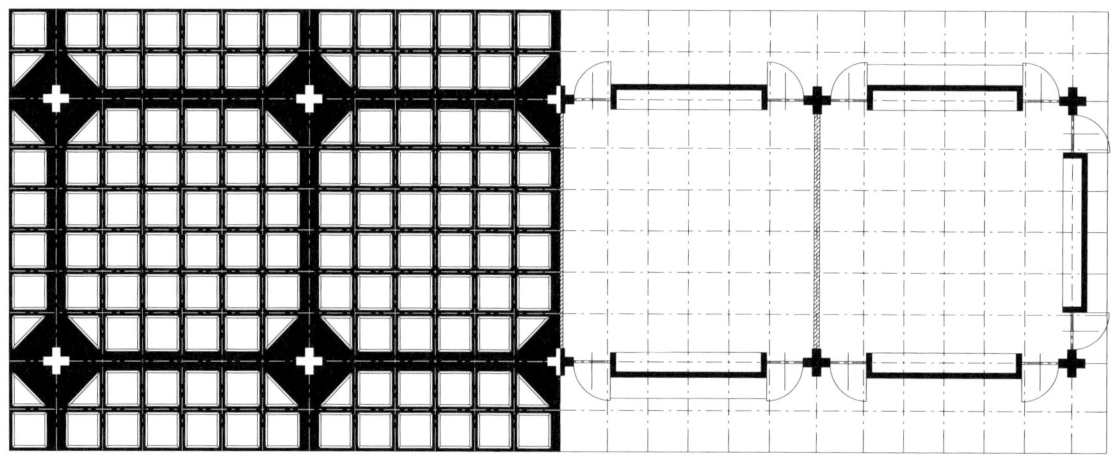

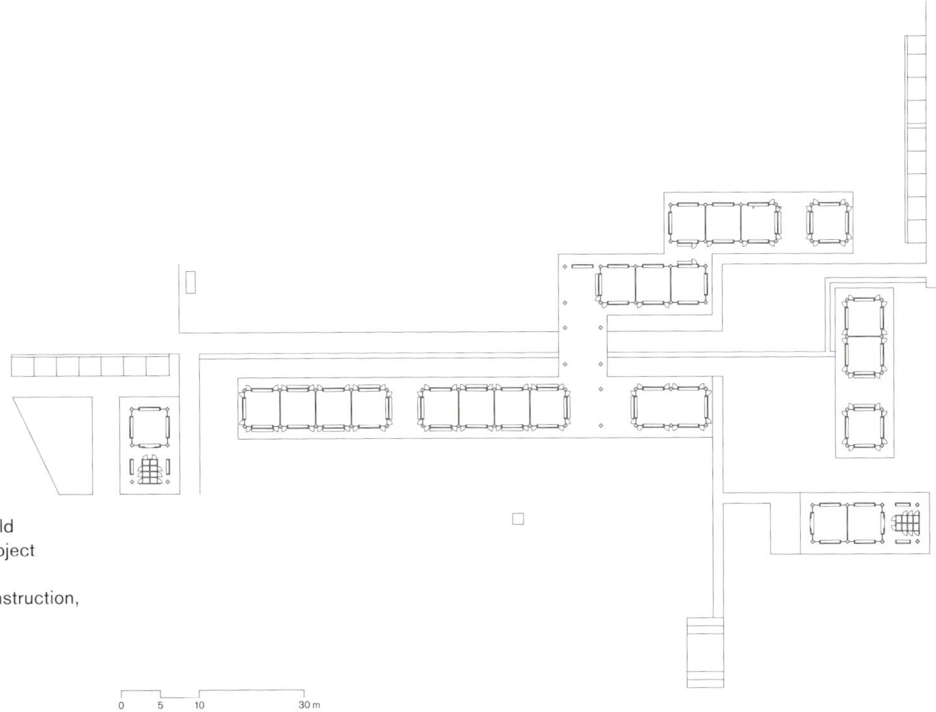

Plans of the One World Foundation school project

The project under construction, 2005

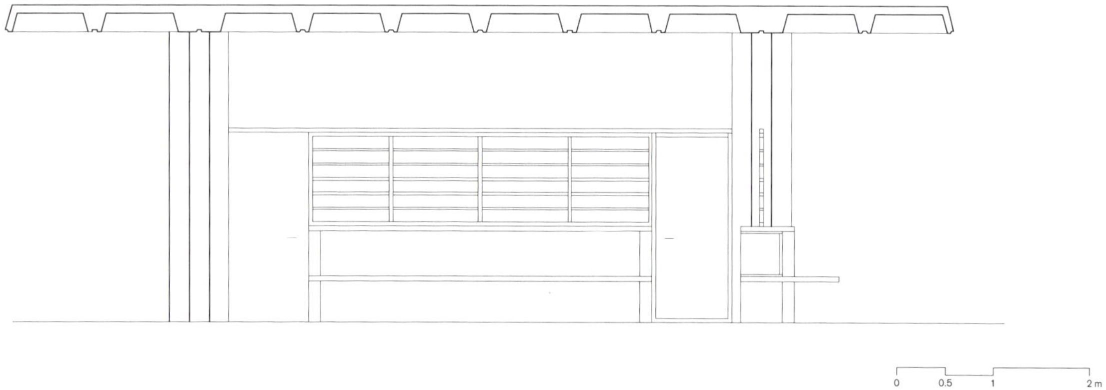

School in Ahungalla, 2008

BUNGALOWS, AHUNGALLA, SRI LANKA, 2001–2002

Traditional construction in Sri Lanka was originally marked by timber structures on stilts and breathable walls, which provided natural ventilation and cooling. But 400 years of colonial history resulted in the loss of this tradition and, in its place, the dominance of massive construction. With these bungalows, Pruscha tried to reinterpret, with modern means, the qualities of the traditional lightweight construction.

See p. 228

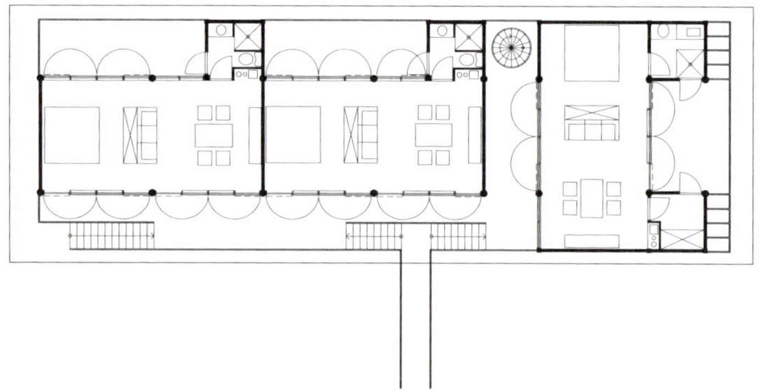

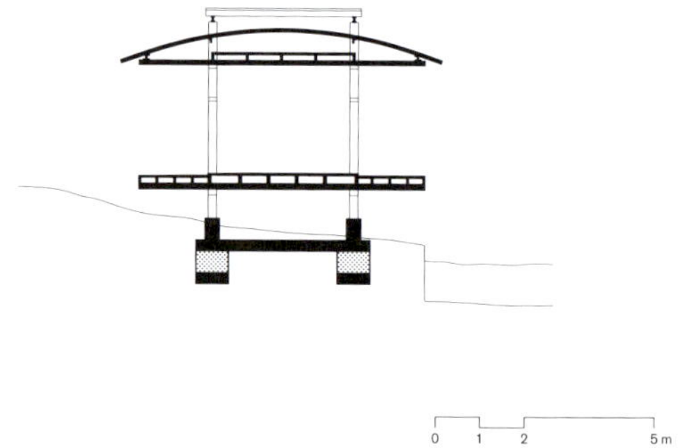

Groundplan and section of the Lagoon Bungalow, 2002

Lagoon Bungalow, 2017

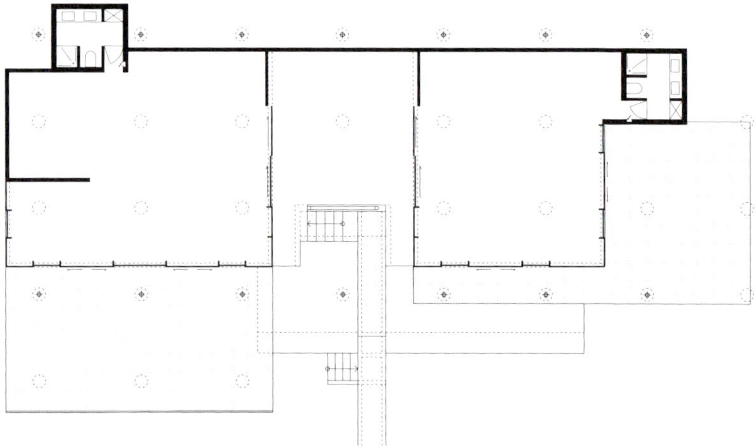

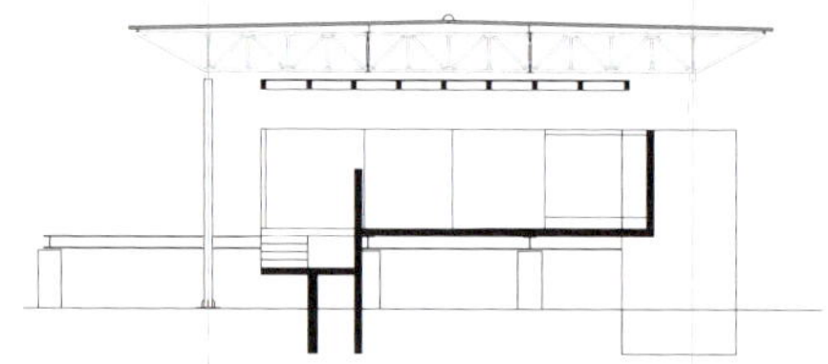

0 1 2 5 m

Groundplan and section of the Palmgrove Bungalow, 2012

Palmgrove Bungalow, 2018

Tower Bungalow under construction, 2019

Section, groundplan and model of the Tower Bungalow, 2018

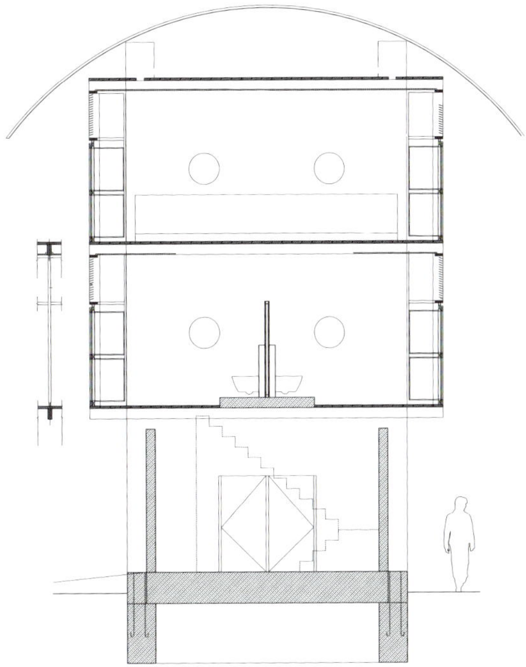

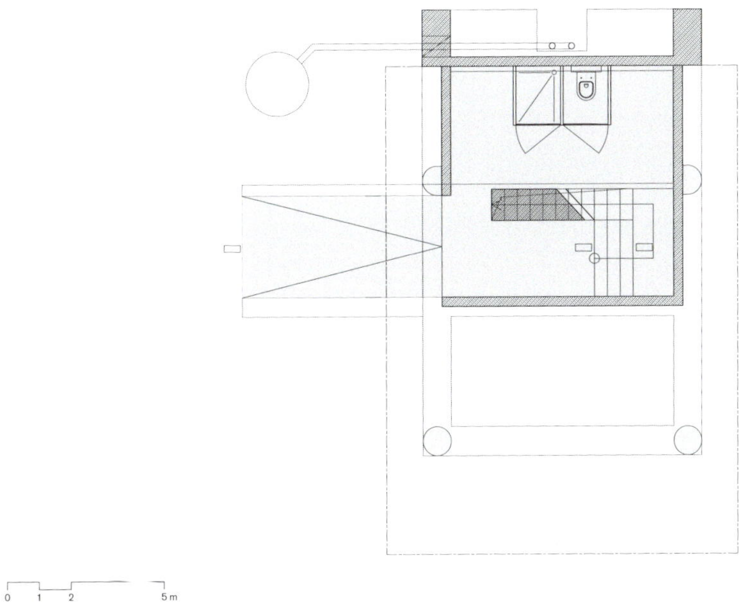

Eva and Carl, 2017

X. EPILOG
CARL PRUSCHA'S BABYLONIAN TOWERS

Giving up my utopian ideas of
making utopian architecture a reality,
I've realized I'll never be able to do that.
So, forget it altogether!
CP

When Pruscha does something, the result is considered out of the ordinary, be it revitalization projects, his own buildings, or urban-renewal visions. Some of his ideas are controversial, some buildings receive high praise and win awards, for instance his MQ West, a multipurpose building erected on a gap site between Vienna's MuseumsQuartier and Breite Gasse in 2004, which was awarded the ZV Bauherrenpreis. See p. 242 His work is never considered a failure, uninteresting, let alone mediocre. Still, very little is ever realized. Why?

His friend and colleague Wolf D. Prix thinks it isn't hard to pinpoint the reason. Pruscha is just too good and visionary, especially for the "toy poodle city of Vienna." For Prix, Pruscha is the "the man who set out to climb the Himalayas walking backwards,"[62] which is to say, one who doesn't take the easy route and insists on doing everything differently than everyone else. Prix and Pruscha have a fundamentally different approach to architecture, yet they hold each other in high regard. They have fun at each other's expense, Prix calling Pruscha the "lil' checker architect," or a concrete fundamentalist, and Pruscha carping about Prix' Gasometer conversion in Vienna. But, Prix explains, one thing is clear, "There is such a thing as solidarity in quality." And quality is exactly where the problem lies. "It's a shame that in Vienna truly talented people not only have nothing to do, but are also met with hostility." An architect who thinks for himself is regarded as difficult.

Pruscha, too, sees himself as a difficult person and is well aware of his contradictions. On the one hand, he aims to prove himself as an architect and wants his projects to be realized. On the other hand, he fears not being able to muster the necessary pragmatism, the readiness to compromise, and an appetite to deal with the messiness of putting a project into action. And that he lacks the patience to deal with the resistance, incompetence, and sloppiness of the people involved. "This leads to the conclusion that I am, of course, someone with a vision, concepts, and ideas, but they make no concessions to reality." Artist Eva Schlegel, his wife, sees a different problem. As an artist-architect he would need an economic partner, a manager, who takes care of these things for him—a problem that many artists are confronted with. He is simply not good at applying for project funds, following up on potential contractors over and over, cleverly negotiating for his own purposes.

Working for the UN and as rector of the Academy, Pruscha was successful in pushing through difficult projects for others; but on his own behalf, not so much. Fending for himself, he doesn't resort to his legendary "tricks," is unable to come up with smart tactics and explore all possible avenues. Making things happen for an institution, for others, comes naturally to him. His hunch is that in these cases he's "probably more ready to compromise." When it comes to his very own ideas, there are no paths to a middle ground—it's all or nothing. That doesn't surprise Wolf D. Prix in the least: "sure, a creative and sensitive and emotional person is not as good fighting for himself as for others."

However, what Carl Pruscha never calls into question are his ideas and projects themselves. He knows that he hasn't failed, and "quite the opposite is true. I have the feeling that all these things will come." Propelled by his boundless creativity and innovational strength, he has planned not just one, but several Towers of Babel in the course of his life. What may be considered hubris or folly today will be taken for granted tomorrow. Sooner or later, his utopian vision of the future will turn into a feasible, sustainable present. A case in point is that already by the early 1960s, Pruscha was dreaming of underground tunnel systems that would transport people and goods at high speeds without destroying cities and landscapes with highways. Today, visionary investor and entrepreneur Elon Musk is about to make exactly that a reality with his Hyperloop, a high-speed transport system. Pruscha: "At the time, there was no question in my mind that that would have to come." And it actually goes against his grain to complete his Towers of Babel anyway. As ruins and fragments, they harbor the kind of truthfulness he calls for. Thus, Pruscha allows future generations to be inspired by them and continue building them. The important thing is that they should never be completed.

1 Wolf D. Prix in conversation with the author on July 2, 2018, in Vienna.
2 Unless stated otherwise, this and all subsequent quotes of Carl Pruscha are from conversations the author conducted with him at his Vienna studio between January 10 and May 13, 2018.
3 Hannelore Strickner in conversation with the author, Innsbruck and Sistrans, December 8, 2017.
4 This and all subsequent quotes of Hannelore Strickner: Strickner 2017.
5 Susanne Mettauer, "The Institutionalization of American Studies at Austrian Universities: The Innsbruck Model." In Anton Pelinka, Günter Bischof, Michael Gehler (ed.), *Austrian Foreign Policy in Historical Context*, New York, 2005, pp. 280–304.
6 Carl Pruscha in conversation with Bettina M. Busse. In Gerald Matt (ed.), *Österreichs Kunst der 60er-Jahre. Gespräche*, Vienna, Nuremberg, 2011, p. 375
7 Jan Tabor, "Roland Rainer. Kardinal und König." In *Falter. Die Stadtzeitung*, April 21, 2004.
8 See "Roland Rainer and his Biographical Entanglements from 1935 to 1945." Ongoing research project since 2016. https://www.azw.at/en/articles/ongoingprojects/. See also Monika Platzer, "Schatten der Vergangenheit. Wien nach 1945. Eine zweite Fassung der 'Perle'?" In Ingrid Holzschuh, Monika Platzer (eds.), *"Wien. Die Perle des Reiches." Planen für Hitler*, Zurich, 2015, pp. 58–67. Rainer had been a member of the Nazi Party since 1936, when it was still illegal in Austria. During the Nazi era, he supported his architectural theories with race-biology arguments. After 1945 he failed to own up to his Nazi past; architectural historian Dietmar Steiner thus called him the "Waldheim of architecture." Lukas Wieselberg, "This is Roland-Rainer-Platz calling" (2015), In http://sciencev2.orf.at/stories/1758830/index.html
9 Rudolf Minichbauer, *Anton Velim* (2006). In: http://galerie-walfischgasse.com/publikationen/Anton_Velim.pdf
10 Strickner 2017.
11 Roland Rainer, *Anonymes Bauen, Nordburgenland*, Salzburg, 1961. See also Jan Tabor 2004.
12 "Roland Rainer." In *Die Akademie in der Zeitenwende*. Archive of the Academy of Fine Arts Vienna, Vienna, 2002, pp. 87–88: 87.
13 "Carl Pruscha im Gespräch mit Bettina M. Busse." In Matt (ed.) 2011, pp. 378.
14 Ibid., p. 379.
15 Ibid., p. 377.
16 Ibid., p. 376.
17 Ibid., p. 379.
18 Ibid.
19 Carl Pruscha: *The Physical Development Plan for the Kathmandu Valley*, Kathmandu, 1969.
20 http://cpruscha.com/1974-1988/3/
21 https://aut.cc/ausstellungen/carl-pruscha-mein-logbuch
22 Charles Correa, "Introductory Note." In Carl Pruscha, *Himalayan Vernacular*, Vienna, 2004, p. 5.
23 http://taragaonmuseum.com/
24 Wolf D. Prix, "Von dem Mann, der auszog, um verkehrt gehend den Himalaya zu besteigen. Rede anlässlich der Überreichung des Goldenen Ehrenzeichens für Verdienste um das Land Wien an Carl Pruscha," Vienna City Hall, May 26, 2008. Unpublished manuscript.
25 Pruscha–Busse 2011, p. 382.
26 Carl Pruscha, *Kathmandu Valley. The Preservation of Physical Environment and Cultural Heritage. Protective Inventory 1 u. 2.* 1st edition, Vienna, 1975. 2nd edition, Kathmandu, 2015.
27 Hoffmann studied under Walter Gropius at the Bauhaus in Dessau from 1926 to 1930.
28 Carl Pruscha, "Aktuelle Gedanken zu einer Revitalisierung des Neugebäudes." Manuscript, August 28, 1998.
29 Klaus-Jürgen Bauer (ed.), *Mein Haus in Lajtakatta. Carl Pruscha Architect*, Eisenstadt, 2016.
30 Ibid., p. 11.
31 Ibid., p. 17.
32 Gerfried Sperl, "Gelebte Architektur." Interview. In *Konstruktiv*, no. 249 (May/June 2005), p. 46.
33 Bauer (ed.) 2016, p. 23.
34 Pruscha–Busse 2011, p. 380.

MuseumsQuartier-West, multipurpose building, Vienna, 2004

Carl Pruscha with collaborator Walter Kräutler, 2005

35 "Carl Pruscha in an interview with Brigitte Groihofer, spring 2016." Unpublished manuscript. Archive Carl Pruscha.
36 Together with Carl Auböck, among other projects, prefab housing development, Vienna, 13th district, Veitingergasse (1952–54); low-rise development Mauerberg, Vienna 23rd district, Lechthalergasse (1961–63, planning 1956); Garden City Puchenau; Upper Austria (1963– 68).
37 Pruscha–Groihofer 2016.
38 Adolf Loos, "Vernacular Art." In: Yehuda Safran, Wilfried Wang (eds), *The Architecture of Adolf Loos: An Arts Council Exhibition,* London, 1987, pp. 110–113
39 Ibid., p. 141.
40 "Roland Rainer." In *Die Akademie in der Zeitenwende,* 2002, p. 87.
41 Jutta Eiblmayr, "Irrwege in der Traviatagasse? Das intellektuelle Luxusetui im Wiener Wohnbau." In *Perspektiven* 1 (1994), http://www.eiblmayr.at/publikationen/text-irrwege-traviatagasse.htm
42 Ibid.
43 Hans Haider, "Vier Wände um den eigenen Hof." In *Wiener Zeitung*, January 28, 2010, https://www.wienerzeitung.at/nachrichten/archiv/62659_Vier-Waendeum- den-eigenen-Hof.html
44 Sperl 2005, p. 46.
45 Julia Zillinger, "Atmosphären." In: Sabine Pollak (ed.), *Wiener Typologien. Eine Studie zu neuen Wohnungstypologien für Wien im Sinne zukünftiger Lebensformen als Grundlage für ein Handbuch zum zukünftigen Wohnen in Wien. Projekt-bericht,* Vienna, 2008/09, p. 143, www.wohnbauforschung.at/index.php?inc=download&id=5446.
46 All three quotes from Peter Sloterdijk, "Die Jahre Pruscha. Zur Physiognomie eines Ausnahmezustands." In *Die Akademie in der Zeitenwende,* 2002, p. 9–11.
47 These lectures were also published in *Über die Wahrheit in der Malerei. Symposium über Wahrnehmung und Individualität,* Vienna, 1990.
48 Erika Billeter, "Pionierzeit im Institut für Gegenwartskunst." In *Akademie in der Zeitenwende,* 2002, pp. 78–80: 78.
49 Michael Sorkin, "Erinnerungen an Charlie." In *Die Akademie in der Zeitenwende,* 2002, pp. 93–97: 95.
50 Ibid., p. 97.
51 Sloterdijk 2002, p. 11.
52 Sorkin 2002, p. 93.
53 "Edelbert Kob." In *Die Akademie in der Zeitenwende* 2002, pp. 81–82: 81.
54 Professor of Architecture Ernst Hiesmayr, then rector of the Vienna University of Technology, prevented the building from being razed in 1975.
55 Leopold Dungl, "Semper Depot sensibel saniert." In *Kurier*, January 18, 1996, p. 25.
56 Eduard F. Sekler, "Zukunft für ein Altes Meisterwerk." In Carl Pruscha (ed.), *Das Semper-Depot. Die Adaptierung des Semper'schen Kulissendepots zum Atelierhaus der Akademie der bildenden Künste,* Munich, New York, Vienna, 1997, p. 105.
57 For example Martina Kandeler-Fritsch, "Ein beispielhafter Dialog von Alt und Neu." In *Architektur & Bauforum* 2 (1996), pp. 58–59; Doris Krumpl, "Altes Gesicht mit neuer Brille." In *Der Standard*, January 17, 1996, p. 10.
58 "Carl Pruscha im Gespräch mit Arno Ritter." Aut film 2005. https://aut.cc/magazin/aut-film/aut-film-carl-pruscha.
59 During his sabbatical at the Getty Institute, Carl Pruscha was able to appoint young Israeli architect Eyal Weizman as interim head of his Studio at the Academy. Weizman went on to become Director of the Center for Research Architecture at Goldsmith College, London, as well as co-founder and head of the art and research agency Forensic Architecture.
60 Pruscha, *Himalayan Vernacular* 2004.
61 Ibid., p. 126.
62 Wolf D. Prix, speech, May 26, 2008.

In 2017, photographer Hertha Hurnaus visited the buildings realized by Carl Pruscha after his return to Vienna in 1974 and documented their current use.

HOUSING TRAVIATAGASSE, INZERSDORF
Documented 2017
New housing typology developed by Pruscha for suburban courtyard housing.

KINDERSPIELHAUS

WASSERTIEFE
1,55 m

SEMPER DEPOT
Documented 2017
Revitalized and restored by Pruscha for the use of the students of the Academy of Fine Arts in Vienna.

Mitch!

Carl Pruscha with his architecture students in front of a just landed BAe 146 at Paro Airport, Bhutan, 2002

TRAVELS WITH CHARLIE

Michael Sorkin

I was seduced by Charlie Pruscha. For reasons at once clear and obscure, I was invited—nearly thirty years ago—to apply for a professorship at the Academy of Fine Art, where Carl was rector and, as I discovered, energetically engaged in a battle to shove that ossifying institution into the present. I'd been promoted for the job by Wolf Prix, with whom I'd become friendly when we were both briefly teaching at the University of Pennsylvania, and this dual sponsorship, I was to discover, meant that I had already taken sides in a battle of which I was completely unaware and in which I had no stake.

This was something I found out later. My late summer interview visit was deceptively delightful. Cunning Charlie had arranged for me to tour in the company of enthusiastic students and a delightful landscape architect, and introduced me to a friendly circle of sardonic charm. I stayed in a hotel with a window that opened hard on Saint Stefan's filigreed spire. Local wines (and this was long before "Grooner" was the default white in every restaurant in Manhattan) were consumed. The high point in the courtship was a tour of Vienna's lush countryside on a perfect day, including visits to several *Kellergassen*—villages with streets lined not with houses but with earth-covered, vaulted, wine cellars—sublime urbanism, an architecture of pleasure, midway between terrain and building. Descending the stairs into the cool caves, we always found a glass of something tasty awaiting.

This choice of routes was hardly accidental. Not simply was the gentle landscape a marvel, its rare symbiosis with this architecture that grew both into and out of it represented a way of viewing the world that, I was to discover, was central to Carl's sensibility and practice. This was overdetermined: a childhood in the Tyrolean mountains, academic studies of village architectures in the Burgenland, intoxication in Nepal before Kathmandu was overwhelmed by development, an enduring jones for South Asia (ultimately to include a gorgeous holiday house in Sri Lanka). Over the years, a succession of opportunities arose to intervene in historical buildings that themselves radiated the aura and fragility of natural phenomena. Charlie's embrace of this continuity extended deep into the social, its rituals and expressions, the communal and the artistic.

I said yes. The complications came later. After—thanks to Charlie—I'd moved into a vast, haunted apartment (scene of a murder during its previous tenancy—we constantly thought we saw bloodstains emerging from under the paint) above the sculpture school, next to the Prater. I began to journey to the Academy on a route that was bracketed by scenes from *The Third Man.* Near home, the gigantic Riesenrad (we rode it a few times but never got around to organizing one of those famous rotating dinners) loomed, and nearing the Academy (just opposite the Café Museum, the smoke-choked school hangout with its fading Adolf Loos interior and haunting memories of an exterminated culture), I'd see clumps of tourists waiting to descend into the sewers for their *Third Man* experience. These compass points bracketed decadence, corruption, and the dawn of modernity, which should have told me something: this is a town in love with its bad conscience.

Vienna is the city of Freud, and never lets you forget it. Shrouded in a fog equal parts nostalgia and amnesia, the city wears its unconscious on its sleeve: It can't stop talking about itself. On the way in from the airport, the city greeted me with the municipal slogan of the day: *Wien ist anders*—Vienna is different. To carry on a design practice in this marinade of greatness and ghosts feeds a chronic neurosis and worse, yielding architectures of anxiety and denial, both wild and kitsch. A weird, covert legibility burdens the city with a task of accountancy that has ambivalently, if erotically, stuffed its brain. No other city is as dense with monuments soaked in ambiguity or so stinking of crime. This smacked me in the face every day, and no recollection of Vienna escapes the pall: a grotesque bench-scaled, Holocaust memorial across the Ringstrasse from the Academy, depicting, in funereal cast-iron black, the monolithic form of a crouched, stereotypically bearded Jew at the moment of his maximum humiliation, cleaning the sidewalk with a brush at the behest of the enthusiastic Nazis of Vienna, whose literal point of view spectators share. Further along the Ring, a fine statue of Karl Lueger, the famously anti-Semitic turn-of-the-last-century mayor, stands unmolested, and behind the Academy one of the city's gigantic and allegedly indestructible Flakturm looms. Not to mention the *Polizei* with machine guns "guarding" the last synagogue left in the city center.

How Nazi he, she, or it was is a question the city forced in my face and I assayed everyone I met who was old enough to have been there. I even wondered about Charlie—who was ten years old when the war ended—and others of his generation. How had they assimilated the swastika bunting, jackbooted SS men, and military hardware which I know from my own upbringing are so intoxicating to little boys? Carl was a student of the much-loved Roland Rainer (director of his meticulous work on the historical architectures of the Burgenland), who'd been an ardent Nazi but was quickly rehabilitated. Were there "What did you do in the war, Professor?" moments? No place I'd ever been had closets like these. An early trip to the small town where Wolf Prix had grown up, taken to get the sniff of his origins and to keep him company while he shut down the architectural office of his late father, forced an unwelcome confrontation. While Wolf shuffled papers, I wandered the office and soon found a framed picture of Dad and two comrades in their Wehrmacht uniforms, grinning from the porch of the French farmhouse they'd expropriated. Memories.

Although Austria had formally moved on from its postwar "first victim" bullshit, habits of dissembling die hard in this city of hyperaestheticized intrigue, and there was nothing I didn't interrogate—human or architectural—for evidence of complicity and crime. When I was at the Academy (where the ghost of Hitler's desire and disappointment appeared around every corner) an object of veneration and pilgrimage was Otto Wagner's great Kirche am Steinhof. I took many architectural visitors to marvel at that magnificent building, surely an inspiration for Charlie's prismatic handling of mass and exquisite sense of detail. The elegant early white buildings of the surrounding sanitarium (not designed

Carl Pruscha with Michael Sorkin at students' meeting at the Academy, Vienna, 1994

by Wagner but always the intended setting for the church) were a seeming model of compassionate modernity, over which the church was meant to cast its balm. A newly frank biography of Johann Asperger, pioneer of the autism spectrum, reveals that the asylum's children's clinic (where Asperger practiced)—Am Spiegelgrund—was a killing ground for "defective" youngsters, many selected by Asperger himself. Had I known to look for it, I might have found the tepid commemoration at the Central Cemetery, where some of the victims are buried. The *New York Times* recently touted it as a great attraction for visitors.

This may seem a sour preamble to an appreciation of an architect of both formal genius and moral rectitude, but Carl's was a generation called to both psychic and reparative account for the crimes of its parents. Vienna itself had fallen with astonishing speed from the vital center of modern artistic and intellectual illumination into the maw of absolute evil and still felt fat with collusion. However, the enthusiastically Nazi city was also the city of Wagner, Loos, Olbrich, Hoffmann, Schütte-Lihotzky, Gruen, Urban, Kiesler, and those eternally amazing housing estates of the Red Ring. When Pruscha arrived in Vienna to begin his architectural studies, he would have seen a city still pocked with ruins and reconstruction, where the air must have been heavy with hypocrisy, lies, and evasion. Innocent of any actual collaboration, how did Carl's generation navigate this terrain of contradiction, learning about its miracle modernity from those who had been complicit in its assassination or by walking the city's spooky streets? I can't get these thoughts out of my mind. Forgive me.

For this and other reasons, modern architecture in Vienna demands periodization—the inescapable punctuation of world wars and enormous political and economic upheavals—and, in this pressure cooker of a city, no era ever escapes the anxiety of the influence of its predecessors, which continue to frame the circumstances of design, whether in celebration or denial. As I soon discovered, though, compact Vienna holds an astonishing convergence of masterpieces, and within a few minutes' walk of the Academy were Olbrich's Secession, Loos' Goldman & Salatsch shop and building on the Michaelerplatz (so reviled by Hitler that he painted it out of the tacky self-made postcards he lived on), a pair of dazzling entry pavilions for an underground rail line by Otto Wagner as well as his Majolica and Köstlergasse Houses (not to mention a neighbor by Plečnik), among the most gorgeous apartment buildings ever. And, there was Charlie's own exquisite restoration and adaptation of the Semper Depot—the former scene shop for the Vienna Opera, built in 1874 by (who else) Gottfried Semper—into a dramatically concise extension for the school.

The Semper Depot is a complete and clarifying summation of Charlie's architectural DNA. True to his primary perceptions of the architectural environment, Charlie treated the renovation of this building as he might a landscape—not in the sense of a *Bürolandschaft,* with its picturesque deployment of desks, chairs, and potted plants, but as a territory of veneration demanding minimal interference. Carl is no historicist but he is a man of respect who brings to all his work a passionate commitment to divining what he finds to be the critical authenticity of a situation, whether the texture of a village, the intricate terracing of a Himalayan agricultural pattern, or the *genius loci* of a received work of architecture. This commitment does not entail an originalist channeling of the intentions of the architecture nor an attempt to exactingly reproduce period detail, but it does mean letting the found architectural landscape stand in the foreground of a minimal yet extremely and beautifully precise intervention.

The brilliance of Carl's renovation of the Semper Depot—which, when he took it on, was bereft of environmental systems and infrastructure and had suffered many decades of decay—is that on entering its soaring interior, the extensive interventions are initially invisible. Only by probing further, adjusting your eyesight to this new light, can Carl's lapidary moves—which descend to the smallest scale—be discerned: an elegant steel escape stair, a small amphitheater, little mezzanines, beautifully wrought fixtures and fittings. None of the conventional descriptors—sensitivity, adaptive reuse, restoration—fully describe what has happened to this building: it has been reinvented. I don't think it's going too far to suggest that this act of reparation is a form of subtle redress for the city's sins. This same spirit of transformative reoccupation appears to have been always already there in Carl's work. An early example is the theoretical Narrenturm "Fools' Tower" project, an artfully thwarted panopticon in which the animating gaze is no longer projected from the center to the periphery of the interior but outward and beyond the building, from monkish cells contoured not to surveillance but to contemplation.

The same hand and process is visible more dramatically in Carl's loving conversion of his own country house in the village of Gattendorf (itself once rich with Jewish life), in the Burgenland, a much abused palazzo built during the Renaissance as a gatehouse between Austria and Hungary, abandoned, then bought in 1735 by the governor of nearby Bratislava, who fashionably "baroqued" it for his residence. The house continued to change hands among the hereditary and, later, industrial nobility until, in the early twentieth century, a Romanian brewer turned it into a granary. Charlie, who'd had his contemplating, designing eye on it for years, bought the place in 1975 and began his remarkable intervention, preserving remaining fragments of the original. He'd been initially drawn to the house both for its latent magnificence and for its situation. Although it is apparently autonomous as an object, it fronts directly on the village high street, which it gently dominates with the weight of its mass and self-consciously grand expression. Carl has spoken about the Janus-like, interior/exterior character of his renovation and this doubling also defines the site: urban in front and sylvan in the back, where the property line is the river Leitha, now approached though an elegant paradise garden.

At the time the house became Carl's, the forms and elements of its exterior were clearly legible but most of the wooden structure of its interior had fallen on very hard times: it was rotted and required removal. In Charlie's account, this initial move to stabilize the structure also radically transformed its spatiality. Stripping away the ceiling of the house's second story revealed an enormous

Carl Pruscha, Walter Pichler, and Raimund Abraham, 1993

space, an under-roof cathedral, framed seriatim by a Gothic succession of trussed wooden joists. The drama and luminosity of this space—like the soaring interior of the Semper Depot—evoked a reaction that, in turn, led to the conceptual doubling that informed the subsequent design. The decision, in essence, was not to transform the shell of the original by further complication or subdivision but, in effect, to furnish it. Charlie became the house whisperer.

An augmented but delicate flow of space forms a continuum that, in its simple geometries and space/object relations, unites house and garden, a Modernist move—and a Renaissance one. A remarkable cubic "cella" stands in the midst of the long under-roof nave and propels a contraction of living space into an efficient minimum, a concisely compressed freestanding object at the middle of the gallery of the great hall: a machine for sleeping. The rest of the house is kitted out with an inventory of wonderful furnishings that amplify their spaces, rather than detracting from them with claims that are too extravagant or competitive. Even subsidiary objects—books, stacks of plates, wall hangings, the architect's desktop collection of pens and pencils—augment a sense of a place that is perfectly livable for Charlie and Eva.

The house has been compared—by Charlie among others—to the work of Carlo Scarpa and Luis Barragán. Reasonable enough. All share a sense of spatial clarity, perfected detail, and modulated light, and there are surely episodes in the Gattendorf house that are evocative of both. I am reminded, though, of another architect: John Hejduk. Hejduk also worked through the idea of the autonomous object which drew its meanings both from its own poetics or (more rarely) functionality, accreting additional layers from the facts of its situation. His renovation of the Foundation Building at Cooper Union—a Janus that inscribes the austerely modern in a powerful predecessor shell—has deep affinities with Carl's reinhabitations of both the Semper Depot and his own house, and all three describe the passage from an originary condition to another that's contoured to fit the fixed skins they rejuvenate.

But how did Carl reach this point of maturity and control? It's a conceit, but the parallel lives and diverging trajectories of Charlie (born 1936), Raimund Abraham (born 1933), Hans Hollein (born 1934), and Walter Pichler (also born 1936) are in vivid conversation and their careers full of intersections: geographical, formal, political, and academic. The initial parallels between Pruscha and Hollein are especially strong. Both received their architectural training at the Academy, Charlie under Rainer and Hollein with Clemens Holzmeister (like Pruscha, Abraham, and Pichler, originally from the Tyrol—something in the water), who'd been expelled from the Academy at the time of the *Anschluss* for having supported the *previous* fascist government of Engelbert Dollfuss and Kurt Schuschnigg. He repaired to Turkey, where he designed—at the behest of Kemal Atatürk—a number of official buildings in Ankara in a stately eclectic style, returning to Vienna only after the end of the war. An account of the internal politics of reputation and rehabilitation at the Academy from war's end through the fifties and early sixties would surely be fascinating.

Both Hollein and Pruscha left Austria after graduation to study in the United States. After a year at the IIT under Mies van der Rohe, Hollein switched—in 1969—to Berkeley—then run by William Wurster, a regionalist and the antithesis of Miesianism—where he was surely immersed in the aftermath of the free-speech movement and the still efflorescent counterculture, something for which his whimsical, antiarchitectural (rather, expanded architectural) thesis offers clear evidence. For his part, Charlie did a graduate degree at the Harvard Graduate School of Design, which was then under the deanship of Josep Lluís Sert, in devoluted thrall of Le Corbusier (for whom Sert had worked) and the epicenter of the American establishment. Carl studied urban design not long after its invention as an academic and design discipline, something alleged to have been the outcome of a conference Sert had organized at Harvard in 1956 with the aim of recapturing the physical side of planning (then dominated by social science, statistics, and formless methodologies) for architecture. This effective reintroduction of the territorial into the architectural field surely had an impact on Pruscha and was bursting to emerge in Nepal.

After his American schooling and some explorations of pueblo architecture in the southwest, Hollein returned to Vienna in 1963, the year he shared an exhibition of visionary work with Pichler at a gallery in the heart of the city. Pruscha finished at Harvard in 1962, moved to New York, lived the bohemian life in Greenwich Village, and worked for the firms of Paul Lester Wiener and Wallace K. Harrison. For the latter he designed a scheme for Battery Park City in Lower Manhattan that was frankly visionary—and loads of fun—but which surely must have cost him his job with the conservative, upper-crusty Harrison. Carl's project—as well as another proposal for Aspen, Colorado, that moved in the same spirit—was, in fact, an amplification of the theoretical work he was doing in parallel at the time, filled with megalomaniac optimism and rendered in lovely drawings of bilaterally symmetrical systems in the wiring-diagram manner, including one that girded the whole planet and extended into outer space. Those were the days!

This was also the period in which Hollein, Abraham, and Pichler, among others, were engaged in the emergent practices of "radical" architecture, but in very different registers. Hollein was the ironist (that collage of an aircraft carrier sailing through rolling hills remains his signature image) but Abraham and Pichler were developing an elemental tectonics that emerged from their remarkable drawings, weighty with graphite and probing the opaque earth. Hovering over this work was the influence of Louis Kahn, who shared—and extraordinarily executed—their preoccupation with primary, Euclidean forms, although perhaps not with the same imperative to excavate and cocoon. The four Austrians were always close, sharing, for a time, a powerfully reductive sensibility, at least until Hollein diverged to become a stylist and Charlie decamped, in 1965, for his ten revelatory years in Nepal.

While his Himalayan period is covered extensively elsewhere in this volume, several crucial things emerged from the adventure that were at once transformative and affirmative, and bridge from one creative condition to another. The first was Carl's enamored relationship to the Nepali landscape and culture, which he investigated and absorbed with joyful rigor. The documentation and planning that emerged was exemplary in its sensitivity and harmoniousness, deeply respectful of the landscape in the very broadest sense—a genuinely pioneering work of environmental understanding and cultural engagement. The torrid politics, however, were ruinous, and the development of Kathmandu under the regime of free-fire development has been catastrophic. I do so regret not having seen it before the invasion.

This experience also enhanced Charlie's own capacity to lead a double life, to practice many of those very Viennese tactics of duplicity. In Nepal, Charlie had privately (and not so privately!) lived like a hippie at home—and in the field—but daily had to deal with scoundrels, bureaucrats, and incompetents, including his erstwhile neighbor Ellsworth Bunker, a leading Vietnam war criminal, immortalized by Allen Ginsberg's lines "Where is Ambassador Bunker today? / Are his Helios machines gunning children at play?" Until the fatal end, though, Carl showed his canny—and rapidly maturing—ability to get along, to maneuver through the crossfire to produce results, a skill I was able to observe at the Academy in his totally astute—and often histrionic (and hilarious!)—leadership as rector. He loved the role and did energetic battle with the obstructive dinosaurs, sycophants, and assholes who simply couldn't keep up with his dervish whirl of stratagems and his chess-master ability to think many moves ahead. That this was in service of a sharp and progressive intellectual and artistic vision resulted in protective sallies that allowed many fresh and confident voices to flourish. Charlie was himself a calculated Janus, two-faced in the best Viennese style, but with full knowledge of the tragicomic circumstances of the school and how to work through them.

Memories of his vigorous direction of faculty meetings remain vivid. My German was never up to following the argumentative back and forth, and I always tried to sit next to the sardonic but warm, wise, ethical, and generous architectural historian, Otto Graf, who kept me up to speed and had been one of the few professors at the Academy to welcome me warmly. My intermittent understanding of the language allowed me to observe the more purely performative aspects of Carl's leadership, the alternation of pugilistic and soothing comments, the canny manipulation of factions to achieve his desired result, the thespian ability to turn from rage to charm on a *Pfennig.* Like some haplessly obedient comrade at a Soviet Party Congress, I kept my eye on Charlie and raised my arm when he did.

His higher education in cunning notwithstanding, Charlie became a builder in Nepal and quickly understood how to negotiate and merge his own sensibilities with his affinities for the place, where they were formed into very habitable and distinctive architecture. The results were visibly hybrid but embodied both cultures in equitable measure with verve and originality. The influence of Kahn is clear, both in his fascination for the possibilities of brickwork—a densification of the earth itself—and also for a strong and direct geometry that Carl's work had embodied and celebrated from the first. There's an intense dialogue between the work of the two on the subcontinent as both strove for a postcolonial originality that could join wider streams of both tradition and innovation, reflecting the bioclimatic particulars of place. The circles, cylinders, and vaults (which also bear the imprint of those *Kellergassen*) that mark Carl's buildings in Nepal were in conversation with concurrent work by Kahn in Dhaka, Ahmedabad, and Fort Worth.

The character visible in his Nepali projects continued to mature in the work Carl did on his return to Vienna. In particular, the Quadrangle Housing at Traviatagasse—part of a complex masterplanned by Raimund Abraham—channels the intensely distilled geometry that Pruscha shares with Abraham and Kahn but also proposes a dwelling type and site organization that are the subtle derivative of a non-European urban organization. The project, as built, is both beautiful and problematic. To begin, the sheer elegance of both increment and ensemble is, as ever, a signature. Pruscha's design for these compact but spacious-feeling individual houses yields a very high density, unit numbers more normally found in traditional multiple dwellings.

The influence of Rainer, if more attenuated, is also clear. Rainer's most successful—and humane—work was his investigation of both the singular and repetitive—low-rise high-density—possibilities of courtyard housing, and he built gracious examples of both, almost invariably in a string format and with an orientation to the surrounding landscape. Pruscha's project was also based on an arrangement of inner courts—or patios—but they're more compressed in plan, stretched in the vertical axis, and very inwardly focused: contemplative spaces, retreats. With their narrow passageways and unfenestrated public faces, they have a Middle Eastern feeling: very interior, very private.

Pruscha is quite clear about his objective in the project to outperform a more traditional linear typology (like Rainer's), keeping the horizontal individuation of units but creating something more urban from their high density and from the labyrinthine organization of public circulation in narrow, Casbah-like streets. There's an intellectual and formal refinement in the project—a willingness to push typological boundaries—but there's also a hermetic quality and something of a mismatch in latitudes: the feel is of an architecture that wants to be in the heat. But the artistry of the ensemble is peerless, even in the snow.

Pruscha's *Wanderjahren* in Nepal had the effect of affirming his special creative relationship with Abraham and Pichler, but they also led him away from their tough, prismatic, tectonics in the direction of a more culturally and naturally inflected architecture. He also was immersed from afar in the early development of the next generation of architects, those who wanted to be rock stars rather than monks, and formed their groupuscules—Haus-Rucker-Co, Missing Link, Coop Himmelblau and the rest in thrall of the Beatles and the Stones (still playing on Himmelb[l]au's answering machine).

In the broader taxonomy of the architecture of the sixties' and seventies' counterculture, these guys (almost always guys) represent one of two distinct, yin-yang, tendencies (there were also others). The first were those—like these Austrian rockers—who celebrated insubordination in a weirdly apolitical way and whose rebellion against the artistic values of the previous generation stood in for more explicit demands and expressions. In this sense, they were thorough Modernists, looking to reinvent architecture, which was then expected, by sheer force of difference, to reinvent culture. Their work in the later sixties was—foremost—ludic, and it seemed that everyone (including Hollein) with avant-garde ambitions was blowing up inflatables, celebrating nomadism, instability, McLuhanesque globalism, and the thinning of the membrane between body and building. This consciousness of the body as something that exceeded its role as a source of scale (per Leonardo or Le Corbusier) to include—especially—sexuality (another key problematic for the politics of "liberation") was also crucial to tough radicals like Abraham and Pichler, as well as for the concurrent Actionists of the art world, who took up the question with stinking misogyny.

The other strain in this dyad was gentler and included those—like Charlie—who went (at least conceptually) east, seeking more authentic and rooted forms of building: architecture without architects, frankly spiritual, connected to timeless rituals and inner journeys. George Harrison began his sitar lessons with Ravi Shankar in 1965 and took half a generation with him to this gentle nirvana of (relative) quietude and sense. Charlie—reefer mad, hanging out with villagers and monks—left his early, traditionalist avant-gardism behind and—although sympathetic with their project—diverged from the self-identified radical cohort that had so quickly conquered the scene. Charlie never repudiated the primal act of building—brick upon brick—absorbed by the direct simplicity of the ancient fundamentals of construction and their cultural origins or inflections.

Hollein, for all this early radicalism, took a different path and wound up effectively betraying the "gang of four" eventually winning the imprimatur of a Pritzker. He reverted to a version of the whipped cream and waltzing Alt Wien schtick that Austria was so eager to establish as the right past to use to revive its lost innocence and to solidify its new place in the world. No coincidence that *The Sound of Music* premiered in 1965, coating the planet in exculpatory treacle. Hollein began his real architectural practice with a series of jewel-like, high-end shops that were crucial in authorizing a more sprightly global modernity and fertilizing the blossoming of a hundred architectural flowers, as well as reestablishing a connection to earlier modern traditions, especially to Wagner and Loos. Unfortunately, he too soon developed a fascination for the clumsiest branch of postmodernity, culminating in that ungainly, *Schlag*-dripping pastiche the Haas House, reviled by Charlie even as his friendship with Hollein endured. Ornament was not exactly a crime anymore.

As the gang of four (Charlie, alas, is the only survivor now) reached their maturity and as the more publicity-wise subversives aspired to build for more conventional programs—Coop Himmelblau is now Coop Himmelb(l)au, Haus-Rucker-Co has morphed into Ortner and Ortner—they retained their facility but lost their edge, building for well-padded institutions, including museums, corporate headquarters for multinationals, car companies, even the European Central Bank. The forms so often continue to be arresting and original but the sting is gone and the global traffic (Zaha Hadid, Morphosis, MAD, OMA, et al.) in the tendency seriously winnows the bite. Moreover, the *l'art pour l'art* sensibility behind this work clouds most of it in the effete criteria of the gallery and the tastes of elites. While all of this building will surely take an important place in the canon of the transition to a postdigital modernity, it is largely irrelevant to the more urgent challenges (to both architecture and everything else) of climate change; poverty, and the widening income gap; slums; megacities; surveillance, and thought control; and the rest of our extinction-level planetary crisis.

The work of Carl Pruscha, Raimund Abraham, Hans Hollein, and Walter Pichler—in its consistency of imagination, commitment to gravity in both fact and representation, attention to fundamentals, and romance with the tectonic motherhood of Earth itself—offers a vital, resonant, and relevant alternative with a pedigree of millennia. While the members of this quartet can't exactly be called environmental pioneers, they uphold the only approach that can really save us: the idea that it's always better to open the window or rely on the thermal conservation of a thick wall than to lard a building with the latest smart technology. All have preferred concision to volume and all have done projects of a scale they can personally control. And, all have built (and drawn) durably beautiful and original work.

Charlie has been at the center of it all. He has not simply shared the seminal formal and conceptual research of this cohort, he has—as architect, educator, scholar, enthusiast, and friend—led a peerlessly engaged life, combining solitary concentration, deep cross-cultural understanding, subtle taste, remarkable design facility, profound love for his city, and a fine dose of hedonism. This rare combination of geniality and genius has allowed him to build a bridge spanning both backward and forward, connecting with Vienna's great tradition, with the generation that preceded him, with the next generation on, and with the one after that—full of admiration and respect for true strivers, inventors, and people of conscience wherever he has found them. Carl Pruscha is Vienna's indispensable man.

One last anecdote. There was a restaurant near the Academy called Ubl, run by two sisters who commanded the kitchen on alternating nights. It was an old-fashioned place with old-fashioned cuisine—Tafelspitz, Schnitzel, Kaiserschmarrn, *und so weiter*. Charlie loved the joint, and we'd often dine there, generally in the company of one or two of Charlie's close friends. To me, the appeal was the somewhat funky but *echte* quality of the room and the folkish pedigree (and guaranteed indigestion) of the cooking. However, Charlie, ever the connoisseur, insisted that he could tell—after a single bite—which sister was in the kitchen (one was held to be the vastly superior cook). There would be arguments (not from me, who couldn't tell the slightest difference), but Charlie never gave ground after that conclusive first taste. I can't remember if the claim was ever verified by a trip to the kitchen, but here was Charlie in full: the aesthete's eye and palette for both high and low. Confidence in his own discernment. Mirthful joy in arguing for his conclusion. So convivial. So comfortable. Charlie belonged everywhere he went.

Carl Pruscha was born in Innsbruck, Austria, on June 10, 1936. He spent his childhood years during the war in the safety of a remote farmhouse in the Tyrolean Mountains. From 1946 to 1955 he attended secondary school in Innsbruck and then until 1959 studied of architecture at the Academy of Fine Arts Vienna (under Professor Roland Rainer). In 1963 he graduated with a postgraduate degree in urban design at the Harvard University Graduate School of Design (under Professor Josep Lluís Sert and Fumihiko Maki) and gained his first practical experience in New York City, in the offices of Paul Lester Wiener and Wallace Harrison. In 1960, he married Edda Velim, an academic restorer who died in 1992.

In 1964 the United Nations appointed him as a physical planning expert with the duty of advisor to the Government of Nepal. This led to his first activities in the field of regional planning, working together with at team of economic and social planners on behalf of the National Planning Commission in Nepal. He established a Department for Housing and Physical Planning and compiled a *Physical Development Plan* for the region of the capital—the Kathmandu Valley—in 1967 (published in Calcutta, 1969). Pruscha further prepared an inventory of the region's rich cultural heritage as a basis for the Kathmandu Valley to become a UNESCO World Heritage Site.

During these years, Pruscha ran a small architecture studio in Kathmandu, which designed and constructed exemplary building projects such as the CEDA building at the Tribhuvan University for the Ford Foundation and the Taragaon Hostel for a Nepalese women's organization. Several residential buildings were also constructed, in which Pruscha sought to transform basic construction and material elements of vernacular architecture into a contemporary architectural idiom. During his years in Nepal, his two daughters were born: Alexandra (1965) and Czeslavia (1969).

After his return to Vienna in 1974 Pruscha produced the two comprehensive volumes of *Kathmandu Valley I + II. The Preservation of Physical Environment and Cultural Heritage* (published by Anton Schroll, 1975); worked as a registered architect and planner; and prepared his dissertation at the Technical University in Graz, Austria, for a doctorate in technical sciences in the field of regional planning.

In 1976 he became full professor for planning and architectural research at the Academy of Fine Arts Vienna, where he then taught for the next twelve years. In 1988 the Collegium of the Academy elected him rector—a position he held until 2002 (he was re-elected every two years). His activities as rector were documented in a publication titled *Akademie in der Zeitenwende* (Vienna, 2002), which included a preface by Peter Sloterdijk. During his period as a rector and professor he also ran a small architectural studio in Vienna. Among the projects he and his team completed were the revitalization of historical buildings such as the Kulissendepot designed by Gottfried Semper, which was transformed into an atelier house for the Academy of Fine Arts, and the two exemplary settlements at Biberhaufenweg in Aspern and at Traviatagasse in Inzersdorf. After 2002, new university laws were passed foreseeing the future leadership of the university being appointed by special supervisory boards—breaking with the previous policy of a professor being elected rector as *primus inter pares* by the entire Collegium of the respective university. Pruscha thus ended his rector tenure and accepted an invitation by the Getty Institute in Los Angeles to be a visiting scholar in 2003. There he worked on a critical analysis of recent developments in countries of still anonymous, authentic architecture in their natural environments. These thoughts were then compiled in the book *Himalayan Vernacular* (published by Verlag Schlebrügge, 2004) drawing on his experiences there in his early years in Nepal. Since 1979 he has also been engaged in the research of anonymous architecture.

During his final years at the Academy he founded and headed a third design class—the Studio for Habitat, Environment, and Conservation. This class was discontinued after he became professor emeritus. He then decided to continue his work at his own architectural studio. Together with his team, he has planned a number of architectural projects, several of which were realized for the One World Foundation in Sri Lanka. A new, larger school building was constructed following the destruction of the old campus of the foundation by the tsunami in 2004. This construction was even presented as the Austrian contribution to the Architecture Biennale in Venice 2010. At the same time, his office also worked on research projects such as the Quadrangle Housing project and on the multidisciplinary research project "Bhutan Habitat."

Since 2002, he has been married to the artist Eva Schlegel. The couple lives in Vienna and owns a summer residence in the northern part of Burgenland.

AMERICAN PROJECTS 1955–1964
Aspen, 1962 > p. 123
Global Linear City, 1963 > p. 126
Urban Development Boston, 1963
Manhattan Downtown Development, 1963 > p. 124
Austrian Embassy Brasilia, 1967

NEPAL PROJECTS 1964–1974
Pruscha's private house at Bansbari, 1967–1968 > p. 139
CEDA building, 1967–1969 > p. 145
Jagadish Sumsher Rana Residence, 1969 > p. 157
UNHCR Refugee Housing, 1969–1971 > p. 142
Taragaon Hostel, 1970–1972 > p. 150

ARCHITECTURAL PROJECTS 1974–2002
Revitalization Schloss Gattendorf, 1975–2008 > p. 168
Revitalization Neugebäude (project), 1976 > p. 210
Family house Strickner, Tirol, 1976–1977 > p. 166
Adaptation of the Institute for Architectural Research, 1979 > p. 222
Learning from Kathmandu Valley (exhibition), Academy of Fine Arts Vienna, 1979
Housing development, Aspern, 1985 > p. 197
Project for "Arkaneum" competition, Museumsquartier, Vienna, 1986 > p. 216
Revitalization Kunsthaus Horn, 1986–1988 > p. 215
Housing development, Kagran, 1990
C.P.P.N. (CarlPruschaPeterNoever collaboration), Havana project, 1991
Housing development, Traviatagasse, Inzersdorf, 1992 > p. 193
Revitalization Semper Depot, Vienna, 1993–1995 > p. 218
Atelier für Birgit Jürgenssen (project), Vienna, 1995
Revitalization Narrenturm (project), 1997–1999 > p. 212
Lagoon bungalows, Sri Lanka, 2001–2005 > p. 234

ARCHITECTURAL PROJECTS 2002–present
Family housing, Klosterneuburg, 2002
Multipurpose building for MQ, 2004
One World Foundation school, Sri Lanka, 2006 > p. 230
Housing for Liesing – the snake (project), 2006
Project for Simmering, Vienna, 2007
Holy Ghost Church (project), Tyrol, 2007
House with Sea view (project), 2007
Pier One (project), Carinthia, 2008
MQ Attic Appartments (project), 2008
Quadrangle Housing (exhibition and manifesto), MAK – Museum of Applied Art, Vienna, 2009
Quadrangle Housing (project), various sites, 2009 > p. 199
Shrine on the Lake (project), 2009
Penthouse Tower (project), various sites, 2010
Artist in Residence Quarter, Hungary, 2011
Palazzetto Lhotka (project), Styria, 2012
Bodh Gaya Project, India, 2012
Palmgrove Bungalow, Sri Lanka, 2012 > p. 234
House on a slope (project), Austria, 2013
House on the hill, Tyrol, 2014
Taragaon restored, 2014
Taragaon Annex proposal 01, 2014
Taragaon Annex proposal 02, 2015
Family housing (project), Klosterneuburg, 2015
Table for Eva Schlegel, Winterpalais Vienna, 2015
Entrance Pavillion Biennale Kochin, 2017
Renovation Hadres, 2017/2019
CPH-Tower, Sri Lanka, 2019

PUBLICATIONS

The Physical Development Plan for the Kathmandu Valley, published by His Majesty's Government of Nepal, Calcutta, 1969

Kathmandu Valley, the Preservation of Physical Environment and Cultural Heritage. A Protective Inventory, Vol. I and II, Anton Schroll & Co., Vienna, 1975

Contribution by Carl Pruscha in *Umriss* 1/87, Peter Noever Publisher, Vienna, 1987

C.P.P.N. in: *The Havana Project. Architecture Again. International Conference on Architecture, Havana, Cuba,* Prestel, Munich, 1996, pp. 146–160

Das Semper-Depot. Die Adaptierung des Semper'schen Kulissendepots in Wien zum Atelierhaus der Akademie der bildenden Künste, Prestel, Munich/New York, 1997

Die Akademie in der Zeitenwende, Archiv der Akademie der bildenden Künste, Vienna, 2002

Himalayan Vernacular, Schlebrügge Editor, Vienna, 2004

Mein Haus in Lajtakatta. Carl Pruscha Architect, Architektur Raumburgenland, Eisenstadt, 2016

"A contribution to contemporary architecture in Sri Lanka," in: *One World Foundation. A Social Sculpture*, One World Foundation, Vienna, 2015

Kathmandu Valley, the Preservation of Physical Environment and Cultural Heritage, A Protective Inventory, Vol. I and II, second edition, Vajra Books, Kathmandu, 2015

AWARDS AND HONORS

Member of the Austrian Committee for Art and Science

Honorary member of the "Sociedad de Arquitectura, Villa Clara" Cuba, 1999

Honorary member of the Association of Visual Artists Vienna Secession

Honorary member of the Senate of the Academy of Fine Arts Vienna

Honorary professor of the Technical University Vienna

Goldenes Ehrenzeichen für Verdienste um das Land Wien

Preis der Stadt Wien für Architektur 2010

Chairman of the Austrian Committee of the Arts

Lars Müller was born in Oslo in 1955. He has lived and worked in Switzerland since 1963. After training as a graphic designer and studying in the United States and the Netherlands, he founded the studio Lars Müller for visual communication and design. He has been a publisher and editor since 1983 and has released over 800 books on typography, design, art, photography and architecture. Publications on social topics such as human rights and ecology complete the program. Lars Müller has been teaching at various universities in Switzerland and internationally since 1985, for example as a guest lecturer at the Harvard University Graduate School of Design and as a visiting professor at UCLA Design Media Arts.

Arno Ritter was born in Vienna in 1965. He studied journalism, history, and philosophy at the University of Vienna. From 1992 to 1995 he was secretary of the ÖGFA –Austrian Society for Architecture. Since 1995 he has directed and curated the exhibition space aut. architektur und tirol in Innsbruck (formerly Architekturforum Tirol), which he has positioned as a place for the presentation of architecture, art, design, and graphic design as well as a space for interdisciplinary discussion on the design of our living space. Since 1999 he has been a member of the Regional Cultural Advisory Board for Tyrol. From 2000 to 2005 he was a board member of the Austrian Architecture Foundation and from 2005 to 2009 a member of the "Art and Construction" Advisory Board of the province of Vorarlberg. From 2003 to 2012 he taught architectural criticism and curatorial practice at the University of Innsbruck and in 2009/10 lectured at the University of Applied Arts in Vienna at the Institute for Transmedial Art. In 2012 he was commissioner of the Austrian contribution to the Architecture Biennale in Venice and since 2015 has been a member of the advisory board of the Werkraum Bregenzerwald with Peter Zumthor. As editor and author he publishes mainly on architecture, photography, and art.

Eva Schlegel was born 1960 in Hall, Austria. She lives and works in Vienna, where she studied fine arts at the University of Applied Arts. After several stays abroad she was professor of art and photography at the Academy of Fine Arts in Vienna from 1997 to 2006. In 2009 she was announced chairwoman of the council of the Art University in Linz, where she stayed until 2018. In 2011 she was commissioner for the Austrian Pavilion at the 54th Venice Biennale. As a freelance artist, her work in various media such as photography, installation, painting, and film focuses primarily on architectural and immaterial space and its perception by the viewer. Since 1985 her works have been shown in numerous exhibitions in Germany and abroad. In 1988 and 1992 she took part in the Sydney Biennale and in 1990 in the Aperto at the Venice Biennale, a fringe event for emerging artists. She designed the Austrian Pavilion together with Coop Himmelb(l)au as part of the Venice Biennale in 1995 and participated in the Kochin Biennale in India in 2017, together with Carl Pruscha. Besides her exhibitions in galleries and museums, Eva Schlegel also implements permanent, site-specific projects, including in Basel, Copenhagen, Mumbai, Stockholm, Vienna, and San Francisco. Numerous publications of her projects are available.

Natalie Lettner was born in Salzburg in 1965. She lives and works in Vienna as a cultural and art scholar. Since 2000 she has worked at the Kunsthistorisches Museum Vienna. She has teached at Bard College, New York; at Webster University, Vienna; and at the European Forum Alpbach. She researches the interfaces between pre-modern and contemporary art as well as between so-called high and popular culture. In addition to her academic work, Natalie Lettner has worked as a documentary film director (*Malibu Song*, 2006; *Mahlers Stadt*, 2010, both together with Werner Hanak), specializing in conveying art and cultural history in an understandable way. She has written essays on the history of Hollywood (sound film, McCarthy era, New Hollywood, horror film) and on contemporary art (including Maria Lassnig, Jonathan Meese, Nafez Rerhuf) as well as the comprehensive study *Images of Evil? Devils, Snakes, and Monsters in Contemporary Art* (Transcript, 2015). Her work also includes the first comprehensive biography of Maria Lassnig (*Maria Lassnig. Die Biografie,* Brandstätter, 2017).

Manjushree Thapa was born in Kathmandu and lives in Toronto. She is the author of several books of fiction and nonfiction about her homeland, Nepal. She also translates Nepali literature into English. Her most recent books include a novel, *All Of Us in Our Own Lives*, and the English translation of Indra Bahadur Rai's classic novel about Darjeeling, *There's a Carnival Today.* She is currently at work on a novel about citizenship.

Michael Sorkin is principal of the Michael Sorkin Studio, a global practice dedicated to progressive urbanism and green design, and president and founder of Terreform, a non-profit research and advocacy institute dedicated to the forms and practices of equitable, sustainable, and beautiful cities. Its book imprint, UR (Urban Research), was launched in 2015. Sorkin is distinguished professor of architecture and director of the Graduate Program in Urban Design at the City College of New York. He has taught at the Academy of Fine Arts in Vienna, Cooper Union, Yale, Columbia, Pennsylvania, Harvard, SCI-Arc, and the Architectural Association. He is the author or editor of twenty books, and architecture critic for *The Nation.* Sorkin is a fellow of the American Academy of Arts and Sciences and Guggenheim Fellow, as well as winner of the National Design Award as "Design Mind" and the AIA (American Institute of Architects) award for Collaborative Achievement.

IMAGE CREDITS

9–12 © Don Oppedijk
13 © Nick Townsend
16, 27 (center, right) © Archiv Pruscha (USAID)
18, 51, 52, 55 (right), 86–95 © Iwan Baan
19 (left) Photo: © Estate of Evelyn Hofer
19 (center) www.britannica.com, photo: Katrina Thomas
19 (right) Photo: © The Granger Collection Ltd.
20 © Koichi Nagashima
21–26, 27 (left), 28–30, 32, 33, 35 (right), 36, 38 (left), 39–43, 48 (right), 50, 121, 123–127, 136, 138–157, 173, 175, 179, 185 (left), 192, 226–229 © Carl Pruscha
31, 34, 35 (left), 48 (left), 53–54, 58, 113, 114, 119 (right), 120, 128, 131, 133, 135, 137, 158, 165–168, 170, 191 (left), 193, 195, 198, 199, 202 (center, right), 206 (left, center), 207 (left), 210, 211, 212 (bottom), 213–216, 217 (left), 220 (left), 230, 231 (top left), 232 (top), 234 (top), 236 (top), 238, 239, 242 (right), 257 From Carl Pruscha's private archive
38 (right), 175 (right), 180, 191 (right), 203 (center), 204 (left), 224, 231 (top right, bottom), 232 (bottom), 233, 234 (bottom), 235, 236 (bottom), 237 © Eva Schlegel
49 © Monica Correa
55 (left) TCD/Prod.DH/Alamy Stock Photo
55 (center) © Biresh Shah
60, 169, 171, 185 (center, right), 194, 218, 219, 220 (right), 221–223, 242 (left, center) © Gerald Zugmann
63–85 © Carl Pruscha, photos: Ganeshman Chitrakar
98 Photo: Guido Harbers
100–103, 106 © K. F. Pruscha
105 (left, center), 119 (left) © 2019, ProLitteris, Zurich
105 (right) Public domain, photographer unknown
110, 182, 188, 203 (right), 205, 207 (right), 209, 252, 255 © Archiv Akademie der Bildenden Künste Wien
111 Architekturzentrum Wien, collection. Photos: Roland Rainer
112, 132 (right) © Edda Velim
116 (left) Photo: Harvard University, © FLC / 2019, ProLitteris, Zurich
116 (center) Courtesy of Frances Loeb Library, Harvard University Graduate School of Design, photo: Phokion Karas
116 (right) © Generalitat de Catalunya
117 (left) From: Ken Tadashi Oshima (ed.): *Kyonori Kikutake. Between Land and See,* Zurich, 2016, p. 182
117 (center) From: Seng Kuan, Yukio Lippit (ed.): *Kenzo Tange. Architecture for the World,* Zurich, 2012, p. 71, photo: Kawasumi Akio
117 (right) Photo: Hans van Dijk, National Archives of the Netherlands / Anefo
118 © Kiesler Foundation, Vienna
122 (left) Photo: Alfred Nawrath, *Unsterbliches Indien,* Vienna, 1956
122 (center) Photo: Bernard Rudofsky, © The Bernard Rudofsky Estate Vienna
122 (right) © Wilfried Krüger
132 (left), 160 © Peter Noever
134 (left) © Addison Godel
134 (right) © Massachusetts Institute of Technology, photo: Peter Serenyi
162 © KHM (Kunsthistorisches Museum, Wien)
172 (left) © Torsten Pauer, 2016
172 (right), 176, 178, 179 (left), 181, 240 © Marina Faust
174 © Andrea Baczinski
177 © Manfred Horvath
189, 204 (center, right) © Archiv Peter Noever
196 © Archiv Pruscha, Luftbild, Siedlungsgenossenschaft
197 © Photo Kühne
200 © Franz Hubmann
202 (left) © Edelbert Köb
203 (left) © Archive Coop Himmelb(l)au
206 (right) © Akademie der Bildenden Künste Wien, photo: Herbert Fidler
208 (left) © Aleksandra Pawloff
208 (center) © Akademie der Bildenden Künste Wien, photo: Christian Fischer
208 (right) © Akademie der Bildenden Künste Wien, Archive Masahiro Moriguchi
212 (top) © Österreichische Nationalbibliothek Wien
217 (right) © Carl Pruscha, photo: Gerald Zugmann
225 Wikicommons, photo: Dhcarlos2010, CC BY-SA 3.0
244–251 © Hertha Hurnaus
250 (bottom left) © Hertha Hurnaus, painting at the back left: © Negra Bernhard
255 © Akademie der Bildenden Künste, photo: Franz Hubmann

ACKNOWLEDGEMENTS

Such a book can only be created with the help of friends and companions, so our special thank goes to them:

Aradhana Seth, Erika Artaker, Arun and Namita Saraf, Natasha Mittal Saraf, Thomas Schrom, Kathrin Messner, Eduard and Pat Sekler, Wolf Prix, Ursula Krinzinger, Benedikt Erhard, Peter Noever, Sabine Haag, Eva Blimlinger, Herbert Liaunig, Charles and Monica Correa, Elke Rhomberg, Rahul Mehrotra, Elisabeth Ginthör Noever, Edelbert Köb, Sylvia Eisenburger, Klaus Derks, Sabine Dortschy, Melanie Wiener, Eva Schober, Peter Weinhäupl, Sandra Tretter, Raji de Silva, Peter Bogner, Gerd Zillner, Martina Walli, Koichi and Catherine Nagashima, Jan Wampler, Mario Correa, Maya Rüegg, Martina Mullis, Harald Posch, Naveen Mypala, Klaus Jürgen Bauer, Alexandra and Czeslavia Pruscha, Gerald Zugmann, Marina Faust, Rita Nowak, Markus Spiegelfeld, Kathi Rollier, Brigitte Groihofer, Sepp Müller, Elisabeth Samsonow, and Christoph Thun Hohenstein

as well as to Carl Pruscha's asspociates, Anais Meon, Zuzana Ernst, Viki Sandor, Valerie Messini, Damjan Minovski, Leonie Link, Leo Haglmüller, Mathias Mulitzer, Walter Kräutler, Franz Loranzi, Andreas Pfusterer, Valerie Rehulka, and Richard Hilbert.

CARL PRUSCHA—SINGULAR PERSONALITY
Architect, Bohemian, Activist

Edited by Lars Müller, Arno Ritter, and Eva Schlegel
Texts by Natalie Lettner, Michael Sorkin, and Manjushree Thapa
Photographs by Iwan Baan and Hertha Hurnaus

Translations: Matthias Goldmann
Copyediting: Camilla Nielsen, Keonaona Peterson
Proofreading: Ian McDonald
Editorial management: Maya Rüegg
Research/Assistance: Erika Artaker
Design: Integral Lars Müller
Production: Martina Mullis
Lithography: prints professional, Berlin, Germany
Printing and binding: DZA Druckerei zu Altenburg, Germany
Paper: Profibulk 1.1, 135 gsm

Lars Müller Publishers is supported by the Swiss Federal Office of Culture with a structural contribution for the years 2016–2020.

Lars Müller Publishers, Zürich, Switzerland
www.lars-mueller-publishers.com

ISBN 978-3-03778-590-4, English
ISBN 978-3-03778-598-0, German

Distributed in North America by ARTBOOK | D.A.P.
www.artbook.com

Printed in Germany

For their financial support we thank
Land Tirol, the Klimt-Foundation, and the Austrian Federal Chancellery.

LAND TIROL

GUSTAV KLIMT WIEN 1900 FOUNDATION

Bundeskanzleramt